S0-BAN-164

THE FATHERS OF THE CHURCH

A NEW TRANSLATION

VOLUME 64

THE FATHERS OF THE CHURCH

A NEW TRANSLATION

THE WORKS OF SAINT CYRIL OF JERUSALEM

Volume 2

Translated by
LEO P. McCAULEY, S.J.
Boston College
Chestnut Hill, Massachusetts

and

ANTHONY A. STEPHENSON
University of Exeter
England

THE CATHOLIC UNIVERSITY OF AMERICA PRESS
Washington, D. C. 20017

NIHIL OBSTAT:

JOSEPH B. COLLINS, S.S., S.T.D.
Censor Librorum

IMPRIMATUR:

✠PATRICK CARDINAL A. O'BOYLE, D.D.
Archbishop of Washington

February 24, 1970

The *nihil obstat* and *imprimatur* are official declarations that a book or pamphlet is free of doctrinal or moral error. No implication is contained therein that those who have granted the *nihil obstat* and the *imprimatur* agree with the content, opinions, or statements expressed.

Library of Congress Catalog Card No.: 68-55980
S.B.N. 8132-0064-4

FOREWORD

It is my duty to record for our readers the death within the past fourteen months of Martin R. P. McGuire (d. March 15, 1969) and Roy J. Deferrari (d. August 24, 1969), both professors emeriti in the Department of Greek and Latin in the Catholic University of America. The two men were members of the Editorial Board of this series of translations since its inception, and Dr. Deferrari was Editorial Director from Volume 5 (1949) to Volume 58 (1967). Moreover, the volumes that have to date appeared since Dr. Deferrari became Director Emeritus were all planned by him, as were many that will appear subsequently. Not the least of his contributions to the series was his ability to achieve loyal cooperation among the corps of translators, and to this cooperation the continuance of the series is in no small measure due. As translator himself, Dr. Deferrari contributed the whole of Eusebius's *Ecclesiastical History* (Vols. 19, 29), a full volume of Ambrose's theological and dogmatic works (44), the volume of Orosius (50), and a part of the first volume (13) of Basil's letters; and he collaborated in the production of five other volumes (4, 13, 15, 22, 36). From Dr. McGuire, had he lived, the series would have received a full translation of the works of Theodoret, a task left unfinished when he died. Actual contributions from his pen were his eloquent rendering of Ambrose's orations on his brother Satyrus that forms part of Volume 22 and the magisterial essay "The Early Christian Funeral Oration" that opens that volume. These pages, for all their excellence, do not in any way measure the contribution that Dr. McGuire made to the series; the debt that his survivors on the Board owe him lies also in the voice of kindly authority that could always be expected from him and the patience and learning he displayed as he spent long hours assisting fellow translators in their work of revision.

* * * * *

In the present volume, Fathers McCauley and Stephenson bring to an end the translation of St. Cyril of Jerusalem they began in Volume 61. Father McCauley has translated, with a brief Foreword, the remaining *Catecheses*; all else is the work of Father Stephenson. Except for the *Mystagogiae,* for which the recent edition of Piédagnel was used, the two translators have based their work on the Reischl-Rupp edition (Munich 1848/60).

June 1, 1970

BERNARD M. PEEBLES
Editorial Director

ACKNOWLEDGMENT

My thanks are due to my friend and colleague, the Revd M. J. Moreton, who, graciously reading most of my manuscript at the galley-proof stage, saved me from some mistakes.

ANTHONY A. STEPHENSON

CONTENTS

Page

SELECT BIBLIOGRAPHY*

Texts:

A. A. Touttée and P. Maran [Maurists] (Paris 1720; reprinted PG 33.331-1181).

W. K. Reischl and J. Rupp (Munich 1848/1860). Text with improvements based on *Cod. Monac. gr.* 394.

J. Quasten, in *Monumenta eucharistica et liturgica vetustissima* (Bonn 1935-1937) 69-111 (also on these same pages in Florilegium patristicum 7.2 [Bonn 1935]).

F. L. Cross, *St. Cyril of Jerusalem's Lectures on the Christian Sacraments* . . . (S.P.C.K. Texts for Students 51; London 1951). Text and English translation (by R. W. Church), with Introduction, of the *Procatechesis* and the Mystagogical Catecheses.

A. Piédagnel, *Cyrille de Jérusalem, Catéchèses mystagogiques;* with French translation (Sources chrétiennes 126; Paris 1966).

English Translations (in addition, for the *Mystagogiae,* to Cross, above):

R. W. Church, *The Catechetical Lectures of S. Cyril, Archbishop of Jerusalem* (Library of the Fathers of the Holy Catholic Church [LCF] 2; Oxford and London 1839). Contains Dean R. W. Church's classic translation of the Lenten Lectures (the prebaptismal *Catecheses*) and the Easter (Mystagogical) *Catecheses,* and a Preface by J. H. Newman, who apparently (cf. xxx) also revised the translation.

E. H. Gifford; *St. Cyril of Jerusalem and St. Gregory Nazianzen* (Library of Nicene and Post-Nicene Fathers, Second Series 7; London 1894; recently reprinted by Eerdmans, Grand Rapids, Mich.). E. H. Gifford's revision of Church's translation, with useful introduction and notes.

W. Telfer, *Cyril of Jerusalem and Nemesius of Emesa* (Library of Christian Classics 4; London 1955). A new translation of extensive selections from the *Catecheses* with the *Letter to Constantius.* Contains very valuable introduction and notes.

French Translations (in addition, for the *Mystagogiae,* to Piédagnel, above):

J. Bouvet, [Cyrillus Hierosolymitanus] *Catéchèses baptismales et mystagogiques* (Les Écrits des saints; Namur 1962).

M. Véricel, *Cyrille de Jérusalem* (Collection Église d'hier et d'aujourd'hui; Paris 1957). Selections.

---

* This bibliography in part resumes and in part supplements that in Volume 1; see also below, p. 143, n. 2. Where a work is cited only by the name of its author, the reference is to his work listed in this bibliography.

German Translation:

P. Hauser, *Des heiligen Cyrillus . . . Katechesen* [*Cat.* and *Myst.*] (Bibliothek der Kirchenväter; Munich 1922).

Other Works:

Didascalia et Constitutiones Apostolorum. Edited by F. X Funk (Paderborn 1905); translation by J. Donaldson in *Ante-Nicene Christian Library* 17 and in ANF 7.

G. Dix, *The Shape of the Liturgy* (2d ed. London 1945).

———, *The Theology of Confirmation in Relation to Baptism* (London 1946).

Hippolytus, *The Apostolic Tradition.* Edited by G. Dix, revised by H. Chadwick (London 1968).

G. W. H. Lampe, *A Patristic Greek Lexicon* (Oxford 1961 ff.).

———, *The Seal of the Spirit* (London 1951).

B. Neunheuser, *Baptism and Confirmation.* Translated by J. J. Hughes (Montreal 1964).

J. Quasten, *Patrology* III (Utrecht/Antwerp-Westminster, Md. 1960) 362-77, with excellent bibliography.

A. Renoux, "Les Catéchèses mystagogiques dans l'organisation liturgique hierosolymitaine du IVe et Ve siècle," *Le Muséon* 78 (1965) 355-59.

ABBREVIATIONS

ANF	*The Ante-Nicene Fathers.*
ApCo	*Apostolic Constitutions,* ed. F. X. Funk.
ApTrad	Hippolytus, *The Apostolic Tradition,* ed. G. Dix.
Cat.	Cyril of Jerusalem, *Lenten Lectures (Catecheses).*
CSEL	*Corpus scriptorum ecclesiasticorum latinorum.*
Denzinger	H. Denzinger, *Enchiridion symbolorum . . .*, 32nd ed. by A. Schönmetzer, S.J. (Freiburg i. B. 1963).
Dix	G. Dix, *The Shape of the Liturgy.*
Dix, TCB	———, *The Theology of Confirmation in Relation to Baptism.*
DTC	*Dictionnaire de théologie catholique,* ed. A. Vacant *et al.* (Paris 1903-1950).

FOTC	*The Fathers of the Church: A New Translation*
GCS	*Die griechischen christlichen Schriftsteller* (Leipzig 1897ff.).
Hist. Eccl. (H.E.)	Eusebius, *Historia ecclesiastica.*
LCC	*Library of Christian Classics.*
LCF	*Library of the Fathers of the Holy Catholic Church.*
LNPF	*A Select Library of Nicene and Post-Nicene Fathers of the Christian Church.*
LTK	*Lexikon für Theologie und Kirche* (2d ed., Freiburg i. B. 1957ff.).
Myst.	Cyril of Jerusalem, *Easter Lectures* (*Mystagogiae*).
PG	Migne, *Patrologia Graeca.*
PGL	G. W. H. Lampe, *A Patristic Greek Lexicon.*
PL	Migne, *Patrologia Latina.*
RR	The Reischl-Rupp edition of Cyril of Jerusalem.
Telfer	W. Telfer, *Cyril of Jerusalem and Nemesius of Emesa.*

CORRIGENDA TO VOL. 1 (FOTC 61)

Pages vii, ix, 1 n., 38, 41, 76 n., 78 n., 79 n., 83 n., 268: *for* Toutée *read* Touttée.

Page ix, 7th entry (W. Telfer): *for* Letter of Constantius *read* Letter to Constantius.

Page xi, 4th abbreviation: *for* DHG *read* DHC.

Page 61, line 14: *for* to the third clause, and the fourth clause, *read* to the fourth clause, and the third clause, . . .

Page 89, 2nd par.: *for* Ch. 24 *read* Ch. 34.

LENTEN LECTURES

(*Katēchēseis*)

XIII-XVIII

Translated by

LEO P. McCAULEY, S.J.

Boston College
Chestnut Hill, Massachusetts

FOREWORD TO CATECHESES 13-18

HESE LECTURES DEAL with the Crucifixion and Burial of Christ (13), His Resurrection, Ascension and Sitting with the Father (14), His coming as Judge of the living and the dead, of whose kingdom there will be no end (15). Two lectures are devoted to the Holy Spirit (16-17), and the pre-baptismal *Catecheses* close with a discourse on the Holy Catholic Church, the Resurrection of the flesh, and life everlasting. The profusion of Scripture texts is even more marked than in the preceding *Catecheses*. Cyril's own words (13.8) help to explain this emphasis on inspired testimony: "For everything that concerns Christ has been written; there is nothing doubtful, since nothing is unattested. All has been inscribed in prophetic records, clearly written . . . by the Holy Spirit." The accommodation of Scripture texts is often forced and sometimes even strange, and one may doubt whether Cyril's listening audience could follow the evolution of his thought. It is possible also that corruption in the manuscript tradition has been responsible for some of the difficulties in the text.

The Greek text used for the first twelve *Catecheses* has been used also for the last six—that of Reischl and Rupp (Munich 1848-60); and, as before, when the Greek of Cyril's biblical quotations does not require adaptation or new wording, the English renderings of Scripture are taken from the version published under the patronage of the Confraternity of Christian Doctrine.

LEO P. MCCAULEY, S.J.

CATECHESIS XIII

On the Crucifixion and Burial of Christ

"Who would believe what we have heard? To whom has the arm of the Lord been revealed?"[1] *"Like a lamb led to the slaughter or a sheep before his shearers, he was silent and opened not his mouth."*[2]

(1) The Catholic Church glories in every action of Christ, but her glory of glories is the Cross. Knowing this, Paul says: "But God forbid that I should glory, save in the cross of our Lord Jesus Christ."[3] It was a wonderful thing for the man blind from birth to receive his sight in Siloe, but what is that compared to the blind of all the world? It was a marvel beyond nature for Lazarus to rise again after four days; there, with Lazarus, the grace stopped; what was it compared to the raising of all men from the tomb of sin? It was wonderful that five loaves should supply food for five thousand, but what was that compared to the feeding of those famishing in ignorance throughout the world? The release of the woman bound by Satan for eighteen years was a portent, but more wonderful was the release of all of us held fast in the meshes of our sins. The glory of the Cross has at one and the same time led into the light those blind through ignorance, has delivered all bound in sin, and redeemed all mankind.

(2) Do not wonder that the whole world was redeemed, for it was no mere man, but the Only-begotten Son of God

1 Isa. 53.1.
2 *Ibid.* 7.
3 Cf. Gal. 6.14.

who died for it. The sin of one man, Adam, availed to bring death to the world; if by one man's offense death reigned for the world, why should not life reign all the more "from the justice of the one"?[4] If Adam and Eve were cast out of paradise because of the tree from which they ate, should not believers more easily enter into paradise because of the Tree of Jesus? If the first man, fashioned out of the earth, brought universal death, shall not He who fashioned him, being the Life, bring everlasting life? If Phinees by his zeal in slaying the evildoer appeased the wrath of God, shall not Jesus, who slew no other, but "gave himself a ransom for all,"[5] take away God's wrath against man?

(3) Therefore let us not be ashamed of the Cross of our Savior, but rather glory in it; "for the doctrine of the cross" is "to the Jews a stumbling-block and to the Gentiles foolishness,"[6] but to us salvation, "foolishness to those who perish but to those who are saved, that is, to us, it is the power of God."[7] For as I said before, it was not a mere man who died for us, but the Son of God, God made man. If under Moses the lamb kept the destroyer away, did not "the Lamb of God, who takes away the sins of the world,"[8] all the more deliver us from our sins? The blood of a brute sheep accorded salvation; shall not the blood of the Only-begotten much more save us? If any man doubts the power of the Crucified, let him question the devils; if any man doubts words, let him believe the evident facts. Many have been crucified throughout the world, but of none of these are the demons afraid. For these died because of their own sins, but Christ for the sins of others; for He "did not sin, neither was deceit found

4 Rom. 5.18. Though the sin of Adam brought the doom of physical death to man, the emphasis in this chapter is rather on the death of the soul, on original sin and the sins of mankind for which the sin of Adam paved the way.
5 Cf. 1 Tim. 2.6; on Phinees, Num. 25.7.
6 1 Cor. 1.18, 23.
7 *Ibid.*
8 John 1.29.

in his mouth."[9] It was not Peter, who could be suspected of partiality, who said this, but Isaia, who, though not present in the flesh, in spirit foresaw His coming in the flesh. But why do I bring only the prophet as a witness? Take the witness of Pilate himself, who passed judgment on Him, saying: "I find no guilt in this man";[10] and when he delivered Him up and washed his hands, he said: "I am innocent of the blood of this just man."[11] There is also another witness to the sinlessness of Jesus in the robber, the first man to enter paradise; he rebuked his fellow and said: " 'We are receiving what our deeds deserved: but this man has done nothing wrong,' for we were present, you and I, at His judgment."[12]

(4) Jesus truly suffered for all men. For the Cross was no illusion; otherwise our redemption also is an illusion. His death was not imaginary; otherwise our salvation is an idle tale. If His death was imaginary, they were right who said: "We have remembered how that deceiver said, while he was yet alive, 'After three days I will rise again.' "[13] Therefore His passion was real, for He was truly crucified, and we are not ashamed of it. He was crucified and we do not deny it, but rather do I glory in speaking of it. For if I should now deny it, Golgotha here, close to which we are now gathered, refutes me; the wood of the Cross, now distributed piecemeal from Jerusalem over all the world, refutes me. I confess the Cross, because I know of the Resurrection; had the Cross been the end, perhaps I would not have confessed it, but concealed both it and my Master; however, since the Cross was followed by the Resurrection, I am not ashamed to avow it.

---

9 1 Peter 2.22.
10 Luke 23.14.
11 Matt. 27.24.
12 Luke 23.41. That the two robbers were present at the judgment of Christ seems rather unlikely. Cyril assumes perhaps that they were condemned to be crucified at the same time as Christ.
13 Matt. 27.63.

(5) Being in the flesh like other men, He was crucified, but not for sins men commit. He was not led to death for love of gain, for He was a teacher of poverty; He was not condemned for lust, for He said plainly: "Anyone who even looks with lust at a woman has already committed adultery with her";[14] not for smiting or striking impetuously, for He turned the other cheek to the smiter; not for despising the Law, for He was the fulfiller of the Law; not for reviling a prophet, for He was proclaimed by the prophets; not for defrauding men of their hire, for He ministered freely, without recompense; not for sinning in word or deed or thought: "Who did no sin, neither was deceit found in his mouth. Who, when he was reviled, did not revile, when he suffered, did not threaten";[15] who came to His passion, not unwillingly, but willingly; and if anyone even now should attempt to dissuade Him and say: "Far be it from thee, O Lord,"[16] He will say again: "Get behind me, Satan."[17]

(6) Do you wish to be convinced that He came to His passion willingly? Others, ignorant of their fate, die against their will, but He foretold His passion: Behold, "the Son of Man will be delivered up to be crucified."[18] Do you know why this Lover of man did not shun death? To prevent the whole world from perishing in its sins. "Behold we are going up to Jerusalem, and the Son of Man will be betrayed and crucified";[19] and again: "He steadfastly set his face to go to Jerusalem."[20] Would you know clearly that the Cross is a glory to Jesus? Listen to His words, not mine. Judas, grown ungrateful to the Master, was intent on betraying Him. Going forth from the table where he had drunk His cup of blessing, he sought, in return for that draught of salvation, to shed

14 Matt. 5.28.
15 1 Peter 2.22, 23.
16 Matt. 16.22.
17 *Ibid.* 23.
18 Matt. 26.2
19 Matt. 20.18, 19.
20 Luke 9.51.

just blood. "Who ate his bread lifted up his heel against him."[21] He had just received the blessed gifts and at once he was plotting His death for the wages of betrayal.[22] When he had been convicted and heard the words: "Thou has said it,"[23] he went forth again; then Jesus said: "The hour has come for the Son of Man to be glorified."[24] Do you see how He knew the Cross to be his own peculiar glory? If Isaia is not ashamed of being sawn asunder, shall Christ be ashamed of dying for the world? "Now is the Son of Man glorified";[25] not that He lacked glory before, for He was glorified with the glory which He had before the creation of the world. As God He was glorified from eternity; now He was being glorified, having borne the crown of His patience. He did not give up His life perforce, nor was He put to death by violence, but of His own will. Hear what He says: " 'I have the power to lay down my life, and I have the power to take it up again.'[26] I yield it to My enemies of My own choice, for unless I willed it so, it could not be." He came, then, of His own free choice to His passion, rejoicing in His noble deed, smiling at the crown, cheered by the salvation of men; He was not ashamed of the Cross, for it saved the world. It was no ordinary man who suffered, but God in man's nature, striving for the reward of His patience.

(7) The Jews, of course, ever ready to object and slow to believe, deny this; hence the prophet just read says: "Who would believe what we have heard?"[27] The Persians believe but not the Hebrews. "They who have not been told of him

21 Cf. Ps. 40.10.
22 Cyril seems to imply that Judas had received the sacred species before he left the supper room.
23 Matt. 26.25.
24 John 12.23.
25 John 13.31.
26 John 10.18.
27 Isa. 53.1. The Benedictine editor has noted a close parallel between what follows to the end of the lecture and Rufinus' exposition of the same article of the Creed *(Commentarius in Symbolum Apostolorum,* 19 sqq.) and has no doubt that Rufinus borrowed freely from Cyril.

shall see, and they who have not heard shall understand";[28] yes, the people whose study is the Scriptures reject what they study. They answer: "Does the *Lord* then suffer? and did the hands of men prevail over His sovereignty?" Read the Lamentations, for in them Jeremia, lamenting you, has written what is worth a lament. He saw your ruin, he beheld your downfall; he bewailed the Jerusalem that then was, for that which now is shall not be bewailed.[29] For that Jerusalem crucified Christ, but that which now is worships Him. Therefore, lamenting he says: "The breath of our mouth, Christ the Lord is taken in our sins."[30] Do I invent what I say? You see he bears witness to the Christ seized by men. What follows? Tell me, O prophet. But he says: "Of whom we said, under his shadow we shall live among the Gentiles."[31] He indicates that the grace of life will no longer abide in Israel, but among the Gentiles.

(8) Since their denials are manifold, let us attempt to adduce, by the Lord's grace, a few testimonies concerning the passion, with the help of your prayers, and as the shortness of time allows. For everything that concerns Christ has been written; there is nothing doubtful, since nothing is unattested. All has been inscribed in prophetic records, clearly written, not on tablets of stone, but by the Holy Spirit. You have heard the Gospel's account of the deeds of Judas; ought you not to receive testimony of this? You have heard that His side was pierced by a spear; should you not see whether this also is written? You have heard that He was crucified in a garden; ought you not to see if this is written? You have heard that He was sold for thirty pieces of silver; should you not learn what prophet said this? You have

28 Rom. 15.21.
29 By "the Jerusalem that then was" Cyril means the Jerusalem captured and destroyed by Titus and reduced to further ruin by Hadrian. The boundaries of the later Jerusalem did not coincide with those of the old city.
30 Lam. 4.20 (Douay).
31 Cf. *ibid.*

heard that He was given vinegar to drink; learn where even this is written. You have heard that His body was laid in a rock, and a stone placed thereon; should you not get testimony of this also from the prophet? You have heard that He was buried; should you not see whether the circumstances of His burial were written down accurately? You have heard that He rose again; should you not see whether we are mocking you in teaching all this? "My speech and my preaching were not in the persuasive words of human wisdom."[32] No sophistical artifices are being advanced, for sophistry is always unmasked; arguments and counterarguments cancel out. "But we preach a crucified Christ,"[33] proclaimed beforehand by the prophets. Seal these testimonies, when you receive them, in your heart. But since they are many, and the time remaining is short, hear now, when you may, a few testimonies of greater moment; and taking these as a start, be diligent and seek out the rest. Let not your hand be stretched out merely to receive, but let it be ready to work. God bestows all things freely. "If any of you is wanting in wisdom, let him ask it of God who gives,"[34] and he shall receive. Through your prayers may He grant utterance to us who speak, and faith to you who hear.

(9) Therefore let us seek the testimonies to Christ's passion. For we have come together now not to make a speculative exposition of the Scriptures, but rather to be convinced of what we already believe. Previously you received from me testimonies concerning the coming of Jesus and His walking upon the sea; for it is written: "Through the sea was your way."[35] You listened on another occasion to testimony of divers cures. I will now start with the beginning of the passion. Judas the traitor came and stood opposite Him, speaking words of peace but plotting enmity. Of him the

32 1 Cor. 2.4.
33 1 Cor. 1.23.
34 James 1.5.
35 Ps. 76.20.

Psalmist says: "My friends and my neighbors have drawn near and stood against me."[36] Again: "Their words are smoother than oil and the same are darts."[37] "Hail, Rabbi,"[38] and he delivered his master to death; he did not regard the words of His warning: "Judas, dost thou betray the Son of Man with a kiss?"[39] For He had all but said: "Recollect your own name—Judas signifies confession—you have made your bargain, you have received the money, confess quickly." "O God, whom I praise, be not silent, for they have opened wicked and treacherous mouths against me. They have spoken to me with lying tongues; and with words of hatred they have encompassed me."[40] Some of the chief priests were present, and Christ was put in bonds before the gates of the city, as you heard recently, if you recall the exposition of the psalm designating the time and the place; how "they returned at evening, and suffered hunger like dogs and prowled about the city."[41]

(10) Harken now in regard to the thirty pieces of silver. "And I will say to them, 'If it seems good to you, give me my wages, or refuse.' "[42] One recompense is due Me for curing the blind and the lame, and I receive another; instead of thanksgiving, dishonor, and instead of worship, insult. Do you see how Scripture foresaw all this? "And they counted out my wages, thirty pieces of silver."[43] O prophetic accuracy! A great and unerring wisdom of the Holy Spirit! For he did not say ten, nor twenty, but thirty, exactly the right amount. Tell also what happened to this payment, O prophet! Does he who received it keep it or does he give it back? And after its return what becomes of it? The prophet says: "So I

36 Cf. Ps. 37.12.
37 Ps. 54.22 (Douay).
38 Matt. 26.49.
39 Luke 22.48.
40 Ps. 108.1-3.
41 Cf. Ps. 58.7. The exposition of the psalm which Cyril refers to must have occurred in a homily not connected with the catechetical lectures.
42 Zach. 11.12 (Sept.).
43 *Ibid.*

took the thirty pieces of silver, and I cast them into the house of the Lord, into the foundry."[44] Compare with the prophecy the Gospel which says: "Judas repented and flung the pieces of silver into the temple, and withdrew."[45]

(11) Here I seek a precise explanation of the apparent discrepancy. They who disregard the prophets assert that the prophet says: "And I cast them into the house of the Lord, into the foundry," while the Gospel says: "And they gave them for the potter's field."[46] Hear how both statements are true. Those conscientious Jews, of course, the chief priests of that time, seeing Judas repentant and saying: "I have sinned in betraying innocent blood," reply: "What is that to us? See to it thyself."[47] Does it then mean nothing to you, the crucifiers? Shall he who received the price of murder and returned it see to it, but you, the murderers, will not see to it? Then they say among themselves: "It is not lawful to put them into the *corbona,* because it is the price of blood."[48] From your own mouths comes your condemnation. If the price is abominable, the deed also is abominable; but if in crucifying Christ you fulfill justice, why do you not receive the price? But the point of the inquiry was this, how there is no disagreement, when the Gospel on the one hand says "potter's field," but the prophet on the other hand says "foundry." The fact is that goldsmiths and coppersmiths are not the only craftsmen who have foundries, but potters too have foundries for their clay. For they sift the fine, rich and useful earth from the gravel, and setting aside the mass of impure matter, they first soften the clay with water, to work it more easily into the forms intended. Why do you wonder that the Gospel says plainly "potter's field," while the prophet spoke his prophecy in the form of an enigma, since prophecy is generally enigmatical?

44 *Ibid.* 13.
45 Matt. 27.3, 5.
46 *Ibid.* 10.
47 *Ibid.* 4.
48 *Ibid.* 6.

(12) They bound Jesus and led Him to the hall of the high priest. Would you know and see that this also is written? Isaia says: "Woe to their souls, because they have taken evil counsel against themselves, saying: 'Let us bind the just, for he is troublesome to us.' "[49] Truly indeed "Woe to their souls"! Let us see how. Isaia was sawn asunder; yet after this the people was restored. Jeremia was cast into the mire of a dungeon, but the wound of the Jews was healed; for the sin was less, since it was against man. But when the Jews sinned, not against man, but against God become man, "Woe to their souls"!—"Let us bind the just"; but could He not have set Himself free, someone will say, He who freed Lazarus from the bonds of death after four days, and freed Peter from the iron fetters? Angels were ready at hand, saying: "Let us break their fetters," but they hold back, because the Lord willed to suffer thus. Again He was led to the tribunal before the ancients; you have heard the testimony already: "The Lord enters into judgment with his people's elders and princes."[50]

(13) The high priest questioned Him and after hearing the truth, tenses; and the wicked servant of wicked men gives Him a blow; and that face, which had shone as the sun, endured to be struck by impious hands. Others come to spit in the face of Him who by spittle had cured the man blind from birth. Is this the return you make to the Lord? This people is stupid and foolish. The prophet in wonder says: "Who would believe what we have heard?"[51] For it was incredible that God, the Son of God, and the Arm of the Lord should suffer all this. But lest those to be saved disbelieve, the Holy Spirit predicts this in the person of Christ, who says (for He who then spoke these words afterwards fulfilled them): "I gave my back to those who beat me";[52]

49 Isa. 3.9, 10 (Sept.).
50 Isa. 3.14.
51 Isa. 53.1.
52 Isa. 50.6.

for Pilate scourged Him and delivered Him to be crucified; "and my cheeks to blows; and my face I did not shield from the shame of spittings";[53] as though He were to say: "Though I knew beforehand that they would strike Me, I did not even turn aside My cheek; for how could I have nerved My disciples to undergo death for the truth, if I had been afraid? I said: 'He who loves his life shall lose it';[54] if I had loved My life, how could I have taught this, not practicing what I taught?" He who was Himself God first endured these sufferings from men to make us men unashamed to endure like sufferings for Him. You see that the prophets have clearly foretold all this. To repeat, I omit further testimonies from Scripture for want of time; for if one were to track down each point, nothing concerning Christ would be left unattested.

(14) Having been bound, Christ went from Caiphas to Pilate; is this also written? Yes; "And having bound him, they led him away as a present to the King of Jarim."[55] But some keen listener will object: "Pilate was not a king" (let us pass over for the time the main points of the inquiry); "How then, having bound Him, did they lead Him as a present to the king?" But read the Gospel; Pilate, hearing that He was from Galilee, sent Him to Herod; for Herod was then king and was present in Jerusalem. Notice the exactness of the prophet; for he says that He was sent as a present; for "Herod and Pilate became friends that very day; whereas previously they had been at enmity with each other."[56] It was fitting that He, who was to restore peace between earth and heaven, should first put at peace the very men who condemned Him, for the Lord Himself was there

53 *Ibid.*
54 John 12.25.
55 Osee 10.6 (Sept.). The accommodation of the Old Testament text may seem strained, but Cyril had the example of Justin (*Dialogue with Trypho* 103) before him, and Rufinus after him drew the same parallel.
56 Luke 23.12.

present, "who reconciles the hearts of the princes of the earth."[57] Mark the exactness of the prophets, and their truthful testimony.

(15) Contemplate with awe the Lord being judged. He suffered Himself to be led and borne about by the soldiers. Pilate sat in judgment, and He who sits at the right hand of the Father stood and was judged. The people whom he had freed from Egypt and often from other places kept shouting against Him: "Away with him! Away with him! Crucify him!"[58] Why, O you Jews? Because He healed your blind? or because He made your lame to walk, and bestowed His other blessings? The prophet in astonishment speaks of this also: "At whom do you open wide your mouth and put out your tongue?"[59] The Lord Himself says in the prophets: "My heritage has turned on me like a lion in the jungle; because she has roared against me, I treat her as an enemy."[60] "I have not renounced them but they have renounced Me; therefore I say: 'I abandon my house.' "[61]

(16) When He was judged He held His peace, and Pilate was moved in His behalf and said: "Do you not hear what they testify against you?"[62] It was not that he knew Him who was being judged, but he feared his wife's dream which had been reported to him. Jesus held His peace. The Psalmist says: "I am become like a man who neither hears nor has in his mouth a retort,"[63] and again: "But I am like a deaf man, hearing not, like a dumb man who opens not his mouth."[64] You have heard this before, if you recall.

(17) The soldiers who surrounded Him mock Him. Their Lord becomes their plaything, and their Master is made a

---

57 Cf. Job 12.24.
58 John 19.15.
59 Isa. 57.4.
60 Jer. 12.8.
61 *Ibid.* 7.
62 Cf. Matt. 27.13.
63 Ps. 37.15.
64 *Ibid.* 14.

mockery. "When they see me, they shake their heads."[65] Yet the figure of the kingly state is there; though they mock Him, they bow the knee. The soldiers crucify Him after first putting on Him a purple garment; and they place a crown upon His head; what though it be of thorns? Every king is proclaimed by soldiers; it was fitting that Jesus also, in figure, be crowned by soldiers. For this reason Scripture says in the Canticles: "Daughters of Jerusalem, come forth and look upon King Solomon in the crown with which his mother has crowned him."[66] But the crown was also a mystery, for it was a remission of sins, and release from the sentence of condemnation.

(18) Adam received the sentence: "Cursed be the earth in your works, thorns and thistles shall it bring forth to you."[67] So Jesus assumes the thorns to remove the condemnation; so also He was buried in the earth, to have the earth which had been cursed receive a blessing instead of the curse. At the time of the sin Adam and Eve clothed themselves with fig leaves; consequently Jesus made the fig tree the last of His signs. When He was about to go to His passion, He cursed the fig tree—not every fig tree, but that alone for the sake of the figure—saying: "May no one ever eat fruit of thee henceforward forever."[68] Let the doom be canceled. Because of old they clothed themselves with fig leaves, He came at a season when fruit is not found on the tree. Who is unaware that in winter the fig tree does not bear fruit, but is clothed in leaves only? Was Jesus ignorant of that which all know? No, but though He knew, He came as though He were seeking, not unaware that He would not find, but making the figurative curse apply only to the leaves.

(19) We have touched on the story of Paradise, and I am truly amazed at the verisimilitude of the types. In Paradise

65 Ps. 108.25.
66 Cant. 3.11.
67 Cf. Gen. 3.17, 18.
68 Mark 11.14.

(the garden of Eden) was the fall, and in a garden our salvation. From the tree came sin, and until the Tree sin lasted. When the Lord was walking in Paradise in the afternoon Adam and Eve hid themselves; and in the afternoon the robber is brought into Paradise by the Lord. But some one will say: "You are inventing sophistries; show me from a prophet the Wood of the Cross; unless you produce testimony from a prophet, I am not convinced." Harken to Jeremia and be convinced: "I was as a meek lamb that is carried to be a victim; did I not know it?"[69] (For read it thus as a question, as I have put it. For He who said: "You know that after two days the passover shall be here, and the Son of Man will be delivered up to be crucified,"[70] did He not know?) "I was as a meek lamb, that is carried to be a victim; did I not know it?" (What sort of lamb? Let John the Baptist interpret, when he says: "Behold the lamb of God, who takes away the sins of the world!"[71]) "They devised a wicked counsel against me, saying (was it that He who knew the counsels did not know their issue? And what did they say?): 'Come, and let us put wood on his bread.' " (If the Lord shall count you worthy, hereafter you shall learn that His body, according to the Gospel, bore the figure of bread.) "Come, and let us put wood on his bread, and cut him off from the land of the living." (Life is not cut off; why do you toil to no purpose?) "And let his name be remembered no more."[72] Your counsel is vain; for before the sun His name abides in the Church. That it was truly Life which hung upon the Cross Moses declares, weeping: "And thy life shall hang before thine eyes; thou shalt fear night and day, neither shalt thou trust thy life."[73] Apropos is the text just now read: "Lord, who has believed what we have heard?"[74]

69 Jer. 11.19 (Sept.).
70 Matt. 26.2.
71 John 1.29.
72 Jer. 11.19 (Sept.).
73 Deut. 28.66 (Sept.).
74 Cf. Isa. 53.1. See above at n. 51.

(20) The Cross was prefigured by Moses when he fixed the serpent on a pole; anyone bitten by the living serpent who looked upon the brazen serpent was saved by faith. Can salvation come from a brazen serpent, fixed on a cross, but not from the incarnate Son of God crucified? Life ever comes from wood. In the time of Noe the preservation of life came from a wooden ark. In Moses' time the sea, on beholding the figurative rod, gave way before him who struck it; could the rod of Moses be so mighty, and the Cross of the Savior powerless? I pass over most of the types for the sake of brevity. In the time of Moses the wood sweetened the water; and the water from Jesus' side flowed upon the wood.

(21) The first signs under Moses were blood and water, and the last of all the signs of Jesus were the same. First Moses changed the river into blood; and at the end Jesus discharged water with blood from His side. Perhaps it was because of the two utterances, one of His judge, the other of those who shouted against Him; or because of the believers and unbelievers. For Pilate said, "I am innocent," and washed his hands with water; they who shouted against Him said, "His blood be on us";[75] these two, then, came from His side, water perhaps for him who judged Him, but blood for them who shouted against Him. There is still another interpretation: the blood was for the Jews, the water for the Christians; for on the Jews, as plotters, came the sentence of condemnation, but to you who now believe, salvation comes by water. Nothing has been done without purpose. Our fathers gave still another explanation. Since in the Gospels the power of salutary Baptism is twofold, one granted by water to those receiving the sacrament, but a second granted to holy martyrs in the time of persecution by blood, therefore blood and water came forth from the side of the savior to confirm the grace of confession made for Christ, whether in Baptism or on the occasion of martyrdom. There is still another reason

75 Matt. 27.24, 25.

in regard to His side. The originator of sin was a woman, formed from the side of Adam; but when Jesus came to grant pardon freely to men and women alike, he was pierced in the side for woman's sake, to undo the sin.[76]

(22) Further inquiry will discover other reasons, but those given are enough, because of the shortness of the time and to avoid exhausting the attention of my hearers. Yet one should never grow weary of hearing about our crowned Lord, especially on this holy Golgotha. For others merely hear, but we see and touch. Therefore, let no one grow weary; take arms against the adversaries for the sake of the Cross itself; set up the faith of the Cross as a trophy against objectors. When you are to dispute with unbelievers concerning the Cross of Christ, first make with your hand the sign of the Cross of Christ, and the objector will be silenced. Do not be ashamed to confess the Cross. For angels glory in it, saying: We "know that you seek Jesus, who was crucified."[77] Could you not have said, O angel, "I know you seek my Master?" But he says with confidence, "I know the Crucified." For the Cross is a crown, not a dishonor.

(23) Let us return to the proposed proof from the prophets. The Lord was crucified; you have received the testimonies. You see this place of Golgotha. With a cry of praise you assent. See that you never deny it in the time of persecution. Let not the Cross be a joy to you merely in the time of peace, but keep the same faith during persecution. Do not be a friend of Jesus in the time of peace and His foe in the time of wars. You receive now the remission of your sins and the graces of the spiritual bounty of your King. When war comes, strive courageously for your King. Jesus, who did no sin, was crucified for you; will you not face crucifixion for Him in turn? You are not bestowing a favor, for you have first received; you are returning a favor, repaying the debt

76 This curious reason why the side of Christ was pierced (i.e. for woman's sake) is found in many ancient sources.
77 Matt. 28.5.

to Him who was crucified for you on Golgotha. Golgotha is interpreted 'the place of a skull.' Who were they who prophetically named this spot Golgotha, where Christ the true Head endured the Cross? As the Apostle says, "He is the image of the invisible God";[78] and subsequently: "Again, he is the head of his body, the Church."[79] Again: "The head of every man is Christ";[80] and "Who is the head of every Principality and Power."[81] The Head suffered in "the place of the skull." O great and prophetic appellation! The very name all but reminds you, saying: "Think not of the Crucified as a mere man; He is 'the head of every Principality and Power.'" The Head which was crucified is the Head of all power and has the Father for His Head; for "the head of man is Christ; and the head of Christ is God."[82]

(24) Christ, then, was crucified for us; He was judged in the night, when it was cold, and therefore a fire of coals was laid. He was crucified at the third hour; and "from the sixth hour there was darkness until the ninth hour";[83] but from the ninth hour there was light again. Are these details written down? Let us inquire. Zacharia says: "And it shall come to pass in that day, and there shall be no light, but cold and frost through one day, (the cold on account of which Peter warmed himself,) and that day shall be known to the Lord."[84] (What? Did He not know the other days? There are many days, but "this is the day [of the Lord's patience] the Lord has made.")[85] "And that day shall be known to the Lord, and not day nor night."[86] What dark saying does the prophet utter? That day is neither day nor night. What then shall we call it? The Gospel interprets it, telling of the event. It was

78 Col. 1.15.
79 *Ibid.* 18.
80 1 Cor. 11.3.
81 Col. 2.10.
82 1 Cor. 11.3.
83 Matt. 27.45.
84 Zach. 14.6, 7 (Douay).
85 Ps. 117.24.
86 Zach. 14.6, 7 (Douay).

not day, for the sun did not shine without interruption from rising to setting, but from the sixth hour to the ninth there was darkness. The darkness was interposed; but God called the darkness night. Therefore it was neither day nor night; for it was neither all light, so as to be called day, nor all darkness, so as to be called night; but after the ninth hour the sun shone forth. This also the prophet foretells; for after saying "not day nor night," he adds: "And in the time of the evening there shall be light."[87] Do you see the exactness of the prophets? Do you see the truth of the events foretold?

(25) Do you seek at what hour exactly the sun failed? Was it the fifth hour or the eighth or the tenth? Give the exact hour, O prophet, to the unheeding Jews; when did the sun set? The prophet Amos says: "On that day, says the Lord God, I will make the sun set at midday" (for there was darkness from the sixth hour) "and cover the earth with darkness in broad daylight."[88] What season is this, O prophet, and what sort of day? "I will turn your feasts into mourning"[89] (for it was in the Azymes that this event took place, and at the feast of the Pasch); then he says: "I will make them mourn as for an only son, and bring their day to a bitter end."[90] For the day of Azymes and at the time of the feast the women mourned and wept, and the Apostles who had hidden themselves were overwhelmed with anguish. How wonderful the prophecy!

(26) But someone will say: "Give me still another sign; what other exact sign is there of the event?" Jesus was crucified, and He had but one tunic and one cloak. The soldiers cut the cloak into four parts and divided it among themselves; but the tunic was not cut, because, if it were cut, it would no longer be of any use; so lots were cast for it by the soldiers; they divided the cloak, but for the tunic they

87 *Ibid.*
88 Amos 8.9 (Sept.).
89 *Ibid.*
90 *Ibid.* 10.

cast lots. Is this also written about? They know, the zealous cantors of the Church, who imitate the angelic hosts and sing praises to God continually; they are counted worthy to sing psalms here on Golgotha, and to say: "They divide my garments among them and for my vesture they cast lots."[91] The "lots" were cast by the soldiers.

(27) Again, when He was judged by Pilate, He was clothed in red, for there "they put on him a scarlet cloak."[92] Is this also written? Isaia says: "Who is this that comes from Edom, in crimson garments from Bosra?"[93] (Who is that who for shame is clothed in scarlet? For Bosra among the Hebrews has such a meaning.) "Why is your apparel red, and your garments like those of the wine presser?"[94] But He answers and says: "I have stretched out my hands all the day to an unbelieving and rebellious people."[95]

(28) He stretched out His hands on the Cross to encompass the ends of the world; for this Golgotha is the very center of the earth. This is not my saying; it is a prophet who has said: "You wrought salvation in the midst of the earth."[96] He who by spiritual hands had established the heavens stretched out human hands; they were fastened with nails that when His humanity, which bore the sins of men, had been nailed to the tree and died, sin might die at the same time, and we might rise again in justice. For as through one man came death, so also through one Man came life; through one Man, that is, the Savior, dying of His own free choice; remember what He said: "I have power to lay my life down, and I have power to take it up again."[97]

(29) He suffered all this because He had come for the

91 Ps. 21.19; Matt. 27.35. It is quite possible that some of the candidates for Baptism were among the choir who sang the psalms.
92 Matt. 27.28.
93 Isa. 63.1.
94 *Ibid.* 2.
95 Cf. Isa. 65.2.
96 Cf. Ps. 73.12 (Douay). This text surely has no geographical connotations; the accommodation of it to Golgotha is obviously forced.
97 John 10.18.

salvation of all; yet the people returned Him an evil recompense. Jesus says, "I thirst,"[98] He who had brought forth water from the flinty rock for them; He asked fruit of the vine He had planted. What happens? This vine, of holy fathers by nature but of Sodom by inclination (for "they are a branch of Sodom's winestock, from the vineyards of Gomorra"),[99] this vine offers to the Lord, when He was thirsty, a sponge filled with vinegar upon a reed. "They put gall in my food, and in my thirst they gave me vinegar to drink."[100] See how clear was the prediction of the prophets. But what sort of gall did they put in My mouth? "They gave him," it says, "wine mixed with myrrh."[101] Myrrh is like gall in taste, and very bitter. "Is the Lord to be thus repaid by you?"[102] Are these the offerings you make to your Master, O vine? Justly did Isaia bewail you of old, saying: "My friend had a vineyard on a fertile hillside";[103] and (not to cite the whole) "I looked," he says, "for the crop of grapes";[104] I thirsted for it to give wine; "but it brought forth thorns";[105] for you see the crown with which I am wreathed. What shall I now decree? "I will command the clouds not to send rain upon it."[106] For the clouds, that is to say, the prophets, were taken away from them, and thereafter the prophets were in the Church; as Paul says: "Of the prophets, let two or three speak at a meeting, and let the rest act as judges."[107] Again, God gave in the Church "some men as apostles, and some as prophets."[108] Agabus, who bound his own hands and feet, was a prophet.

98 John 19.28.
99 Deut. 32.33 (Sept.).
100 Ps. 68.22.
101 Mark 15.23.
102 Deut. 32.6.
103 Isa. 5.1.
104 *Ibid.* 4.
105 *Ibid.* 4 (Sept.).
106 *Ibid.* 6.
107 1 Cor. 14.29.
108 Cf. Eph. 4.11. For Agabus cf. Acts, 21.10-11.

(30) Of the robbers crucified with Him, it was said: "And he was reckoned among the wicked."[109] Up to this time both were wicked, but one of them was wicked no longer. For one was wicked to the end, yielding not to salvation, and, though his hands were fastened, he struck blasphemously with his tongue. The Jews passing by wagged their heads, mocking the Crucified, and fulfilling the Scripture: "When they see me, they shake their heads."[110]

One robber joined in the reviling, but the other rebuked him; for the second robber it was the end of life and the beginning of restoration, the surrender of his soul, and the anticipation of salvation. After rebuking his fellow robber, he says: " 'Lord, remember me';[111] to You I direct my speech; never mind him, for the eyes of his understanding are blinded; but remember me. I do not say: 'Remember my deeds,' for I am afraid of these. Every man is well disposed to his fellow traveler; I am traveling with You towards death; remember me, your fellow wayfarer. I do not say: 'Remember me now,' but 'When thou comest into thy kingdom.' "[112]

(31) What power, O robber, enlightened you? Who taught you to worship that despised man crucified along with you? O Eternal Light, which illumines those lying in darkness! Therefore he justly heard the words: "Be of good cheer,"—not that your deeds should cause you to be of good cheer, but because the King is here, dispensing favors. The request was for something distant in time, but the grace was very speedy. " 'Amen I say to thee, this day thou shalt be with me in paradise,'[113] because this day you have heard My voice, and have not hardened your heart. Swiftly I passed sentence against Adam; swiftly I pardon you. To Adam it was said:

109 Mark 15.28; Isa. 53.12.
110 Ps. 108.25.
111 Luke 23.42.
112 *Ibid.*
113 *Ibid.* 43; in what follows cf. Ps. 94.8.

'For the day you eat of it, you must die';[114] today you have been faithful; today will bring you salvation. The tree brought ruin to Adam; it shall bring you into paradise. Fear not the serpent; he shall not cast you out, for he has fallen from heaven. I say not to you, 'This day thou shalt depart,' but 'This day thou shalt be with me.' "[115] Take heart; you shall not be cast out. Fear not the flaming sword; it stands in awe of its Lord. O mighty and ineffable grace! The faithful Abraham has not yet entered, but the robber enters! Moses and the prophets have not entered, but the lawless robber enters. Even before you Paul marvelled at this, saying: "Where the offense has abounded, grace has abounded yet more."[116] They who had borne the heat of the day had not yet entered; and he who came at the eleventh hour entered. Let no one murmur against the Master of the house, for he says: " 'Friend, I do you no injustice. Have I not a right to do what I choose'[117] with my own? The robber has the will to do just deeds, but death prevents him; I wait not for the work only, but faith too I have accepted. I have come who feed my sheep 'among the lilies'; I have come to feed them in the gardens. I have found a sheep that was lost; I take it upon my shoulders. For he believes, since he has asked: 'I have gone astray like a lost sheep';[118] 'Lord, remember me when thou comest into thy kingdom.' "[119]

(32) In the Canticles I sang of this garden of old to my spouse, and I said this to her: "I am come to my garden, my sister, my bride."[120] ("Now in the place where he was crucified there was a garden.")[121] And what do You take from

114 Gen. 2.17.
115 Luke 23.43.
116 Rom. 5.20. It is difficult to understand just how the good thief anticipated the patriarchs and others awaiting the redemption, in entering into paradise.
117 Matt. 20.13, 15.
118 Ps. 118.176.
119 Luke 23.42.
120 Cant. 5.1.
121 John 19.41.

there? "I have gathered my myrrh";[122] for He drank wine mingled with myrrh, and vinegar; and having taken these, He said: "It is consummated."[123] The mystery has been accomplished; Scripture has been fulfilled; sins are forgiven. For "when Christ appeared as high priest of the good things to come, he entered once for all through the greater and more perfect tabernacle, not made by hands (that is, not of this creation), nor again by virtue of blood of goats and calves, but by virtue of his own blood; into the Holies, having obtained eternal redemption. For if the blood of goats and bulls, and the sprinkled ashes of a heifer sanctify the unclean unto the cleansing of the flesh, how much more will the blood of Christ?"[124] Again: "Since, then, brethren, we have confidence to enter the Holies in virtue of the blood of Christ, a new and living way which he inaugurated for us through the veil (this is, his flesh)."[125] Because His flesh, His veil, was dishonored, the figurative veil of the temple was rent asunder, as it is written: "And behold the curtain of the temple was torn in two from top to bottom,"[126] for not a particle of it was left. Since the Master said: "Behold, your house is left to you desolate,"[127] the house itself was shattered.

(33) The Savior endured all this, "making peace through the blood of the cross, for all things whether in the heavens or on the earth."[128] For we were enemies of God through sin, and God had decreed the death of the sinner. One of two things, therefore, was necessary, either that God, in His truth, should destroy all men, or that in His loving-kindness, He should remit the sentence. But see the wisdom of God; He preserved the truth of His sentence and the exercise of His loving-kindness. Christ took our sins "in his body upon

122 Cant. 5.1.
123 John 19.30.
124 Heb. 9.10-14.
125 Heb. 10.19, 20.
126 Matt. 27.51.
127 Matt. 23.38.
128 Col. 1.20.

the tree; that we, having died to sin," by His death "might live to justice."[129] He who died for us was of no small worth; He was no material sheep; He was no mere man; He was more than an angel, He was God made man. The iniquity of sinners was not as great as the justice of Him who died for them; the sins we committed were not as great as the justice He wrought, who laid down His life for us; He laid it down when He willed, and took it up again when He willed. He did not lay down His life perforce, or yield up His spirit against His will, as you may learn from His words to His Father: "Father, into thy hands I commend my spirit."[130] I commend it, to take it up again. "And having said this, he expired,"[131] not for long, since He quickly rose again from the dead.

(34) The sun was darkened because of the Sun of Justice. The rocks were rent, because of "the spiritual rock."[132] Tombs were opened, and the dead arose, because of Him who was "free among the dead."[133] He "sent forth his prisoners out of the pit, wherein there is no water."[134] Do not be ashamed, then, of the Crucified, but say with confidence: "He beareth our sins and carrieth our sorrows, and by his bruises we are healed."[135] Let us not be ungrateful to our Benefactor. Again: "For the wickedness of my people was he led to death; and I shall give the ungodly for his burial, and the rich for his death."[136] And Paul says clearly: "that Christ died for our sins, according to the Scriptures, and that he was buried, and that he rose again the third day, according to the Scriptures."[137]

(35) But we seek to know expressly where He was buried.

129 1 Peter 2.24.
130 Luke 23.46.
131 *Ibid.*
132 I Cor. 10.4.
133 Ps. 87.6 (Douay).
134 Cf. Zach. 9.11.
135 Cf. Isa. 53.4, 5.
136 Cf. *ibid.* 8, 9.
137 1 Cor. 15.3, 4.

Was His tomb made with hands? Does it rise above the ground, like the tombs of kings? Was the sepulchre made of stones joined together? And what is laid upon it? Tell us exactly, O prophets, about his tomb also, where it lies, and where we shall look for it. But they answer: "Look upon the solid rock which you have hewn";[138] look and see. You have in the Gospels: "In a rock-hewn tomb."[139] What next? What kind of door has the sepulchre? Again the prophet says: "They have ended my life in the pit, and they have laid a stone over me."[140] I, who am "the chief corner stone, chosen, precious,"[141] lie for a while within a stone, I, who am "a stone of stumbling"[142] to the Jews, but of salvation to them that believe. The Tree of Life, then, was planted in the earth, to bring blessing for the earth, which had been cursed, and to bring release for the dead.

(36) Let us not be ashamed to confess the Crucified. Let the Cross, as our seal, be boldly made with our fingers upon our brow, and on all occasions; over the bread we eat, over the cups we drink; in our comings and in our goings; before sleep; on lying down and rising up; when we are on the way and when we are still. It is a powerful safeguard; it is without price, for the sake of the poor; without toil, because of the sick; for it is a grace from God, a badge of the faithful, and a terror to devils; for "he displayed them openly, leading them away in triumph by force of it."[143] For when they see the Cross, they are reminded of the Crucified; they fear Him who has "smashed the heads of the dragons."[144] Despise not the seal as a free gift, but rather for this reason honor your Benefactor all the more.

(37) If ever you fall into disputation, and arguments fail

---

138 Isa. 51.1 (Sept.).
139 Luke 32.53.
140 Lam. 3.53 (Sept.).
141 1 Peter 2.6; Isa. 28.16.
142 1 Peter 2.8.
143 Col. 2.15.
144 Ps. 73.13.

you, let your faith still remain unshaken. Rather become well informed and silence the Jews from the prophets and the Greeks from their own fables. The Greeks worship men struck by thunderbolts, but the bolt from heaven does not come at random. If they are not ashamed to worship men struck by lightning and abhorred by God, will you be ashamed to worship the beloved Son of God, who was crucified for you? I am ashamed to speak of their so-called gods, and I omit mention of them to save time, but let them that know speak out. Let the mouths of all heretics be stopped. If any man should say that the Cross is only an illusion, turn away from him. Abhor those who say that Christ was crucified in fancy only. For if He was crucified in fancy only, salvation is a fancy also, since our salvation comes from the Cross. If the Cross is a fancy, the Resurrection is a fancy also; and "if Christ has not risen we are still in our sins."[145] If the Cross is a fancy, the Ascension also is a fancy; and if the Ascension is a fancy, then the second coming is likewise an illusion, and everything, finally, is unsubstantial.

(38) First, therefore, take as an indestructible foundation the Cross, and build upon it the rest of your faith. Do not deny the Crucified, for if you deny Him you have many to confute you. First Judas the traitor will confute you; for he who betrayed Him knew that He was condemned to death by the chief priests and the ancients. The thirty pieces of silver bear witness; Gethsemane bears witness, where the betrayal took place; not yet do I speak of the Mount of Olives, where they who were with Him that night were praying. The moon in the night bears witness; the day bears witness, and the failing sun, for it endured not to look upon the crime of the conspirators. The fire, where Peter stood and warmed himself, confounds you; if you deny the Cross, the eternal fire awaits you; I speak of harsh consequences that you may not experience them. Remember the swords

145 Cf. 1 Cor. 15.17.

that came against Him in Gethsemane, that you may not feel the eternal sword. The house of Caiphas will convince you, which by its present desolation manifests the power of Him who once was judged in it.[146] Caiphas himself will rise up against you in the day of judgment; the servant too who gave Jesus the blow will rise up, and those who bound Him, and those who led Him away. Herod and Pilate will rise up against you, all but saying: "Why do you deny Him who was maligned before us by the Jews, and who we knew well had done no wrong? For I, Pilate, then washed my hands." The false witnesses will rise up against you, and the soldiers who put the purple cloak upon Him, set the crown of thorns on His head, crucified Him on Golgotha, and cast lots for His tunic. Simon of Cyrene, who carried the Cross after Jesus, will confound you.

(39) Of the heavenly bodies the sun in eclipse will convict you; of the products of the earth the wine mingled with myrrh; of grass plants the reed; of herbs, the hyssop, of the products of the sea, the sponge; of trees, the wood of the Cross. Add the soldiers too, as I have said, who nailed Him to the Cross and cast lots for His vesture; the soldier who opened His side with a spear; the women who were then present; the veil of the temple then rent asunder; the pretorium of Pilate, now desolate by the power of Him who was then crucified; this holy Golgotha rising on high and visible to this day, displaying even now how the rocks, because of Christ, were then rent; the sepulchre nearby, where He was laid; and the stone placed upon the door, which to this day lies next to the sepulchre; the angels who were then present; the women who worshipped Him after His resurrection; Peter and John, who ran to the sepulchre; and Thomas, who put his hand into His side, and his fingers

146 Apparently the site of the house of Caiphas and that of the pretorium of Pilate (mentioned in chapter 39) were well known, though these buildings had been utterly destroyed. The pretorium is one of the best authenticated sites today.

into the print of the nails. For it was for our sake that he touched them so carefully; for what you, who were not present, would have sought, he who was present did seek by God's dispensation.

(40) You have twelve Apostles witnesses of the Cross, and the whole earth, and the world of men who believe in Him who was crucified. Let your very presence here now persuade you of the power of the Crucified. For who brought you to this assembly? What soldiers? With what bonds were you constrained? What sentence drove you here now? No, it was the saving emblem of Jesus, the Cross, that has brought you all together. This reduced the Persians to bondage, and civilized the Scythians; this gave to the Egyptians, in place of cats and dogs and their manifold errors, the knowledge of God. To this day the Cross heals diseases, puts devils to flight, and overcomes the deceptions of philters and incantations.

(41) The Cross will appear again with Jesus from heaven;[147] for His emblem will precede the King; and the Jews, seeing Him whom they pierced, and recognizing by the Cross Him whom they dishonored, will repent and mourn (and they shall mourn tribe by tribe, for they shall repent then, when there shall be no time for repentance); and we shall glory, taking pride in the Cross, worshipping the Lord who was sent, and was crucified for us, worshipping also God the Father who sent Him, with the Holy Spirit; to whom be glory forever and ever. Amen.

147 In *Catechesis* 15.22 Cyril speaks of a luminous cross preceding the second coming of Christ, and the development of thought is similar in both sections.

CATECHESIS XIV

On the Resurrection of Christ, His Ascension into Heaven and His Sitting at the Right Hand of the Father

"Now I recall to your minds, brethren, the gospel that I preached to you, . . . that he rose the third day, according to the Scriptures."[1]

(1) "Rejoice, O Jerusalem, and hold festival together, all you who love" Jesus, for He is risen; "rejoice all you who mourned before,"[2] on hearing of the rash, wicked deeds of the Jews. For He whom they treated here with insult is risen again; and as the discourse on the Cross brought sorrow, so let the tidings of the Resurrection bring joy to all present. Let mourning be turned into gladness and lamentation into joy; and let our mouth be filled with joy and gladness because of Him who after His Resurrection cried: "Rejoice."[3] I realize the sorrow of Christ's friends during the past days; our discourse ended with the death and burial without telling the glad news of the Resurrection, and so your mind was in suspense to hear what it desired to hear. Therefore the Dead is risen, He who was "free among the dead,"[4] and deliverer of the dead. He patiently endured the shame of the crown of thorns; He has risen to crown Himself with the diadem of victory over death.

1 1 Cor. 15.1-4.

2 Cf. Isa. 66.10.

3 Matt. 28.9. The original Greek word is a greeting, and it is generally translated 'Hail,' or 'All hail,' but Cyril's context seems to require the translation 'Rejoice.'

4 Ps. 87.6 (Douay).

(2) Just as we advanced the testimonies concerning His Cross, so let us now verify the proofs of His Resurrection; the Apostle, whose text is before us, says: "He was buried, and He rose again the third day, according to the Scriptures."[5] An Apostle has sent us back to the testimony of the Scriptures; from the same source we will do well to discover the hope of our salvation. First we must learn if the Sacred Scriptures tell us the exact time of the Resurrection, that is, whether it comes in summer, or in autumn, or after winter; from what sort of place the Savior rose; what the place of the Resurrection is called in the admirable prophets; whether the women who sought and did not find Him afterwards rejoiced in finding Him; thus when the Gospels are read, their holy narratives will not be considered fables or fantasies.

(3) In my last discourse you heard an account of our Savior's burial; in the words of Isaia, "His burial shall be in peace"[6] (for in His burial He made peace between heaven and earth, bringing sinners to God); and "the just man is taken away before the face of evil,"[7] and "His burial shall be in peace," and "I will give the ungodly for his burial."[8] There is also the prophecy of Jacob in the Scriptures: "He lay down and couched as a lion, and as a lion's whelp; who will disturb him?"[9] Similarly in Numbers: "Lying down he has slept as a lion, and as a lion's whelp."[10] You have often heard also the words of the Psalm: "To the dust of death you have brought me down."[11] We indicated the place, when we quoted the words: "Look unto the rock which you have hewn."[12] It

5 1 Cor. 15.4.
6 Isa. 57.2 (Sept.). The citation from Isaia does not occur in *Cat.* 13. There may have been a slip of memory, or the reference may be to the homily of the preceding day (cf. below, Ch. 24).
7 *Ibid.* 1 (Sept.).
8 Isa. 53.9 (Sept.).
9 Gen. 49.9.
10 Num. 24.9.
11 Ps. 21.16.
12 Isa. 51.1 (Sept.).

remains for us to add the testimonies concerning the Resurrection itself.

(4) First of all He says in the eleventh Psalm: "Because they rob the afflicted and the needy sigh, now will I arise, says the Lord."[13] For some this testimony remains doubtful, since He rises often in anger to exact vengeance of His enemies. Therefore consider the fifteenth Psalm, which says plainly: "Keep me, O God, for in you I take refuge,"[14] and "Blood libations to them I will not pour out, nor will I take their names upon my lips,"[15] since they renounced Me, and acknowledged Caesar as their King; and in the words which follow: "I set the Lord ever before me; with him at my right hand I shall not be disturbed";[16] and: "Even in the night my heart exhorts me";[17] afterwards He says clearly: "Because you will not abandon my soul to the nether world, nor will you suffer your faithful one to undergo corruption."[18] He did not say: "nor will you suffer your faithful one to undergo death"; otherwise, He would not have died; but "corruption," He says, "I see not, and in death I shall not abide." "You will show me the path to life."[19] You see life after death is clearly proclaimed. Take the twenty-ninth Psalm: "I will extol you, O Lord, for you drew me clear and did not let my enemies rejoice over me."[20] What came to pass? Were you freed from your enemies, or released when about to be smitten? He Himself says clearly: "O Lord, you brought me up from the nether world."[21] In the text above He says prophetically, "You will not abandon," but here He speaks of what was to be as though it had already happened: "You brought me up," "You have preserved me from among those

13 Ps. 11.6.
14 Ps. 15.1.
15 *Ibid.* 4.
16 *Ibid.* 8.
17 *Ibid.* 7.
18 *Ibid.* 10.
19 *Ibid.* 11.
20 Ps. 29.2.
21 *Ibid.* 4.

going down into the pit."[22] When shall this take place? "At nightfall, weeping enters in, and with the dawn, rejoicing";[23] for in the evening there was the grief of the disciples, and in the morning the joy of the Resurrection.

(5) You wish to know the place? He says in the Canticles: "I came down to the nut garden";[24] for it was a garden where He was crucified. Though now richly adorned with kingly gifts, it was formerly a garden, and tokens and traces of this still remain. "An enclosed garden, a fountain sealed,"[25] that is, by the Jews, who said: "We have remembered how that deceiver said, while he was yet alive, 'After three days I will rise again.' Give orders, therefore, that the sepulchre be guarded"; and then: "So they went and made the sepulchre secure, sealing the stone, and setting the guard."[26] Clearly directed against the Jews are the words: "And in rest will you judge them."[27] Now who is the "fountain sealed," or who is signified by the "wellspring of living water"?[28] It is the Savior Himself, of whom it is written: "For with you is the fountain of life."[29]

(6) What does Sophonia say to the disciples in the person of Christ? "Prepare yourself, rise up at dawn; all their gleaning is destroyed";[30] He means the gleaning of the Jews, for whom remains neither a cluster nor a gleaning of salvation; for their vine is cut down. See how he says to the disciples, "Prepare yourself, rise up at dawn"; at dawn expect the Resurrection. Afterwards, in the same context of Scripture he says: "Wherefore expect me, says the Lord, in the day of my resurrection at the martyry."[31]

---

22 *Ibid.* 4.
23 *Ibid.* 6.
24 Cant. 6.11.
25 Cant. 4.12.
26 Matt. 27.63-66.
27 Job 7.18 (Sept.).
28 Cant. 4.15.
29 Ps. 35.10.
30 Soph. 3.7 (Sept.).
31 *Ibid.* 8 (Sept.). Churches built over the tombs of the martyrs were

You see that the prophet foresaw that the place of the Resurrection was to be called "the martyry." Now for what reason is this place of Golgotha and of the Resurrection called, not a church like the rest of the churches, but a martyry? It was perhaps because of the prophet who said: "in the day of my resurrection at the martyry."

(7) Who is this and what is the sign of his resurrection? It is clearly told, in the very next verse of the prophet: "For then I will change a tongue for peoples"—since after the Resurrection, with the sending of the Holy Spirit, the gift of tongues was granted—"that they may serve the Lord with one accord."[32] What other sign is added in the same prophet that they would "serve the Lord with one accord"? "From beyond the rivers of Ethiopia they shall bring me offerings."[33] Recall the story in the Acts of the Ethiopian eunuch, who came "from beyond the rivers of Ethiopia."[34] Therefore the Scriptures tell the time, the peculiar features of the place, and the signs following the Resurrection; henceforth have a firm belief in the Resurrection and let no one cause you to waver in confessing Christ risen from the dead.

(8) Accept an additional testimony from the eighty-seventh Psalm, where Christ speaks in the prophets—for He who then spoke afterwards came among us—: "O Lord, the God of my salvation: I have cried in the day, and in the night before thee";[35] and subsequently: "I am become as a man without help, free among the dead."[36] He did not say, "I am become a man without help," but "as a man without help"; for He was crucified, not because of helplessness, but because He willed it; His death was not a result of invol-

called martyries. 'Martyry' would be an appropriate title for the church built over the tomb of the Chief of martyrs. There is some evidence that it was called the Great Martyry or the Martyry of the Savior.

32 *Ibid.* 9 (Sept.).

33 *Ibid.* 10 (Sept.).

34 Acts 8.27.

35 Ps. 87.2 (Douay).

36 *Ibid.* 5, 6 (Douay).

untary weakness. "I am numbered with those who go down into the pit."[37] What is the sign? "You have taken my friends away from me"[38] (for the disciples fled away). "Will you work wonders for the dead"?[39] Then: "But I, O Lord, cry out to you; with my morning prayer I wait upon you."[40] See how these verses manifest the actual circumstances of the Passion and the Resurrection.

(9) From what place did the Savior rise? He says in the Canticle of Canticles: "Arise, come, my neighbor";[41] and in a later verse: "in a cleft of the rock."[42] For He calls a cleft of the rock the hollow place originally in front of the sepulchre; this had been hewn of the rock itself, a practice customary in front of sepulchres. It is not visible now, it is true, because the outer hollowed-out rock was hewn away to make room for the present adornment. Before royal magnificence embellished the monument, there was a hollow place before the tomb. Now where is the rock with its hollow? Is it situated in the middle of the city or by the walls and the outskirts? Is it inside the ancient walls or inside the outer walls afterwards constructed? It says in the Canticles: "In a cleft of the rock, near the outer walls."[43]

(10) At what season does the Savior rise? Is it in summer or at another time? In the same Canticles, just before the words quoted above, He says: "The winter is past, the rains are over and gone. The flowers appear on the earth, the time of pruning has come."[44] Is not the land now full of flowers, and are not the vines being pruned? You see how He said also that the winter was past. For in this month Xanthicus spring is already come. This is the time, the first month among

37 *Ibid.* 5.
38 *Ibid.* 9.
39 *Ibid.* 11.
40 *Ibid.* 14.
41 Cant. 2.10 (Sept.).
42 *Ibid.* 14. It would seem that the complete tomb consisted of two chambers both hollowed out of the natural rock.
43 *Ibid.* 14 (Sept.).
44 *Ibid.* 11, 12.

the Hebrews, in which is celebrated the feast of the Pasch, formerly the figurative Pasch, but now the true. This is the season of the creation of the world; for God then said: "Let the earth bring forth vegetation, yielding seed according to its kind and according to its likeness."[45] Now, as you see, every herb is in seed. At that time God made the sun and the moon and gave them courses of equal day and night; just a few days ago we had the equinox. Then God said: "Let us make man in our image and likeness";[46] he received the image, but he obscured the likeness by his disobedience. Man's loss of grace and his restoration took place in the same season. At the season created man, by his disobedience, was cast out of Paradise, then, he who believed, by his obedience, was brought in. Salvation came about in the same season as the Fall, when "the flowers appeared," "and the time of pruning was come."[47]

(11) The place of His burial was a garden, and a vine was planted there; He has said: "I am the vine."[48] He was planted in the earth, to root out the curse that came from Adam. The earth was doomed to thorns and thistles; from the earth sprang the true Vine, to fulfill the words: "Truth shall spring out of the earth, and justice shall look down from heaven."[49] What is He going to say who was buried in the garden? "I gather my myrrh, and my spices";[50] and again: "Myrrh and aloes with all the finest spices."[51] These were the tokens of His burial, and in the Gospels it is said: "The women came to the tomb, taking the spices they had prepared";[52] "and there also came Nicodemus, bringing a mixture of myrrh

---

45 Gen. 1.11 (Sept.).

46 Gen. 1.26. Image and likeness generally connote the same thing. Cyril makes a distinction between them as though image meant nature, and likeness virtue, or something similar.

47 Cf. Cant. 2.12.

48 John 15.5.

49 Ps. 84.12.

50 Cant. 5.1.

51 *Ibid.* 4.14.

52 Luke 24.1.

and aloes."[53] And next, it is written: "I have eaten my bread with my honey":[54] the bitter before the Passion, and the sweet after the Resurrection. After He was risen He entered through the closed doors; the Apostles did not believe, for "they thought they saw a spirit."[55] But He said: "Feel me, and see";[56] put your fingers into the print of the nails, as Thomas demanded. "But as they still disbelieved and marvelled for joy, He said: 'Have you anything here to eat?' And they offered Him a piece of broiled fish and honeycomb."[57] Do you see the fulfillment of the text: "I have eaten my bread with my honey."?

(12) Before He entered through the closed doors He was sought by those noble and courageous women; He was sought, the Bridegroom and Suitor of souls. These blessed women came to the sepulchre and sought Him who was risen; and tears were still flowing from their eyes, though it was more fitting for them to dance with joy for Him who had risen. Mary came seeking Him, according to the Gospel, but she did not find Him; afterwards she heard from the angels and finally saw Christ. Does Scripture testify to this? It says in the Canticle of Canticles: "On my bed I sought him whom my heart loves." At what time? "On my bed *at night* I sought him whom my heart loves."[58] Mary came, it says, "while it was still dark."[59] "On my bed I sought him—sought him but I did not find him."[60] In the Gospel Mary says: "They have taken away my Lord, and I do not know where they have laid him."[61] The angels present dispelled her ignorance, for they said: "Why do you seek the living one among the dead?"[62]

53 John 19.39.
54 Cant. 5.1 (Sept.).
55 Luke 24.37.
56 *Ibid.* 39.
57 Luke 24.41, 42.
58 Cant. 3.1.
59 John 20.1.
60 Cant. 3.1.
61 John 20.13.
62 Luke 24.5.

Not only did He rise but the dead accompanied Him in His resurrection. Mary did not know it; in her person the Canticle of Canticles says to the angels: "Have you seen him whom my heart loves? I had hardly left them (that is, the two angels), when I found him whom my heart loves. I took hold of him and would not let him go."[63]

(13) After the vision of the angels Jesus came, announcing Himself, and the Gospel says: "And behold Jesus met them, saying, 'Hail!' And they came up and embraced his feet."[64] They took hold of Him and the text was fulfilled: "I will hold him, and will not let him go."[65] Though weak in body the women were courageous in spirit. "Many waters cannot quench charity, neither can floods drown it."[66] He whom they sought was dead, but their hope of the Resurrection was not quenched. The angel said to them again: "Do not be afraid";[67] I say, not to the soldiers, "Do not be afraid," but to you; let them fear, and being taught by experience, let them bear witness and say: "Truly he was the Son of God";[68] but you must not be afraid, for "perfect love casts out fear";[69] going forth, "tell his disciples that he has risen."[70] They departed with joy, yet full of fear. Is this in Scripture? Yes, the second Psalm, prophetic of the Passion of Christ, says: "Serve the Lord with fear, and rejoice before him with trembling";[71] rejoice, to be sure, for the Lord who has risen, but with trembling, because of the earthquake, and the angel who appeared like lightning.

(14) The chief priests and the Pharisees, through the agency of Pilate, sealed the tomb; but the women saw Him who was risen. Now Isaia, who knew the impotency of the chief priests and the women's firmness of faith, says: "You women, who

63 Cant. 3.3, 4.
64 Matt. 28.9.
65 Cf. Cant. 3.4.
66 Cant. 8.7.
67 Matt. 28.5.
68 Matt. 27.54.
69 1 John 4.18.
70 Matt. 28.7.
71 Ps. 2.11.

come from the vision, approach: for the people has no understanding."[72] The chief priests lack understanding, but the women behold with their own eyes. When the soldiers came into the city and told the chief priests what had happened, they said to the soldiers: "Say, his disciples came by night and stole him while we were sleeping."[73] Well did Isaia foretell this also, in their persons: "But tell us, and relate another deceit."[74] Christ has risen and come back from the dead, and by a bribe they persuade the soldiers; but they do not persuade the kings of our day. The soldiers then betrayed the truth for silver; the emperors of our times have built this holy Church of the Resurrection of God our Savior, inlaid with silver and wrought with gold, where we are assembled, and they have beautified it with treasures of silver and gold and precious stones. "And if the procurator hears of this, we will persuade him."[75] Though you persuade the soldiers, you will not persuade the world. Why were the guards who watched Jesus not condemned, as the guards of Peter, when he escaped from prison? Peter's guards had no defense in their ignorance, and were sentenced by Herod; the guards of Jesus, though they knew the truth and concealed it for money, were protected by the chief priests. A few of the Jews of that time were persuaded, but the world hearkened to the truth. Those who concealed the truth were buried in oblivion, but those who received it were made manifest by the power of the Savior, who rose from the dead and raised the dead with Himself. In the person of the risen dead the prophet Osee says plainly: "He will revive us after two days; on the third day he will raise us up, to live in his presence."[76]

(15) The Sacred Scriptures do not convince the unheeding

72 Isa. 27.11 (Sept.).
73 Matt. 28.13.
74 Isa. 30.10 (Sept.).
75 Matt. 28.14. The phrase "the emperors of our times" at the opening of the sentence certainly refers to Constantine, but the plural may include his sons or indirectly his mother, Helena.
76 Osee 6.2 (Sept.).

Jews, who disregard all that is written, and impugn the Resurrection of Jesus; it is best to meet them thus: Why do you assert that Eliseus and Elia raised the dead, but deny the Resurrection of our Savior? Is it because we have no living witnesses of what we assert? Well, produce witnesses of those earlier events. But that was written about? So is this. Why do you accept one and reject the other? Hebrews wrote the earlier history; the Apostles also were all Hebrews. Why, therefore, do you disbelieve Jews? Matthew, who wrote the Gospel, wrote it in the Hebrew tongue; and Paul the preacher was a Hebrew of the Hebrews; and the twelve Apostles were of Hebrew stock; besides, fifteen Bishops of Jerusalem in succession were appointed from the Hebrews. Why do you accept your own accounts but reject ours, though these too were written by Hebrews among you?

(16) But it is impossible, someone will say, for the dead to rise. Eliseus twice raised the dead, both when he was alive, and after his death. We believe that when a dead man had been cast upon the corpse of Eliseus he rose again on contact; but Christ has not risen from the dead? When the dead man touched Eliseus he rose again, though Eliseus who raised him remained dead as before; but in this case the Dead of whom we treat rose, and many dead who did not even touch Him rose. For "many bodies of the saints who had fallen asleep arose; and coming forth out of the tombs after his resurrection, they came into the holy city" (manifestly the city we are in), "and appeared to many."[77] Eliseus indeed raised a dead man, but he did not conquer the world; Elia raised the dead, but demons are not driven out in the name of Elia. We do not speak ill of these prophets, but we praise their Master more. We do not belittle their marvels to magnify our own, for their miracles are ours also; but from their deeds we win credit for our own.

77 Matt. 27.52, 53. Cyril's interpretation is the common one, but some of the Fathers think that the saints who rose were assumed into the celestial Jerusalem, heaven.

(17) They further object: A dead man recently deceased was raised by the living; but show us that it is possible for a man dead and buried for three days to rise again. The testimony we seek is supplied by the Lord Jesus Himself in the Gospels, when He says: "For even as Jona was in the belly of the fish three days and three nights, so will the Son of Man be three days and three nights in the heart of the earth."[78] Now when we study the story of Jona the force of the resemblance becomes striking. Jesus was sent to preach repentance; so was Jona. Though Jona fled, not knowing what was to come, Jesus came willingly, to grant repentance for salvation. Jona slumbered in the ship and was fast asleep amid the stormy sea; while Jesus by God's will was sleeping, the sea was stirred up, for the purpose of manifesting thereafter the power of Him who slept. They said to Jona: "What are you doing asleep? Rise up, call upon your God! that God may save us";[79] but the Apostles say: "Lord, save us!"[80] In the first instance they said: Call upon your God, and in the second, Save us. In the first Jona said to them: "Pick me up and throw me into the sea, that it may quiet down for you";[81] in the other Christ Himself "rebuked the wind and the sea, and there came a great calm."[82] Jona was cast into the belly of a great fish, but Christ of His own will descended to the abode of the invisible fish of death. He went down of His own will to make death disgorge those it had swallowed up, according to the Scripture: "I shall deliver them from the power of the nether world, and I shall redeem them from death."[83]

(18) Here let us pose the question: Is it more difficult for a man dead and buried to rise again from the earth, or for a man in the belly of a fish, where he has come into contact

78 Matt. 12.40.
79 Jona 1.6 (Sept.).
80 Matt. 8.25.
81 Jona 1.12.
82 Matt. 8.26.
83 Cf. Osee 13.14.

with the extreme heat of a living creature, to suffer no corruption? Everyone knows that the heat of the belly is so intense that even bones that have been swallowed are decomposed. How was it possible for Jona to be three days and three nights in the belly of the fish without suffering corruption? How could Jona live for three days without breathing our air, since according to man's nature we cannot live without breathing it? The Jews answer: "The power of God went down with Jona when he was tossed about in the depths." But if the Lord granted His servant life by sending His power with him, can he not grant it to Himself? If one is credible, the other is credible; if one is incredible, the other also is incredible; to me both are equally credible. I believe also that Christ rose from the dead. I have many testimonies of this, from the Sacred Scriptures, and from the power of the risen Christ working to this day. He descended alone into the nether world, but ascended therefrom with a numerous company; for He went down to death, "and many of the bodies of the saints who had fallen asleep arose"[84] by His power.

(19) Death was panic-stricken on seeing a new visitant descending into the nether world, One not subject to the bonds of the place. Why, O you porters of hell, were you terrified on seeing Him? What unaccustomed fear seized upon you? Death fled away and his flight convicted him of cowardice. The holy prophets ran forward, and Moses the Lawgiver, and Abraham, Isaac, and Jacob; David also and Samuel; Isaia and John the Baptist, who bore witness to Him when he said: "Art thou he who is to come, or shall we look for another?"[85] All the Just, whom death had swallowed up, were ransomed; for it was fitting that the King who had been heralded should be the Redeemer of His noble heralds. Then each of the Just said: " 'O death, where is thy victory? O death, where is thy sting?'[86] For the Conqueror has ransomed us."

84 Matt. 27.52.
85 Matt. 11.3.
86 1 Cor. 15.55.

(20) Jona fulfilled a type of our Savior when he prayed from the belly of the fish and said: "I cried for help from the midst of the nether world."[87] He was in fact in the fish, yet he says that he is in the nether world. In a later verse he manifestly prophesies in the person of Christ: "My head went down into the chasms of the mountains."[88] Yet he was still in the belly of the fish. What mountains encompass you? But I know, he says, that I am a type of Him who is to be laid in the sepulchre hewn out of the rock. While he was in the sea Jona says: "I went down into the earth";[89] for he typified Christ, who went down into the heart of the earth. Foreseeing also the deceit of the Jews, who persuaded the soldiers to lie by saying to them, "Say," that they "stole him away,"[90] Jona says: "They that observe lying vanities have forsaken their own mercy."[91] For He who showed them mercy came, was crucified and rose again, when He had shed His precious blood for the Jews and the Gentiles. But they say: "Say," that they "stole him away," "observing lying vanities." Concerning His Resurrection Isaia says: "He who brought from the earth the great shepherd of the sheep."[92] He has added the word 'great,' lest He be esteemed merely equal in honor with the shepherds before Him.

(21) Therefore, since we have the prophecies, let our faith be firm. Let them fall, who fall from disbelief, for they will it so; but you have taken your stand upon the rock of faith in the Resurrection. Even to this day the Manichaeans say that the Resurrection of the Savior was imaginary and not real, paying no heed to Paul, who writes: "Who was born according to the flesh of the offspring of David'; and afterwards: "by resurrection from the dead, Jesus Christ our

87 Jona 2.3.
88 *Ibid.* 2.6, 7 (Sept.).
89 *Ibid.* 2.7 (Sept.).
90 Cf. Matt. 12.40.
91 Cf. Jona 2.9.
92 Isa. 63.11 (Sept.).

Lord."[93] Again his words are directed against them when he says: "Do not say in thy heart: Who shall ascend into heaven? or, Who shall descend into the abyss? that is, to bring up Christ from the dead."[94] In like manner, by way of confirmation he has written elsewhere: "Remember that Jesus Christ rose from the dead";[95] and again: "and if Christ has not risen, vain then is our preaching, vain too is your faith. Yes, and we are found false witnesses as to God, in that we have borne witness against God that he raised Christ whom he did not raise."[96] Subsequently he says: "But as it is, Christ has risen from the dead, the firstfruits of those who have fallen asleep."[97] "And he appeared to Cephas; and after that to the twelve"[98] (for if you disbelieve one witness, you have twelve witnesses); "then he was seen by more than five hundred brethren at once"[99] (if they disbelieve the twelve, let them heed the five hundred); "after that, he was seen by James,"[100] His own brother, and first bishop of this diocese. Since so famous a bishop was privileged to see the risen Christ, as his disciple, do not disbelieve. But you may say that His brother is a biased witness; thereafter "he was seen by me,"[101] Paul, His enemy; can testimony be doubted when it is proclaimed by an enemy? "I formerly was a persecutor,"[102] but now preach the glad tidings of the Resurrection.

(22) There are many witnesses of our Savior's Resurrection: the night, and the light of the full moon (for that night was the sixteenth); the rock of the sepulchre which received Him; the stone also shall set itself against the face of the Jews, for

---

93 Rom. 1.3, 4.
94 Rom. 10.6, 7.
95 2 Tim. 2.8.
96 1 Cor. 15.14, 15.
97 *Ibid.* 20.
98 *Ibid.* 5.
99 *Ibid.* 6.
100 *Ibid.* 7. Here and in *Cat.* 4.28 Cyril seems to single out James from the rest of the Apostles, perhaps because of his episcopal dignity.
101 *Ibid.* 8.
102 1 Tim. 1.13.

it saw the Lord; even the stone which was rolled back, lying there to the present day, testifies to the Resurrection. The Angels of God who were present bore witness to the Resurrection of the Only-begotten; Peter and John, and Thomas, and the rest of the Apostles; some of them ran to the sepulchre, and saw the linen and the burial cloths, in which He had been wrapped, lying there after the Resurrection; and others touched His hands and feet and beheld the prints of the nails; and all of them were breathed upon by the Savior, and were deemed worthy of the power of forgiving sins in virtue of the Holy Spirit. Witnesses too were the women, who took hold of His feet, who beheld the mighty earthquake and the shining angel standing by; the linen cloths also, which enveloped Him and which He left behind when He rose; the soldiers and the money they received; the spot itself, still to be seen; and this holy Church, which from his deep love of Christ was built by the Emperor Constantine of happy memory, and embellished as you see.

(23) Another witness to the Resurrection of Jesus is Tabitha, who in His name was raised from the dead. For how can one disbelieve in the risen Christ, when even His name has raised the dead? The sea too is a witness to the Resurrection of Jesus, as you have already heard. The draught of fish also bears witness, and the hot coals laid there, and the fish thereon. Peter is also a witness, who before had denied Him thrice, but afterwards confessed Him thrice, and was charged to feed His spiritual sheep. Yonder stands even to this day Mount Olivet, all but showing even now to the eyes of the faithful Him who ascended, and the heavenly gate of the Ascension. For He descended from heaven to Bethlehem, but from Mount Olivet He ascended to heaven;[103] He began in Bethlehem His struggles for men, but on Olivet He was crowned for them. You have many witnesses, therefore; you

---

103 According to the Gospel of St. Luke (24.50, 51) the Ascension took place at Bethany, but Cyril is following an accepted tradition that it occurred on the top of Mount Olivet (Acts 1.12).

have this place of the Resurrection itself; you have to the east the place of His Ascension. You have as witnesses the angels also, who bore testimony at His Resurrection, and the cloud on which He ascended, and the disciples who came down from the place of the Ascension.

(24) The sequence of the Creed would naturally lead me on to speak of the Ascension; but God's grace has so disposed it that you heard most fully about it, according to the measure of my weakness, yesterday, on the Lord's day; for the course of the lessons in church, by the ordination of divine grace, comprised the narrative of our Savior's Ascension into heaven. What was then said was spoken mainly for all and for the assembled faithful, but especially for you. The question is whether you paid attention to what was said. For you know that the sequence of the Creed teaches you to believe in Him "who rose on the third day, and ascended into heaven, and sits at the right hand of the Father." I take it for granted that you remember our exposition; still I shall remind you, in passing, of what was then said. Remember what is clearly written in the Psalms: "God mounts his throne amid shouts of joy";[104] remember that the divine Powers also said to one another: "Lift up your gates, you princes";[105] remember too the Psalm which says: "He has ascended on high, he has led captivity captive";[106] remember the prophet who said: "He that builds his ascension in heaven";[107] recall also the other points mentioned yesterday in connection with the objections of the Jews.

(25) When they deny the possibility of the Resurrection, recall what was said of the carrying away of Habacuc; for if Habacuc was transported by an angel, who lifted him up by the hair of his head, much more could the Lord of both prophets and angels, mounting a cloud from Mount Olivet, ascend into heaven by His own power. You may well recall

104 Ps. 46.6.
105 Cf. Ps. 23.7.
106 Cf. Ps. 67.19; Eph. 4.8.
107 Cf. Amos 9.6.

such wonders, yet reserve the supremacy for the Lord, the Worker of wonders, for while they were borne up, He "upholdeth all things."[108] Recall that Henoch was translated; but Jesus ascended. Recall yesterday's account of Elia, how he was taken up in a fiery chariot; but the chariot of Christ is "ten thousandfold thousands of them that rejoice."[109] Recall that Elia was taken up to the east of the Jordan, but Christ ascended to the east of the brook Cedron; that Elia ascended *as* into heaven, but Jesus, into heaven; that Elia promised that a double portion in the Holy Spirit would be given to his holy disciple; but Christ granted so full a share of the Holy Spirit to His disciples that besides having the Holy Spirit themselves, by the laying on of hands, they communicated the Spirit to those who believed.

(26) When you have wrestled with the Jews and have overcome them by parallel examples, then come to the surpassing glory of the Savior: His predecessors were the servants, but He was the Son of God. You will be reminded of His preeminence when you reflect that a servant of Christ was caught up to the third heaven. For if Elia reached the first heaven but Paul the third, the latter surely attained to a more honorable dignity. Be not ashamed of your Apostles; they are not inferior to Moses, or second to the prophets; but they are noble among the noble, and indeed, nobler still. For Elia, it is true, was taken up into heaven; but Peter has the keys to the kingdom of heaven, after hearing the words: "Whatever thou shalt loose on earth shall be loosed in heaven."[110] Elia was taken up to heaven only, but Paul into heaven and paradise (for it was but fitting that the disciples of Jesus should receive more manifold grace) and "heard secret words that man may not repeat."[111] But Paul came down again from heaven, not because he was unworthy to abide in the third heaven, but (after enjoying gifts beyond man's lot and

108 Heb. 1.3.

109 Cf. Ps. 67.18.

110 Matt. 16.19.

111 2 Cor. 12.4.

descending in honor) to receive the crown of martyrdom, when he had preached Christ and suffered for Him. I pass over the other points I treated yesterday in the Lord's day assembly, for to understanding hearers a mere reminder is sufficient for instruction.

(27) Recall also what I have often said regarding the sitting of the Son at the right hand of the Father, according to the sequence of the Creed: "and He ascended into heaven, and sits at the right hand of the Father." Let us not too curiously inquire into the precise nature of this sitting, for it surpasses our understanding. Let us not endure those who perversely assert that it was only after His Cross and Resurrection and Ascension into heaven that the Son began to sit at the right hand of the Father. For He did not gain His throne by way of advancement; but from the time He is—and He is eternally begotten—He sits with the Father. The prophet Isaia, having beheld this throne before the coming of the Savior in the flesh, says: "I saw the Lord seated on a high and lofty throne."[112] For the Father "no man has at any time seen,"[113] and He who then appeared to the prophet was the Son. The Psalmist also says: "Your throne stands firm from of old; from everlasting you are."[114] There are many testimonies on this point, but we will content ourselves with these only, because of the lateness of the hour.

(28) Now I must recall a few of my many remarks concerning the sitting of the Son at the right hand of the Father. The hundred and ninth Psalm says clearly: "The Lord said to my Lord: Sit at my right hand, till I make your enemies your footstool."[115] Our Savior, confirming this text in the Gospels, says that David did not speak of his own will, but by the inspiration of the Holy Spirit: "How then does David in the Spirit call him Lord, saying: 'The Lord said to my

112 Isa. 6.1.
113 John 1.18.
114 Ps. 92.2.
115 Ps. 109.1, 2.

Lord, Sit at my right hand.' "[116] In the Acts of the Apostles, on Pentecost day, Peter, standing with the Eleven, and discoursing to the Israelites, cites in express words this testimony from the hundred and ninth Psalm.

(29) I must remind you of a few similar testimonies regarding the sitting of the Son at the right hand of the Father. There is the passage in Matthew: "Nevertheless I say to you, hereafter you shall see the Son of Man sitting at the right hand of God."[117] Writing in similar vein the Apostle Peter says: "Through the resurrection of Jesus Christ; who is at the right hand of God, having gone into heaven."[118] The Apostle Paul, writing to the Romans, says: "Christ who died, yes, and rose again, he who is at the right hand of God."[119] Writing to the Ephesians, he speaks thus: "Its measure is the working of his mighty power, which he wrought in Christ, in raising him from the dead, and setting him on his right hand."[120] The Colossians he taught thus: "Therefore, if you have risen with Christ, seek the things that are above, where Christ is seated at the right hand of God."[121] In the Epistle to the Hebrews he says: "Who has effected man's purgation from sin and taken his seat at the right hand of the Majesty on high."[122] And: "Now to which of the angels has he ever said, Sit at my right hand, until I make thy enemies the footstool of thy feet?"[123] Also: "But he, having offered one sacrifice for sins, has taken his seat forever at the right hand of God, waiting thenceforth until his enemies be made the footstool under his feet."[124] Again: "Looking towards the author and finisher of faith, Jesus, for the joy set before him, endured a cross, despising shame, and sits at the right hand of the throne of God."[125]

---

116 Matt. 22.43.
117 Matt. 26.64.
118 1 Peter 3.21, 22.
119 Rom. 8.34.
120 Eph. 1.19, 20.
121 Col. 3.1.
122 Heb. 1.3.
123 *Ibid.* 1.13.
124 Heb. 10.12, 13.
125 Heb. 12.2.

(30) Though there are other testimonies to the sitting of the Only-begotten at the right hand of God, let these suffice at the moment; let me repeat, however, my observation that it was not after His coming in the flesh that He obtained the dignity of this seat; for before all ages the Only-begotten Son of God, our Lord Jesus Christ, ever holds the throne at the right hand of the Father. May the God of all Himself, the Father of Christ, and our Lord Jesus Christ, who descended and ascended, and sits with the Father, guard your souls; may He preserve unshaken and unchangeable your hope in Him who rose again; and may He raise you up together with Him from your dead sins to His heavenly gift, and deem you worthy to "be caught up in clouds to meet the Lord in the air,"[126] in His good time; and until that time of His glorious second coming arrives, may He write all your names in the book of the living, and after writing them, never blot them out. For the names of many who fall away are blotted out.[127] May He grant to all of you to believe in Him who rose again, and to look for Him who ascended and is to come again; He will come, but not from the earth (be on your guard, then, because of the impostors who are to come); who sits on high, and is present here with us, observing the order and steadfastness of faith in each. Do not think that because He is absent in the flesh He is therefore absent in the spirit; He is here in the midst of us, listening to what is said of Him, seeing our thoughts, searching our hearts and souls; He is ready even now to present all of you, as you come forward for Baptism in the Holy Spirit, to the Father, and say: "Look at me and the children whom the Lord has given me";[128] to whom be glory forever. Amen.

126 1 Thess. 4.16.

127 Cyril probably has in mind the phrase "erased from the book of of the living" (Ps. 68.29), but the idea appears also in Apoc. 3.5, "blot his name out of the book of life."

128 Isa. 8.18.

CATECHESIS XV

On the Words: "And He Is to Come with Glory to Judge the Living and the Dead, of Whose Kingdom There Shall Be No End"

"As I watched, thrones were set up and the Ancient One took his throne. . . . As the visions during the night continued, I saw one like a son of man coming, on the clouds of heaven."[1]

(1) We preach not one coming of Christ, but a second as well, far more glorious than the first. The first gave us a spectacle of His patience; the second will bring with it the crown of the Kingdom of God. In general all things are twofold in our Lord Jesus Christ. His birth is twofold, one of God before the ages, and one of a virgin in the consummation of the ages. His descent is twofold, one lowly, "like the rain upon the fleece,"[2] and a second, His manifest coming, which is yet to be. In His first coming He was wrapped in swaddling clothes in the manger; in His second He will be "robed in light as with a cloak."[3] In His first coming He "endured a cross, despising shame";[4] in His second He will come in glory, attended by a host of angels. We do not rest, therefore, in His first coming, but we look also for His second. Just as we said of His first coming: "Blessed is he who comes in the name of the Lord,"[5] so we shall repeat the same at His second

1 Dan. 7.9, 13.
2 Cf. Ps. 71.6.
3 Ps. 103.2.
4 Heb. 12.2.
5 Matt. 21.9.

coming, saying with the angels in adoration, as we meet our Master: "Blessed is he who comes in the name of the Lord." The Savior will come this time, not to be judged, but to judge those who then judged Him. He who then was silent before His judges will remind those wicked men of their cruelty at the Cross, and say: "Such and such you did, and I was silent."[6] Then He came by divine condescension, seeking to win men by His teaching; but this time they will of necessity, whether they will or no, submit to Him as King.

(2) Of these two comings the Prophet Malachia says: "And suddenly there will come to the temple the Lord whom you seek";[7] that is one coming. Of the second coming he says: "And the messenger of the covenant whom you desire. Yes, he is coming, says the Lord of hosts. But who will endure the day of his coming? And who can stand when he appears? For he is like the refiner's fire, or like the fuller's lye. He will sit refining and purifying."[8] In what immediately follows the Savior Himself says: "I will draw near to you for judgment, and I will be swift to bear witness against the sorcerers, adulterers, and perjurers."[9] It was with this in view that Paul says in due warning: "But if anyone builds upon this foundation, gold, silver, precious stones, wood, hay, straw—the work of each will be made manifest, for the day of the Lord will declare it, since the day is to be revealed in fire."[10] Paul indicates these two comings also in writing to Titus in these words: "The grace of God our Savior has appeared to all men, instructing us, in order that, rejecting ungodliness and worldly lusts, we may live temperately and justly and piously in this world; looking for the blessed hope and glorious coming of our great God and Savior, Jesus Christ."[11] Do you see how he speaks of a first coming, for which he gives thanks,

6 Cf. Ps. 49.21.
7 Mal. 3.1.
8 *Ibid.* 1-3.
9 *Ibid.* 5.
10 1 Cor. 3.11, 12.
11 Titus 2.11-13.

and of a second we are to look for? We find the same lesson in the wording of the Creed we profess, as delivered to us, that is, to believe in Him who "ascended into heaven and sat down on the right of the Father, and is to come in glory to judge living and dead, of whose kingdom there will be no end."[12]

(3) Our Lord Jesus Christ, therefore, is to come from heaven, and to come with glory at the end of this world, on the last day. For an end of this world there will be; this created world will be made new again. Corruption, theft, adultery and sins of every kind have flooded the earth, and bloodshed has been paid with blood; so to prevent this wondrous dwelling place from continuing forever filled with iniquity, this world is to pass away, to make room for a fairer world. You want proof of this from Scripture? Hearken to Isaia: "The heavens shall be rolled up like a scroll, and all their hosts shall wither away as the leaf on the vine, or as the fig withers on the fig tree."[13] And the Gospel says: "The sun shall be darkened, and the moon will not give her light, and the stars will fall from heaven."[14] Let us not grieve as though we alone were to die, for the stars also will die; but perhaps they will rise again. The Lord shall fold up the heavens, not to destroy them, but to raise them up more beautiful. Listen to David the Prophet: "Of old you established the earth, and the heavens are the work of your hands. They shall perish but you remain."[15] But someone will say: "Behold, he says plainly that 'they shall perish.' " Ah, but hear in what sense he says, "they shall perish"; it is clear from what follows: "though all of them grow old like a garment. Like clothing you change them, and they are changed."[16] For just as man is said to perish, according to the text: "The

12 The Creed was given in *Cat.* 5.12, but evidently the part of the Creed being explained was repeated by Cyril and his hearers in turn.
13 Isa. 34.4.
14 Matt. 24.29.
15 Ps. 101.26, 27.
16 *Ibid.* 27, 28.

just perishes, and no one takes it to heart,"[17] and this is said, though the resurrection is expected, so we look for a "resurrection" of the heavens. "The sun will be turned to darkness, and the moon to blood."[18] Let the converts from the Manichaeans be instructed and no longer make these luminaries their gods, nor impiously think that this sun which is darkened is Christ. Listen to the Lord's words: "Heaven and earth will pass away, but my words will not pass away";[19] for the Master's creatures are less precious than His words.

(4) The things that are seen, therefore, will pass away, and there shall come the things to be looked for, a fairer world. "It is not for you," He says, "to know the times or dates which the Father has fixed by his own authority."[20] Essay not to declare when these things shall be, nor yet supinely slumber. For He says: "Watch, therefore, because at an hour you do not expect, the Son of Man will come."[21] But since looking for Christ we need to know the signs of the consummation, to save us from deception, destruction and delusion by the false Antichrist, the Apostle, divinely inspired, came by God's dispensation to the True Teacher and said: " 'Tell us, when are these things to come, and what will be the sign of thy coming and the end of the world?'[22] We look for You to come again; but 'Satan disguises himself as an angel of light.' "[23] Keep us, therefore, from worshipping another than You. He, opening His divine and blessed lips, says: "Take care that no one leads you astray."[24] You also, my hearers, seeing Him now with the eyes of the mind, listen to Him repeating the same words to you: "Take care that no one leads you astray." This saying counsels you to pay heed to our

17 Isa. 57.1.
18 Joel 3.4.
19 Matt. 24.35.
20 Acts 1.7.
21 Matt. 24.42, 44.
22 *Ibid.* 3.
23 2 Cor. 11.14.
24 Matt. 24.4.

words. For it is not a history of what is past, but a prophecy of the future, and what will surely come to pass. Not that we prophesy, for we are unworthy, but we bring before you what is written and we declare the signs. Observe how much of the prophecy has come true, how much still remains, and put yourself on guard.

(5) "Take care that no one leads you astray. For many will come in my name, saying, I am the Christ, and they will lead many astray."[25] These words have been fulfilled in part. For already Simon Magus made this claim; Menander too, and other impious heresiarchs.[26] Yet others will make the same claim in our time, and after us.

(6) A second sign: "For you shall hear of wars and the rumors of wars."[27] Are not the Persians and Romans warring for Mesopotamia right now? Does nation rise against nation, or kingdom against kingdom,[28] or not? "And there will be pestilences and famines and earthquakes in various places."[29] These calamities have already come to pass. Again: "And terrors from heaven, and great storms."[30] "Watch, therefore," He says, "for you do not know at what hour your Lord is to come."[31]

(7) But we seek our own sign of His coming. We who are of the Church seek the Church's sign. The Savior says: "And then many will fall away, and will betray one another, and will hate one another."[32] If you should hear of bishops in conflict with bishops, clergy against clergy, and flock against

---

25 *Ibid.* 4, 5.

26 Simon Magus claimed at different times to be Father, Son and Holy Spirit (*Cat.* 6.14). According to Irenaeus (*Adv. haer.* 1.23.5) Menander claimed to be the savior sent for the salvation of men.

27 Matt. 24.6.

28 After the death of Constantine there was a series of wars between the Persians and the Romans for the possession of Mesopotamia.

29 Matt. 24.7. Jerome in his *Chronica* testifies to the occurrence of these calamities in the first half of the fourth century.

30 Cf. Luke 21.11.

31 Matt. 24.42.

32 *Ibid.* 10.

flock even unto blood, do not be troubled.[33] It has been prophesied. Fix your attention, not on the events themselves, but on the fact that they have been foretold. Even if I who teach you should be lost, you must not perish along with me. It is quite possible for a disciple to surpass his master, for the last to become the first, for the Master receives those who come even at the eleventh hour. If treason was found among the Apostles, do you wonder if hatred of the brethren is found even among bishops? But this sign concerns not only the rulers but also the flock. For He says: "And because iniquity will abound, the charity of the many will grow cold."[34] Will anyone present boast that he has a sincere friendship for his neighbor? Is it not true that often the lips kiss, the countenance smiles, the eyes are cheerful, while the malicious heart is plotting guile with smooth words?

(8) You have this sign also, "The gospel of the kingdom shall be preached in the whole world, for a witness to all the nations; and then will come the end."[35] As we see, nearly the whole world is now filled with the doctrine of Christ.

(9) What is to come to pass next? "Therefore when you see the abomination of desolation, which was spoken of by Daniel the prophet, standing in the holy place—let him who reads understand." Again: "Then if anyone say to you, 'Behold here is the Christ,' or 'There he is,' do not believe it."[36] Fraternal hatred is followed by the Antichrist. For the devil prepared divisions among the people to bring about a favorable reception when the Antichrist comes. God forbid that any of Christ's servants, here or elsewhere, should side with the enemy. Writing of this, the Apostle Paul has given a

33 The conflict between bishops centered perhaps on the opposition of Athanasius and his followers, and those opposed to him. The factions accused each other in turn of Arianism or Sabellianism.

34 Matt. 24.12.

35 *Ibid.* 14. The pilgrims coming to Jerusalem from near and far would give the impression to the inhabitants that the Christian faith had been spread through the known world. (Cf. also *Cat.* 8.27 and *Cat.* 10.16.)

36 The two quotations: Matt. 24.15, 23.

manifest sign: "For the day of the Lord will not come unless the apostasy comes first, and the man of sin is revealed, the son of perdition, who opposes and is exalted above all that is called God, or that is worshipped, so that he sits in the temple of God and gives himself out as if he were God. Do you not remember that when I was still with you, I used to tell you these things? And now you know what restrains him, that he may be revealed in his proper time. For the mystery of iniquity is already at work; provided only that he who is at present restraining it, does still restrain, until he is gotten out of the way. And then the wicked one will be revealed, whom the Lord Jesus will slay with the breath of his mouth and will destroy with the brightness of his coming. And his coming is according to the working of Satan with all power and signs and lying wonders, and with all wicked deception to those who are perishing."[37] These are Paul's words. The apostasy has come, for men have forsaken the true faith.[38] While some preach the identity of the Son with the Father, others dare to say that Christ was brought into being from nonbeing.[39] While formerly heretics were manifest, the Church is now filled with secret heretics. Men have fallen away from the truth and have itching ears. Is the discourse charming? All listen to it gladly. Does it aim at amendment? All turn aside. Many have forsaken sound doctrine; they choose the evil rather than prefer the good. The apostasy is at hand, therefore, and the Enemy's coming is to be looked for; already to some extent he has begun to send his precursors; now he has only to swoop upon his prey. So stand upon your defense, and guard your soul. The Church now charges you before the living God; before the event it briefs you about the Antichrist. Whether all this will come to pass in your time, we do

37 2 Thess. 2.3-10.
38 In speaking of the apostasy here and below, Cyril has in mind defection from the true faith, not the advent of the Antichrist or the collapse of the Roman Empire.
39 The two heresies referred to are Sabellianism and Arianism.

not know. But it is good to be aware of these events and to be on your guard.

(10) The True Christ, the Only-begotten Son of God, comes no more from the earth. If somebody should come with vain show in the desert, do not go out. If they say: "Lo, here is Christ, lo, there," do not believe them. No more look downwards or to the earth; for it is from heaven that the Lord is to come; not alone, as before, but with a countless host of angels in His train; not secretly, like rain upon the fleece, but like blazing lightning. For He Himself has said: "As lightning comes forth from the east and shines even to the west, so also will the coming of the Son of Man be."[40] Again: "And they will see the Son of Man coming upon the clouds of heaven with great power and majesty. And he will send forth his angels with a great trumpet."[41]

(11) When the Incarnation was at hand and God's birth from a virgin was expected, the devil created prejudice against the holy mystery by the crafty invention among idol worshippers of fables in which gods begot and were begotten of women; thus, he felt that the truth, coming after the false, would win no credence. So, too, when the second coming of the True Christ is imminent, the adversary will take advantage of the simple, and especially of those of the circumcision, by advancing a mysterious wizard, highly skilled in the guileful craft of sorceries and enchantments; he will seize the power of the Roman Empire and falsely call himself Christ. By this title he will deceive the Jews, who await the Messiah, and by his magical illusions he will lead astray the Gentiles as well.

(12) The Antichrist is to come when the termination of the Roman Empire and the end of the world are imminent.[42]

40 Matt. 24.27.
41 *Ibid.* 30, 31.
42 It was a common opinion that the Roman Empire was the fourth kingdom of Daniel (7.23), as Cyril indicates in the next chapter, and that it would last to the coming of the Antichrist and the end of the world.

Ten kings of the Romans will rise up together, ruling in different places perhaps, but at the same time. Following these an eleventh, the Antichrist, seizing the Roman power by his magical arts, will humble three of the kings before him, while reducing to subjection the remaining seven. At first, posing as a learned and prudent man, he will pretend to be moderate and benevolent; he will take in the Jews as their hoped-for Messiah by deceitful signs and wonders of his magical craft; afterwards he will be so marked by the variety of his cruel and lawless crimes as to surpass all the workers of injustice and impiety before him; he will display against all men, but especially against us Christians, a sanguinary, relentless, merciless, and crafty spirit. After three and a half years of such wickedness he will be destroyed by the glorious descent of the Only-begotten Son of God, our Lord and Savior Jesus, the True Christ; He will slay the Antichrist with the breath of His mouth, and consign him to the fire of Gehenna.

(13) Our teaching is no invention on our part, but derived from the Sacred Scriptures, particularly from the prophecy of Daniel just read; the Archangel Gabriel has interpreted it thus: "The fourth beast shall be a fourth kingdom on earth, which shall be greater than all the kingdoms."[43] According to the traditional interpretation of the Fathers, this is the kingdom of the Romans. The first famous kingdom was the Assyrian, the second that of the Medes and the Persians; next came the kingdom of the Macedonians; the fourth is the present kingdom of the Romans. Subsequently, by way of interpretation Gabriel says: "The ten horns shall be ten kings rising out of that kingdom; another shall rise up after them, who shall surpass all those before him in wickedness"[44] (not only these ten, he says, but all who were before him). "And he shall lay low three kings";[45] clearly he refers to the ten

43 Cf. Dan. 7.23.
44 Cf. *ibid.* 24.
45 Cf. *ibid.*

former kings, and, dethroning three of them, he will doubtless rule with the remaining seven. "He shall speak against the Most High,"[46] Gabriel says; he is a blasphemer and a transgressor of the law, who has not received the kingdom from his fathers but has seized the power by his magical arts.

(14) Can we identify this character or his deeds? Be our interpreter, O Paul. "And his coming is according to the working of Satan with all power and signs and lying wonders";[47] this means that Satan will use him as his personal instrument. Realizing that his own condemnation will be no longer deferred, he will no longer wage war through his ministers in his usual way, but now openly, in person. "With all signs and lying wonders"; for the father of falsehood will display his lying works and cheating fancies, to make the people think they see a dead man raised, when he is not raised, and the lame walking, and the blind receiving sight, when there have been no such cures.

(15) Again Paul says: "Who opposes and is exalted above all that is called God, or that is worshipped" (that is, above every god; Antichrist, then, is to abhor idols), "so that he sits in the temple of God."[48] What temple? He means the ruined temple of the Jews, already destroyed. God forbid that it be the one in which we are! Not with the idea of favoring ourselves do we say this. For if he is to come as Christ to the Jews, and wants their worship, with a view to deceiving them further, he will manifest the greatest zeal for the temple; he will create the impression that he is the descendent of David who is to restore the temple of Solomon. Antichrist will come when in the temple of the Jews not a stone upon a stone will be left, as our Savior foretold.[49] For when the decay of time, or demolition with a view to rebuilding, or other causes

46 *Ibid.* 25.
47 2 Thess. 2.9.
48 *Ibid.* 4.
49 Cyril seems to believe that the Antichrist and the end of the world would follow the *total* destruction of the temple as prophesied by Christ (Matt. 24.2).

have overthrown all the stones both of the outer circuit and the inner shrine of the Cherubim, the Antichrist will appear amid all signs and lying wonders, lifting himself up against all idols; in the beginning he will pretend to be kindly, but afterwards he will display a cruel spirit against the saints of God. For Daniel says: "As I watched, that horn made war against the holy ones";[50] and elsewhere: "It shall be a time unsurpassed in distress since nations began until that time."[51] He is the terrible beast, a mighty dragon, unconquerable by man, ready to devour; we have more from the Sacred Scriptures to narrate concerning him, but we shall observe due measure and content ourselves for the time with what we have said.

(16) The Lord, realizing the might of the adversary, grants indulgence to the devout saying: "Then let those who are in Judea flee to the mountains."[52] But let the man who is confident that he can resist Satan take his stand (for I do not despair of the sinews of the Church) and say: "Who shall separate us from the love of Christ?"[53] Let the timid among us secure their safety, but let the courageous take a bold stand. "For then there will be great tribulation, such as has not been from the beginning of the world until now, nor will be."[54] Thanks be to God, who has confined the severe tribulation to a few days, for He says: "But for the sake of the elect those days will be shortened."[55] The Antichrist will reign but three and a half years; this assertion rests, not on apocryphal books, but on Daniel, who says: "And they shall be delivered into his hands until a time, and times, and half a time."[56] A "time" is the one year in which the Antichrist's

50 Dan. 7.21.
51 Dan. 12.1.
52 Matt. 24.16.
53 Rom. 8.35.
54 Matt. 24.31.
55 *Ibid.* 22.
56 Dan. 7.25 (Douay). When Cyril mentions apocryphal books as opposed to Daniel, some see a reference to the Apocalypse, which Cyril did not include in his canon.

power will increase; but "times" signify two more years of iniquity, making a total of three years; and the "half a time" is six months. Elsewhere Daniel repeats the same words: "And he swore by him that lives forever, that it should be for a time, and times, and half a time."[57] Some may have interpreted in the same sense the following: "There shall be one thousand two hundred ninety days,"[58] and also the words: "Blessed is the man who has patience and perseverance until the one thousand three hundred and thirty-five days."[59] It may be necessary, therefore, to hide and flee; for perhaps we "will not have gone through the towns of Israel before the Son of Man comes."[60]

(17) What blessed men will then bear devout witness to Christ? I maintain that the martyrs of that time will surpass all martyrs. Previous martyrs would have wrestled with men only, but they will engage with Satan personally in the time of the Antichrist. Kings in former persecutions merely put men to death; they did not pretend to raise the dead or display apparent signs and marvels. But in this time the seduction of terror and deceit will be such "as to lead astray, if possible, even the elect."[61] Let no one then alive entertain the thought: "What more did Christ do? By what power does this man work these wonders? Unless God so willed, He would not have permitted them." The Apostle warns you beforehand: "Therefore God sends them a misleading influence,"[62] ("sends," that is, allows to happen,) not to give them an excuse, but for their condemnation. Why? "Who have not believed the truth," that is, in the true Christ, "but have consented to iniquity,"[63] that is, to the Antichrist. But in the various per-

57 Cf. Dan. 12.7.
58 *Ibid.* 11. St. Hippolytus and others have interpreted the 1290 days as the extent of the reign of the Antichrist.
59 *Ibid.* 12.
60 Matt. 10.23.
61 Matt. 24.24.
62 2 Thess. 2.11.
63 Cf. *ibid.* 10.

secutions that arise God permits and will even then permit such happenings, not because He cannot prevent them, but as is His wont, He crowns His champions through suffering, as He crowned His Prophets and Apostles; thus toiling for a short time they inherit the eternal kingdom of heaven, according to the words of Daniel: "At that time all your people shall be saved, everyone who is found written in the book." (Clearly the book of life is meant.) "Many of those who sleep in the dust of the earth shall awake; some shall live forever, others shall be an everlasting horror and disgrace. But the wise shall shine brightly like the splendor of the firmament; and those who lead the many to justice shall be like the stars forever."[64]

(18) Be on your guard, therefore; you know the signs of the Antichrist; do not keep them to yourself but share them generously with all. If you have a natural son admonish him now; if you have begotten one by catechizing,[65] put him also on guard against accepting the false Christ as the true. "For the mystery of iniquity is already at work."[66] I fear the wars of the nations, I fear the schisms of the Churches, I fear the mutual hatred of the brethren. But enough on these evils; God forbid that they be brought to pass in our days; yet let us be wary. So much for the Antichrist.

(19) Let us look hopefully for the Lord's coming upon the clouds of heaven. The angelic trumpets will then be sounded; the dead in Christ shall rise first; the living faithful shall be taken up in the clouds, receiving more than human honor as the reward of their superhuman efforts; thus the Apostle writes: "For the Lord Himself with cry of command, with voice of archangel, and with trumpet of God will descend from heaven; and the dead in Christ will rise up first. Then we who live, who survive, shall be caught up together with

---

64 Dan. 12.2, 3.

65 It is clear that some of the baptized faithful were present at Cyril's lectures. There were catechists deputed in the various churches.

66 2 Thess. 2.7.

them in clouds to meet the Lord in the air, and so we shall ever be with the Lord."[67]

(20) Ecclesiastes knew of the Lord's coming at the end of the world when he said: "Rejoice, O young man, while you are young";[68] and subsequently: "Ward off grief from your heart, and put away trouble from your presence; remember your Creator, before the evil days come, before the sun is darkened, and the light, and the moon, and the stars; and they who look through the windows grow blind" (this signifies the power of sight); "before the silver cord is snapped" (he means the cluster of the stars, silvery in appearance); "and the golden fillet shrinks back" (here is indicated the sun with its golden aspect, for the fillet-like flower [the anthemis] is a well-known plant, with ray-like shoots of foliage circling it); "and they shall rise up at the voice of the sparrow, and they shall see from the height, and terrors shall be in the way."[69] What shall they see? "Then they will see the Son of man coming upon clouds of heaven"[70] and they will mourn, tribe by tribe. What happens when the Lord comes? "The almond tree will bloom, and the locust will grow sluggish and the caper berry will be scattered abroad."[71] According to the interpreters the blooming of the almond tree signifies the passing of winter; our bodies, after the winter, then, are to flourish with a heavenly bloom.[72] "And the locust will grow sluggish," signifies the winged soul clothing itself with the body; "and the caper berry will be scattered abroad"; this suggests that the wicked, like thorns, will be scattered.

(21) You see how all proclaim the coming of the Lord; you see how they know the voice of the sparrow. Let us learn the nature of this voice. "For the Lord Himself with cry of

67 1 Thess. 4.16-17.
68 Eccles. 11.9.
69 Cf. Eccles. 11.10; 12.1-6.
70 Matt. 24.30.
71 Cf. Eccles. 12.5.
72 Cyril seems to believe that the general resurrection will take place in the spring.

command, with voice of archangel, and with trumpet of God will descend from heaven."[73] An Archangel will utter a proclamation, saying to all: "Rise to meet the Lord." Awesome indeed will be that descent of the Master. David says: "God shall come manifestly: our God shall come, and shall not keep silence. A fire shall burn before him: and a mighty tempest shall be round about him."[74] According to the Scripture just read, the son of Man will come to the Father,[75] in the clouds of heaven, trailing a stream of fire, which shall try men. A man whose works are golden shall be made more splendid; if a man's actions have been unsubstantial like stubble, he shall be burned by fire. The Father sits, having "his clothing snow white, and the hair on his head as white as wool."[76] This is said after the manner of men. Why? Because He is King of those undefiled by sins. For He says: "I shall make your sins as white as snow and as wool,"[77] signifying forgiveness of sins, or actual sinlessness. The Lord who ascended on clouds will come from heaven on clouds. For He has said: "And they shall see the Son of Man coming upon the clouds of heaven with great power and majesty."[78]

(22) But what is the sign of His coming—to prevent a hostile power from daring to imitate it? "And then will appear," He says, "the sign of the Son of Man in heaven."[79]

73 1 Thess. 4.16.

74 Ps. 49.3 (Douay).

75 Since Cyril is here speaking of the coming of our Lord from heaven, the expression "will come *to* the Father" is unsettling, since "*from* the Father" would appear to be what is meant. But, as he states, Cyril has in mind the Biblical reading that preceded this Lenten Lecture, and there (Dan. 7.13) the "son of man" is described as having come *to* "the ancient of days" "on the clouds of heaven." Cyril's concern appears to be with the image rather than the direction of movement. Perhaps also, by way of parallel with the context in Daniel (cf. 7.14), there is the suggestion that Christ comes to the Father first to receive the commission to judge all men.

76 Cf. Dan. 7.9.

77 Cf. Isa. 1.18.

78 Matt. 24.30.

79 *Ibid.* Cf. Letter to Constantius 4 and 6, where Cyril records an appearance of a luminous cross at Jerusalem and predicts it will be seen again at the second coming of Christ.

The true sign, Christ's own, is the Cross. A sign of a luminous cross precedes the King, showing Him who was formerly crucified; and so the Jews, who before had pierced Him and plotted against Him, on seeing it, will mourn tribe by tribe, saying: "This is He who was struck with blows, this is He whose face they spat upon, this is He whom they fastened with bonds; this is He whom of old they crucified and held in derision. Where," they will say, "shall we flee from the face of Your wrath?" Surrounded by the angelic hosts, they can never escape. The sign of the Cross will terrify His foes but will give joy to His faithful friends, who have heralded Him or suffered for Him. How blessed the man who will then be found a friend of Christ! That great and glorious King, attended by angels and sharing His Father's throne, will not despise His faithful servants. To prevent His elect from being confused with His enemies, "He will send forth his angels with a great trumpet, and they will gather his elect from the four winds."[80] He did not despise one man, Lot; how then will He despise the multitude of the just? "Come, blessed of my Father,"[81] He will say to those who will then ride upon chariots of clouds and be gathered together by angels.

(23) But someone present will say: "I am poor," or "I may be sick in bed at the time," or "I shall be taken, a woman in the mill"; "Shall we be overlooked?" Take heart; the Judge is no respecter of persons. "Not by appearance shall he judge nor by hearsay shall he decide."[82] He does not esteem the learned above the simple, nor the rich above the poor. Though you be in the fields the angels will take you. Do not think that He will take the lords of the land but will leave you, the husbandman. Though you be a slave, though you be poor, have no anxiety; He who took the form of a servant will not despise servants. Though you lie sick in bed, it is written: then "there will be two on one bed; one will be taken, and

80 *Ibid.* 31.
81 Matt. 25.34.
82 Cf. Isa. 11.3.

the other will be left."[83] Though you be forced to grind in the mill, man or woman, though you be in bonds and attached to the mill, yet He "who leads forth those bound in strength,"[84] will not overlook you.[85] He brought Joseph out of bondage and prison to a kingdom; He will redeem you too from your afflictions and lead you into the kingdom of heaven. Only take courage, toil and strive zealously, for nothing will be lost. Every prayer you make, every psalm you sing is recorded; every alms, every fast is recorded, every lawful marriage as well as continence for God's sake, is recorded. First in the lists are the crowns for virginity and purity, and you shall shine as an angel. You have listened gladly to the good; listen patiently now to the opposite. Your every act of covetousness is recorded, and every act of fornication; every false oath is recorded, every blasphemy, sorcery, theft and murder. All these are henceforth recorded, if after Baptism you commit the same faults; for what went before is blotted out.

(24) "But when the Son of Man," He says, "shall come in his majesty, and all the angels with him."[86] Just imagine before how many witnesses you will come to judgment. The whole human race will then be present. Consider the magnitude of the Roman Empire; consider how many barbarian tribes are now in existence, and how many have disappeared in the last hundred years; reckon the number buried in the last thousand years; compute the total number of men from Adam to the present day. It is a huge multitude but smaller in number than the angels. The ninety-nine sheep and the one constitute the ratio of angels to men.[87] For we must calculate their number according to the total extent of space.

83 Luke 17.34.
84 Cf. Ps. 67.7.
85 Cyril, like so many saints before and after him, thought he saw at hand the signs of the end of the world and the second coming of Christ. He speaks as though some of his hearers might be alive at the second coming.
86 Matt. 25.31.
87 Where Cyril got the idea that space is crowded with angels is not clear—possibly from Origen.

The entire earth may be compared to a point in the middle of one heaven; the multitude dwelling in this vast encircling heaven must be enormous. The numbers in the heaven of heavens are beyond all reckoning. Indeed it is written: "Thousands of thousands were ministering to him, and myriads upon myriads attended him";[88] the multitude is not exactly expressed, because the prophet could not express a larger number. Present then at the judgment will be God, the Father of all, Jesus Christ sitting with Him, present too, the Holy Spirit. The angelic trumpet will summon us all, bringing our deeds with us. Ought we not henceforth be touched with anxiety? Consider the added penalty, apart from punishment, of being condemned in the presence of so many. Should we not prefer to die many times over than to be condemned by friends?

(25) Let us be fearful, my dear brethren, of God's condemnation. He needs no examination or proofs for condemnation. Do not say: "At night I committed fornication," or "I made use of magical arts," or "I committed a certain other deed, and there was no man at hand." From your own conscience you will be judged, as your conflicting thoughts accuse or defend you, "on the day when God will judge the hidden secrets of men."[89] The awe-inspiring countenance of the Judge will compel you to speak the truth, or rather, though you are silent, it will convict you. For you will rise clothed in your sins or your just deeds. The Judge Himself declared this. (For it is Christ who judges. "For neither does the Father judge any man, but all judgment he has given to the Son";[90] the Father does not deprive Himself of His power, but judges through the Son. Therefore by the will of the Father the Son judges; for the wills of the Father and the Son are not different, but one and the same.) What, then, does the Judge say about your bearing or not bearing your deeds? "And before

88 Dan. 7.10.
89 Rom. 2.15, 16.
90 John 5.22.

him will be gathered all the nations."[91] In the presence of Christ "every knee should bend of those in heaven, on earth and under the earth."[92] "And he will separate them one from another, as the shepherd separates the sheep from the goats."[93] How does the shepherd do this? Does he seek from a book which is a sheep and which a goat? or does he decide from the evident facts? Does not the wool manifest the sheep, and the hairy and rough skin the goat? So with you too, once you have been cleansed of your sins, your deeds will be as pure wool, your robe unstained, and you will say always: "I have taken off my robe, how shall I put it on?"[94] By your vesture you will be recognized as a sheep. But if you shall be found hairy, like Esau, who was shaggy of body and wicked of mind, who lost his birthright for food, and sold his prerogative, you will be among those on the left hand. God forbid that anyone present fall from grace, or because of evil deeds be found in the ranks of sinners on the left hand!

(26) The judgment will be awesome, the sentence an occasion for dread. The kingdom of heaven lies before us, everlasting fire has been prepared. Some one will ask, how can we escape the fire, how can we enter into the kingdom? "I was hungry," He says, "and you gave me to eat."[95] Learn the way now; have done with allegory and fulfill what is said. "I was hungry and you gave me to eat; I was thirsty and you gave me to drink; I was a stranger and you took me in; naked and you covered me; sick and you visited me; I was in prison, and you came to see me."[96] If these words describe your conduct, you will reign with Him; if not, you will be condemned. Therefore begin now to act thus; persevere in the faith; avoid being shut out like the foolish virgins, who delayed to buy oil. It is not enough that you have the lamp, you must keep

91 Matt. 24.32.
92 Phil. 2.10.
93 Matt. 25.32.
94 Cant. 5.3.
95 Matt. 25.35.
96 *Ibid.* 35, 36.

it burning. Let the light of your good deeds shine before men; let not Christ be blasphemed because of you. Put on an incorruptible garment, bright with good works. Administer well any stewardship entrusted to you by God. Have you been granted riches? Then dispense them rightly. Has the task of teaching been committed to you? Carry it out zealously. Many are the portals of good stewardship. Only let none of us be condemned and cast out, but rather may we with confidence meet Christ the eternal King, who reigns forever. For He reigns forever, who judges living and dead, having died for the living and the dead. As Paul says: "For to this end Christ died and rose again, that he might be Lord both of the dead and of the living."[97]

(27) If you hear anyone say that the kingdom of Christ will have an end, abhor this assertion as heresy. It is another head of the dragon, which sprang up recently in Galatia.[98] A certain reckless fellow maintained that after the end of the world Christ will reign no longer. He added that the Word, which issued from the Father, will be resolved again into the Father, and will exist no more—uttering such blasphemies to his own destruction. For he paid no heed to the Lord's words: "The Son abides forever."[99] He did not hearken to Gabriel, who said: "He shall be king over the house of Jacob forever, and of his kingdom there shall be no end."[100] Consider whether you would rather believe the Archangel Gabriel, who taught that our Savior will abide forever, or the heretics who teach the contrary. Gabriel, of course. Listen to the apt testimony of Daniel: "As the visions during the night continued, I saw one like a son of man coming in the clouds of heaven; when he reached the Ancient One and was presented before him, he received dominion, glory and kingship; nations and peoples of every

97 Rom. 14.9.
98 The reference is to Marcellus, Bishop of Ancyra in Galatia.
99 John 8.35.
100 Luke 1.32, 33.

language serve him. His dominion is an everlasting dominion that shall not be taken away, his kingship shall not be destroyed."[101] Hold fast to these truths and believe them, and cast aside all heresy. For you have been given clear proof that the kingdom of Christ will never end.

(28) The stone hewn without hands from the mountain—this is Christ according to the flesh—carries a similar interpretation. "And his kingdom shall not be delivered up to another people."[102] And David says: "Your throne, O God, stands forever and ever";[103] and elsewhere: "Of old you established the earth," and subsequently: "They shall perish, but you remain," and then: "But you are the same and your years have no end";[104] these words Paul has interpreted as referring to the Son.[105]

(29) Learn how they who teach heresy came to such madness. They read wrongly the words of the Apostle: "For he must reign, until he has put all his enemies under his feet";[106] they say that when His enemies have been put under His feet He will reign no longer, a foolish and perverse assertion. For surely He who is King before He has subdued His enemies will be King after He has overcome them.

(30) They have recklessly asserted also that the text, "When all things are made subject to him, then the Son himself will also be made subject to him who subjected all things to him,"[107] signifies that the Son is to be absorbed into the Father. Tell me, you most impious men, will you, the creatures of Christ, endure, but Christ, through whom you and all things were made, perish? This would be downright blasphemy. Again, how will all things be subject to Him? By

101 Dan. 7.13, 14 (Sept.).
102 Cf. Dan. 2.44.
103 Ps. 44.7.
104 Ps. 101.26-28.
105 Cf. Heb. 1.8-12.
106 1 Cor. 15.25. In what follows Cyril explains the source of Marcellus' error, as he conceives it.
107 *Ibid.* 28.

perishing or enduring? Or will all else that is subject to the Son abide, but the Son, subject to the Father, not abide? He will be subject, not as though beginning to obey the Father (for from all eternity "he does always the things that please him"[108]), but because then too He will tender not a forced obedience, but a self-chosen conformity. For He is not a servant subject to necessity, but a Son, obeying from choice and affection.

(31) Let us ask the heretics the meaning of "until," or "as far as." For with these words I shall engage them at close quarters and attempt to refute their error. They have dared to assert that the text, "Until he has put all his enemies under his feet," signifies His end; they would limit His eternal kingdom and literally terminate his never-ending dominion. Let us further consider similar phrases in the Apostle. For example: "Yet death reigned from Adam until Moses."[109] Are we to believe that men up to Moses died, but none thereafter? or that after the Law there was death no longer among men? You see that the word "until" does not denote a limit of time; rather Paul has shown clearly that though Moses was a just and admirable man, nevertheless the sentence of death pronounced against Adam affected him also and those who came after him, even though they had not committed sins like Adam's disobedience in eating of the tree.

(32) Consider another similar text: "Down to this day, when Moses is read, the veil covers their hearts."[110] Does "down to this day" mean until Paul only? Is it not until this present day and unto the end? If Paul can say to the Corinthians: "Since we reached as far as you with the gospel of Christ, but we hope, as your faith increases, to preach the gospel in places that lie beyond you,"[111] you see clearly that "as far as"

---

108 Cf. John 8.29.
109 Rom. 5.14.
110 Cf. 2 Cor. 3.14.
111 2 Cor. 10.14, 15.

does not denote the end, but has something following it. How then should you take the text, "Until he has put his enemies"? Just as Paul in another place says: "But exhort one another every day, while it is still Today,"[112] that is, continually. For just as one should not speak of the beginning of the days of Christ, so suffer no one at any time to speak of the end of His kingdom. For it is written: "His kingdom is an everlasting kingdom."[113]

(33) I have more testimonies from the Sacred Scriptures about the everlasting kingdom of Christ, but I shall be content with what I have advanced, since it is late. Worship Christ only as King, my dear brethren, and shun all error of heresy. With God's grace you will get an explanation of the remaining articles of the faith in good time. May the God of all protect you all, ever mindful of the signs of the consummation, and unvanquished by the Antichrist. You have heard the signs of the impostor to come; you have received the proofs of the True Christ, who will come down openly from heaven. Therefore shun him who is false, and look for Him, who is the True. You have been taught the way, how in the judgment you may be found among those on the right hand. Guard what has been committeed to you concerning Christ, and be conspicuous for good works; thus you will stand confidently before your Judge and inherit the kingdom of heaven: through whom and with whom be glory to God with the Holy Spirit, forever and ever. Amen.

112 Heb. 3.13.
113 Dan. 3.100.

CATECHESIS XVI

On the Holy Spirit (1)

"Now concerning spiritual gifts, brethren, I would not have you ignorant. Now there are varieties of gifts, but the same Spirit."[1]

(1) Spiritual grace is surely needed to discourse about the Holy Spirit; I do not mean, to speak in keeping with His dignity, for that is impossible, but to run our course without danger, when we adduce the words of Sacred Scripture. For that is a truly awesome statement in the Gospels, where Christ has said plainly: "But whoever speaks against the Holy Spirit, it will not be forgiven him, either in this world or in the world to come."[2] A man must often fear to say, either from ignorance or assumed reverence, what is improper about the Holy Spirit, and thereby come under this condemnation. Jesus Christ, the Judge of living and dead, has declared that such a man has no pardon; what hope is there for a man guilty of the offence?

(2) Therefore we must rely on the grace of Jesus Christ to grant us the faculty of speaking without defect, and to grant you the gift of hearing with understanding; for there is need of understanding, not only for those who speak, but also for those who hear; else they may hear one thing and wrongly conceive another in mind. Let us assert of the Holy Spirit, therefore, only what is written; let us not busy ourselves about what is not written. The Holy Spirit has authored the Scrip-

1 1 Cor. 12.1, 4.
2 Matt. 12.32.

tures; He has spoken of Himself all that He wished, or all that we could grasp; let us confine ourselves to what He has said, for it is reckless to do otherwise.

(3) There is One Holy Spirit, the Advocate. As there is One God, the Father, and there is no second Father, and as there is one Only-begotten Son and Word of God, and He has no brother, so there is one only Holy Spirit, and there is no second Spirit equal in honor to Him. The Holy Spirit is a mighty Power, a being divine and unsearchable. He is living and rational, the Sanctifier of all things made by God through Christ. He enlightens the souls of the just; He inspired the prophets; he inspired the Apostles in the New Testament. Let them be abhorred who dare to divide the operation of the Holy Spirit. There is One God, the Father, Lord of the Old and the New Testament, and One Lord Jesus Christ, who was prophesied in the Old, and came in the New Testament, and One Holy Spirit, who heralded Christ through the Prophets, and when Christ came, descended and showed him forth.[3]

(4) Let no one, therefore, separate the Old from the New Testament, and say that the Spirit in the Old is one and in the New another; to do so is to offend the Holy Spirit Himself, who is honored with Father and Son, and on the occasion of holy Baptism is included with them in the Holy Trinity. For the Only-begotten Son of God said in express terms to the Apostles: "Go, therefore, and make disciples of all nations, baptizing them in the name of the Father, and of the Son, and of the Holy Spirit."[4] Our hope is in Father, Son and Holy Spirit. We do not proclaim three gods; let the Marcionists be put to silence; but with Holy Spirit, through

3 In the opening chapters there is a sound statement of Christian doctrine very carefully phrased in the light of current heresies. After the third chapter in one manuscript there is an interpolation of about forty lines. Part of this has been identified as a passage from a catechetical oration of Gregory of Nyssa; the rest is of unknown origin.

4 Matt. 28.19.

one Son, we preach one God. The faith is indivisible, the worship inseparable. We do not divide the Holy Trinity, like some, nor do we confuse the Persons, like Sabellius.[5] In true piety we know one Father, who sent His Son to be our Savior; we know one Son, who promised to send the Advocate from the Father; we know the Holy Spirit, who spoke in the prophets, and on Pentecost descended upon the Apostles in the form of fiery tongues here in Jerusalem, in the Upper Church of the Apostles. The most honored privileges are ours. Here Christ descended from heaven; here the Holy Spirit descended from heaven. It is particularly fitting that as we speak of Christ and Golgotha here on Golgotha, so also we should speak of the Holy Spirit in the Upper Church; but since He who descended there shares the glory of Him who was crucified here, therefore we speak here also of Him who descended there, for their worship is indivisible.

(5) We wish, then, to speak of the Holy Spirit; not indeed to describe His essence in exact detail, for that would be impossible, but to note the various errors of certain men concerning Him, and so save us from ever being carried away through ignorance; to cut off the paths of error, and so thereby travel the one royal highway. If by way of caution we repeat any statement of these heresies, may this be turned upon the heads of the heretics; and let us be guiltless, both us who speak, and you who hear.

(6) For the heretics, impious always, have sharpened their tongues against the Holy Spirit, and have recklessly uttered abominations, as Irenaeus has recounted in his books against the heretics.[6] Some have even said that they themselves were the Holy Spirit; the first of these was Simon the magician, mentioned in the Acts of the Apostles; for when he was cast

5 The reference in "some" is mainly to the Arians, who reduced the Son to a creature, and who held the Holy Spirit was inferior even to the Son.

6 In his work *Adversus haereses* St. Irenaeus details the peculiar doctrines of the Gnostics and others on the Holy Spirit (1.2.5f.). For Simon in the next sentence see Acts 8.9ff.

out he did not hesitate to teach such heresy. The so-called Gnostics, impious men, uttered other falsehoods against the Holy Spirit, and the wicked Valentinians still others. The accursed Mani had the audacity to say that he was the Advocate sent by Christ. Others again have asserted that there is one Spirit in the Prophets, and another in the New Testament; so diverse is their error, or rather their blasphemy. Abhor such men, therefore, and shun the blasphemers of the Holy Spirit, for whom there is no pardon. For what fellowship have you with men without hope, you, who are about to be baptized even now in the Holy Spirit? If he who attaches himself to the thief and runs with him is liable to punishment, what hope will he have who offends against the Holy Spirit?

(7) Let the Marcionists also be detested, who have stripped from the New Testament the words of the Old. For the abominable Marcion, who first asserted three gods,[7] knowing that testimonies of the Prophets concerning Christ are inserted in the New Testament, cut out these Old Testament testimonies, to leave the King without witness. The Gnostics also, mentioned above, are to be abhorred; their name signifies knowledge, though their ignorance is profound. They have rashly spoken about the Holy Spirit fables such as I do not dare to repeat.

(8) Abominate the Cataphrygians also and Montanus, their ringleader in evil, and his two prophetesses, Maximilla and Priscilla. This man, who was out of his mind and truly mad (for otherwise he would not have said such things), dared to say that he himself was the Holy Spirit. He was a miserable creature, sunk in all impurity and wantonness; I can only hint at his corruption, out of respect for the women here present. When he had seized upon Pepusa, a tiny village in Phrygia and falsely named it Jerusalem, on the pretext of

7 Of the three gods of Marcion one was good, the father of Christ, another bad, the devil who rules the nations, and a third in between, the creator of the world, the God of the Jews.

their so-called mysteries, he cut the throats of wretched little children and chopped them into pieces for their unholy banquets; because of this, until rather recent times, in the periods of persecution, we were suspected of these crimes; for these Montanists are also called, falsely, it is true, by the common name of Christians; Montanus, I repeat, went so far as to call himself the Holy Spirit, though he was a monster of impiety and cruelty, and subject to inexorable condemnation.

(9) Not otherwise was the nefarious Mani, a veritable garbage bin of all heresy; reaching the lowest depths of perdition, he collected the worst features of all the heresies, and developed and preached a more novel error. He did not hesitate to assert that he was the Advocate whom Christ had promised to send. Now the Savior, in promising Him, said to the Apostles: "But wait here in the city" of Jerusalem "until you are clothed with power from on high."[8] What follows? Did the Apostles, dead two hundred years, wait for Mani, "until they should be clothed with power"?[9] Will anyone dare to assert that they were not filled with the Holy Spirit from Pentecost on? For it is written: "Then they laid hands on them and they received the Holy Spirit."[10] This happened many years before Mani, once the Holy Spirit descended on the day of Pentecost.

(10) Why was Simon Magus condemned? Was it not because he came to the Apostles and said: "Give me this power, so that on whomever I shall lay my hands he may receive the Holy Spirit"?[11] He did not say, "Give me also the participation in the Holy Spirit," but "Give me this power," with a view to selling to others what could not be sold—something he himself did not possess. He offered money to men without pos-

8 Luke 24.49.

9 Mani appeared A.D. 277 (*Cat.* 6.20); so according to Cyril's reckoning the death of the last Apostle would be roughly A. D. 77.

10 Acts 8.17.

11 *Ibid.* 19.

sessions, and that too after seeing men bring the price of what they sold and lay it at the feet of the Apostles. He did not realize that they who trod underfoot the wealth offered for the sustenance of the poor would surely never sell him the power of the Holy Spirit for a price. But what do they say to Simon? "Thy money go to destruction with thee, because thou hast thought that the gift of God could be purchased with money."[12] For in hoping to sell the grace of the Spirit you are another Judas. If Simon, who wished to purchase this power for a price, merits perdition, how monstrous is the impiety of Mani, who asserted that he was the Holy Spirit? Let us loathe those worthy of hatred; let us shun those from whom God turns away. Let us confidently say to God regarding all heretics: "Did I not hate, O Lord, those who hated you: and did I not pine away because of your enemies?"[13] For there is an enmity that is laudable, as it is written: "I will put enmity between you and the woman, between your seed and her seed."[14] Friendship with the serpent produces enmity with God, and death.

(11) Enough about these outcasts. Let us return to the Sacred Scriptures and "drink water from our own cisterns and running water from our own wells."[15] Let us drink of the living water, "springing up unto life everlasting."[16] The Savior "said this of the Spirit whom they who believed in him were to receive."[17] Consider what He says: "He who believes in me," and not simply this, but "as the Scripture says"—He has referred you back to the Old Testament—"from within him there shall flow rivers of living water";[18] not visible rivers merely watering the earth with its thorns and trees, but enlightening souls. Elsewhere He says: "But the

12 *Ibid.* 20.
13 Ps. 138.21.
14 Gen. 3.15.
15 Cf. Prov. 5.15.
16 John 4.14.
17 John 7.39.
18 *Ibid.* 38.

water I shall give him shall become in him a fountain of water, springing up into life everlasting";[19] a new kind of water, living and springing up, springing up for those who are worthy.

(12) Why has He called the grace of the Spirit water? Because all things depend on water; water produces herbs and living things; water of the showers comes down from heaven, and coming down in one form, has manifold effects; one fountain waters the whole of Paradise; one and the same rain comes down on all the world, yet it becomes white in the lily, red in the rose, purple in the violets and hyacinths, different and many-colored in manifold species; thus it is one in the palm tree and other in the vine, and all in all things, though it is uniform, and does not vary in itself. For the rain does not change, coming down now as one thing and now as another, but it adapts itself to the things receiving it and becomes what is suitable to each. Similarly the Holy Spirit, being One and of One Nature and indivisible, imparts to each man His grace "according as he will."[20] The dry tree when watered brings forth shoots; so too the soul in sin, once it is made worthy through penance of the grace of the Holy Spirit, flowers into justice. Though the Spirit is One in nature, yet by the will of God and in the name of the Son, He brings about many virtuous effects. For He employs the tongue of one man for wisdom, He illumines the soul of another by prophecy, to another He grants the power of driving out devils, to another the gift of interpreting the Sacred Scriptures; He strengthens the self-control of one man, teaches another the nature of almsgiving, and still another to fast and mortify himself, another to despise the things of the body; he prepares another man for martyrdom, acting differently in different men, though He Himself is not diverse, as it is written: "Now the manifestation of the Spirit is given

19 John 4.14.
20 1 Cor. 12.11.

to everyone for profit. To one through the Spirit is given the utterance of wisdom; and to another the utterance of knowledge, according to the same Spirit; to another faith, in the same Spirit; to another the gift of healing, in the one Spirit; to another the working of miracles; to another prophecy; to another the distinguishing of spirits; to another various kinds of tongues; to another interpretation of tongues. But all these things are the work of one and the same Spirit, who divides to everyone according as he will."[21]

(13) There are many statements of spirit in general in the Sacred Scriptures, and a man could easily become confused from ignorance, if he did not know to what sort of spirit the particular text refers; therefore, we must be sure of the nature of the Holy Spirit according to Scripture. For example Aaron is called Christ (anointed), and David also, and Saul and others are called Christs, yet there is only one True Christ; similarly since the name of spirit has been given to many things, we must determine what in particular is called the Holy Spirit. Many things are called spirits; our soul is called spirit; this wind which is blowing is called spirit; great valor is called spirit; impure action is called spirit; and a hostile devil is called spirit. Take care, therefore, when you hear such things, not to mistake one for another because of the similarity of name. Scripture says of the soul: "When his spirit departs he returns to the earth";[22] and again of the soul: "Who forms the spirit of man within him."[23] It says in the Psalms of the angels: "Who make your angels spirits";[24] it says of the wind: "With a vehement spirit thou shalt break in pieces the ships of Tharsis";[25] and: "As the trees of the woods are moved with the spirit";[26] and: "Fire, hail, snow, ice, spirit of storm."[27] Our Lord says of His blessed teaching: "The words that I have spoken to you are spirit and life,"[28] that is,

21 *Ibid.* 7-11.
22 Ps. 145.4.
23 Zach. 12.1.
24 Ps. 103.4.
25 Ps. 47.8 (Douay).
26 Isa. 7.2 (Douay).
27 Cf. Ps. 148.8.
28 John 6.64.

they are spiritual. The Holy Spirit is not an utterance of the tongue; He is living, granting wise speech, speaking and discoursing Himself.

(14) Do you wish to learn of His speaking and discoursing? Philip by the revelation of an angel went down into the way leading to Gaza, when the eunuch was approaching, "and the Spirit said to Philip: 'Go near and keep close to this carriage.' "[29] Note how the Spirit speaks to one who listens. Ezechiel says: "The spirit of the Lord fell upon me, and he told me to say: 'Thus says the Lord' ";[30] and again: "The Holy Spirit said" to the Apostles at Antioch: " 'Set apart for me Saul and Barnabas unto the work to which I have called them.' "[31] You see the Spirit living, setting apart, calling and sending with authority. And Paul: "Except that in every city the Holy Spirit warns me, saying that imprisonment and persecution are awaiting me."[32] This is the good Sanctifier of the Church, her Helper and Teacher, the Holy Spirit, the Advocate, of whom our Savior said: "He will teach you all things," and He did not say merely "He will teach," but also: "and he will bring to your mind whatever I have said to you";[33] for the teaching of Christ and that of the Holy Spirit are the same, not different. The Spirit testified to Paul beforehand of the future, to confirm him in heart by that foreknowledge. All this has special reference to the text: "The words that I have spoken to you are spirit,"[34] and so you must not consider these words a mere utterance of the lips, but sound doctrine.

(15) Sin, as I said before, is called spirit, but in another and contrary sense, as when it is said: "For the spirit of harlotry has led them astray."[35] The name "spirit" is applied

29 Acts 8.29.
30 Ezech. 11.5.
31 Acts 13.2.
32 Acts 20.23.
33 John 14.26.
34 John 6.64.
35 Osee 4.12.

to the unclean spirit, the devil, but with the addition, "the unclean": for the epithet is attached in each case, to signify its particular nature. When Scripture refers to the soul of a man as a "spirit," it is with the addition "of man"; if to the wind, it says, "spirit of storm"; if to sin, "spirit of harlotry," if to the devil, "an unclean spirit"; in this way we know to what particular thing the term refers, and need not think that it means the Holy Spirit. God forbid! For this word spirit is common to many things; everything that does not have a solid body is generally called spirit. Since the devils do not have such bodies they are called spirits; but there is a great difference. When the unclean devil comes upon a man's soul—may the Lord deliver from him every soul of those who hear me, and of those who are not present—it is like a wolf upon a sheep, greedy for blood, ready to devour. His advent is fierce; there is a sense of oppression; the mind is darkened; his attack is unjust, a seizure of another's possession. He forcibly uses another's body and another's bodily member as his own. He casts down him who stands upright—for he is kin to him who fell from heaven—; he perverts the tongue, he twists the lips; foam comes instead of words; the man is blinded; his eye is open, yet through it the soul sees nothing, and wretched man quivers and trembles at the point of death. The devils are truly enemies of men in abusing them so foully and pitilessly.

(16) Not such is the Holy Spirit; God forbid! His actions on the contrary, effect what is good and salutary. First of all, His coming is gentle, the perception of Him fragrant, His yoke light; rays of light and knowledge shine forth before His coming. He comes with the heart of a true guardian; He comes to save, to cure, to admonish, to strengthen, to console, to enlighten the mind, first of the man who receives Him, then through him the minds of others also. As a man previously in darkness and suddenly seeing the sun gets the faculty of sight and sees clearly what he did not see before, so the man

deemed worthy of the Holy Spirit is enlightened in soul, and sees beyond human sight what he did not know. Though his body is upon the earth his soul beholds the heavens as in a mirror. He sees, like Isaia, "the Lord seated on a high and lofty throne";[36] he sees, like Ezechiel, "him who is above the cherubim";[37] he sees, like Daniel, "thousands upon thousands and myriads upon myriads";[38] and little man sees the beginning and the end of the world, the times in between, the successions of kings; in short, things he had not learned, for the True Enlightener is at hand. The man is confined within walls; yet his power of knowledge ranges far and wide, and he perceives even the actions of others.

(17) Peter was not at hand when Ananias and Sapphira sold their possessions, but he was present by the Spirit. "Why," he says, "has Satan tempted thy heart, that thou shouldst lie to the Holy Spirit?"[39] There was no accuser; there was no witness; how did he know what had happened? "While it yet remained, did it not remain thine; and after it was sold, was not the money at thy disposal? Why hast thou conceived this thing in thy heart?"[40] Peter, an unlettered man, by the grace of the Spirit came to know what not even the wise men of the Greeks knew. You have the like in the case of Eliseus. When he had freely healed the leprosy of Naaman, Giezi accepted the reward, taking for himself the reward of another's success. Giezi took the money from Naaman and put it in a dark place. But the darkness is not dark to the saints. When he returned Eliseus questioned him; and just as Peter, when he said: "Tell me, did you sell the land for so much,"[41] so Eliseus asks: "Whence comest thou, Giezi?[42] Not in ignorance do I ask, 'Whence comest thou?' You have come from darkness

36 Isa. 6.1.
37 Cf. Ezech. 10.1.
38 Dan. 7.10.
39 Acts 5.3.
40 *Ibid.* 4.
41 *Ibid.* 8.
42 4 Kings 5.25.

and into darkness you will go. You have sold the cure of the leper, and you will inherit the leprosy yourself. I have fulfilled," he says, "the command of Him who said to me: 'Freely you have received, freely give.'[43] But you have sold the grace; receive also the wages of the sale." But what does Eliseus say to him? "Did not my heart go forth with you?[44] I was here shut up in the body, but the spirit given to me by God saw even things far away, and showed me what was happening elsewhere." Consider how He removes ignorance and instills knowledge. You see how the Holy Spirit enlightens souls.

(18) Isaia lived almost a thousand years ago, and saw Sion as a hut. The city was still standing, beautified with public squares and clothed in honor; yet he says: "Sion shall be plowed like a field";[45] foretelling what has been fulfilled in our day. Observe the exactness of the prophecy; for he said: "Daughter Sion shall be left like a hut in a vineyard, like a shed in a melon patch."[46] Now the place is full of melon patches. Do you see how the Holy Spirit enlightens the saints? Therefore do not be distracted by a common term, but hold fast to what is exactly true.

(19) Whenever a goodly thought on chastity or virginity occurs to you as you sit here, it is due to His teaching. Has it not often happened that a maiden, on the very threshold of the bridal chamber, has fled away, through the inspiration of His teaching on virginity?[47] Or that a man distinguished at court has scorned wealth and honor, on being taught by the Holy Spirit? Is it not true that often a young man on beholding beauty has closed his eyes and fled the sight, and thus escaped defilement? How did this come to pass, you ask? The Holy Spirit taught the young man's soul. Covetous desires

43 Matt. 10.8.
44 Cf. 4 Kings 5.26.
45 Mich. 3.12. A slip on the part of Cyril, who assigns this text to Isaia.
46 Isa. 1.8.
47 Some have thought that Cyril has in mind St. Thecla, whose fame was great in Jerusalem, though undoubtedly there were other examples in the lives of the saints.

abound in the world; yet Christians live in poverty. Why? Because of the prompting of the Holy Spirit. The Holy Spirit, the Good Spirit is truly worthy of honor, and it is fitting that we are baptized into Father, Son and Holy Spirit. A man still encumbered with the body wrestles with many cruel demons; often the demon, unconquerable by iron bonds, is conquered by the man through prayer, by virtue of the Holy Spirit within him.[48] The simple breathing of the exorcist becomes as fire to the invisible foe. We have from God, therefore, a strong Ally and Protector, a mighty Teacher and Champion in our behalf. Let us not fear the demons nor the devil, for our Defender is mightier; let us but open up the doors to Him; for He goes about seeking those worthy, seeking to whom He may impart His gifts.

(20) He is called Comforter, because He comforts and encourages us, and "helps our weakness. For we do not know what we should pray for as we ought, but the Spirit Himself pleads for us with unutterable groanings,"[49] that is, clearly, to God. Often a man for Christ's sake has been treated with contumely and unjustly dishonored; martyrdom is at hand, tortures on every side, fire, swords, wild beasts, and the abyss; but the Holy Spirit gently whispers to him: "Wait for the Lord,"[50] for your present sufferings are slight, while your rewards will be great; endure for a little while and you will be with the angels forever. "The sufferings of the present time are not worthy to be compared with the glory to come that will be revealed in us."[51] He portrays for the man the kingdom of heaven, and even gives him a glimpse of the Paradise of pleasure; and the martyrs, who must present their bodily countenances to their judges, are in spirit already in Paradise, and despise what appear to be hardships.

48 The wrestling with demons refers to the various activities of the exorcists.
49 Rom. 8.26.
50 Ps. 26.14.
51 Rom. 8.18.

(21) You must know too that the Holy Spirit empowers the martyrs to bear witness. The Savior says to His disciples: "When they bring you before the synagogues and the magistrates and the authorities, do not be anxious how or wherewith you shall defend yourselves, for the Holy Spirit will teach you in that hour what you ought to say."[52] A man cannot testify as a martyr for Christ's sake except through the Holy Spirit. For if "no man can say 'Jesus is Lord,' except in the Holy Spirit,"[53] shall any man give his life for Jesus' sake except through the Holy Spirit?

(22) The Holy Spirit is indeed mighty, all-powerful in gifts, and wonderful. Consider how many of you sit here now, how many souls we are here present. He adapts Himself to each, and being present in our midst, He sees the dispositions of each, He sees our reasoning and our conscience, what we say, what we think, what we believe. This may seem a strong assertion, but actually it is quite weak. For just consider, enlightened in mind by Him, how many Christians there are in this whole diocese, how many in the whole province of Palestine. Again let your mind range from this province to the whole Roman Empire; then fix your gaze on the whole world; there are races of Persians, nations of Indians, Goths, Sarmatians, Moors, Libyans, Aethiopians and others whose names are unknown to us; for the names of many nations have not even reached us. Consider each nation's bishops, priests, deacons, solitaries, virgins, all the laity; contemplate their mighty Protector, the Dispenser of their gifts, how throughout the whole world He bestows on one chastity, on another perpetual virginity, inspires one to almsgiving, another to poverty, and grants to another the power of driving out evil spirits. As the light with one casting of its rays brightens everything, so too the Holy Spirit enlightens those who have eyes. For if any man because of blindness is not deemed

52 Luke 12.11, 12.
53 1 Cor. 12.3.

worthy of His grace, let him not blame the Spirit but his own disbelief.

(23) You have seen His power, exercised throughout the world. Tarry no longer on the earth, but mount on high. Ascend now in thought to the first heaven, and contemplate the countless myriads of angels. Rise still higher in thought, if you can; contemplate the Archangels too, behold the Spirits[54] also, the Virtues, the Principalities, the Powers, the Dominations. Set over all these by God as their Ruler, their Teacher and their Sanctifier is the Paraclete. Among men Elia has need of Him, as also Eliseus and Isaia; among angels Michael and Gabriel have need of Him. No created being is equal in honor to Him. Not all the classes of angels, not all their hosts together have equality with the Holy Spirit. The all-perfect power of the Paraclete overshadows them all. While they are sent to minister, He searches even the deep things of God, according to the Apostle: "For the Spirit searches all things, even the deep things of God. For who among men knows the things of a man save the spirit of the man which is in him? Even so, the things of God no man knows but the Spirit of God."[55]

(24) He heralded Christ in the Prophets; He wrought in the Apostles; and to this day He seals souls in Baptism. The Father gives to the Son, and the Son shares with the Holy Spirit. Not I but Jesus says: "All things have been delivered to me by my Father";[56] and of the Holy Spirit He says: "When he, the Spirit of truth, has come, he will teach you all the truth," and what follows; "He will glorify me, because he will receive of what is mine and declare it to you."[57] The Father, through the Son, with the Holy Spirit, bestows all gifts. The gifts of the Father are not different from the gifts of the Son

54 Cyril seems to count the Spirits as a distinct angelic order, though elsewhere the traditional nine choirs are named (*Myst.* 5.6).

55 1 Cor. 2.10, 11.

56 Matt. 11.17.

57 John 16.13, 14.

or those of the Holy Spirit. For there is one Salvation, one Power, one Faith. There is One God, the Father; One Lord, His Only-begotten Son; One Holy Spirit, the Advocate. It is enough for us to know this much; inquire not curiously into His nature and substance. For if it had been written, we would have spoken about it; what is not written let us not essay. It is enough for salvation for us to know that there is Father, Son and Holy Spirit.

(25) This Spirit descended upon the seventy elders in the time of Moses. (May the length of my discourse, dear brethren, not prove tedious to you. But may He of whom we discourse impart strength to everyone, to us who speak and to you who listen.) To repeat, this Spirit descended upon the seventy elders in Moses' day; my object is to prove that He knows all things and works as He will. The seventy elders were chosen: "The Lord then came down in the cloud, and taking some of the spirit that was on Moses, he bestowed it on the seventy elders";[58] not that the Spirit was divided, but His grace was divided according to the vessels and the capacity of the recipients. Now there were sixty-eight present, and they prophesied; Eldad and Medad were not present. To make it clear that it was not Moses who bestowed the gift, but the Spirit who wrought, Eldad and Medad, who had been called but had not yet presented themselves, also prophesied.

(26) Josue, the son of Nun and successor of Moses, was amazed, and coming to Moses said to him: Have you heard that Eldad and Medad are prophesying? They were called and did not come forward; "Moses, my lord, stop them."[59] I cannot forbid them, he said, for the grace is from heaven. So far am I from forbidding them that I consider it a favor. But I think you have not spoken thus in envy. Be not over-zealous on my account, because they have prophesied, and you do not yet prophesy. Await the proper time. "Would

58 Num. 11.25.
59 *Ibid.* 28.

that all the people of the Lord might prophesy, whenever the Lord shall give them his spirit."[60] He spoke the words "whenever the Lord shall give," prophetically. For He has not given it as yet; so you do not have it yet. Did not Abraham, Isaac, Jacob and Joseph have His spirit? Did not the men of old have it? It is clear that the words, "whenever the Lord shall give," means "give to all"; now the grace is partial, then it shall be granted profusely. He intimated what was to come to pass among us on the day of Pentecost; for He Himself came down among us. He had come down before upon many, it is true; for it is written: "Now Josue, the son of Nun, was filled with the spirit of wisdom, since Moses had laid his hands upon him."[61] Note the same ceremonial everywhere, both in the Old and the New Testament. In Moses' day the Spirit was given by the imposition of hands; and Peter imparted the Spirit by the imposition of hands. Upon you also, who are to be baptized, the grace will come. In what manner I do not say, for I do not anticipate the proper time.[62]

(27) The Spirit came upon all the just and the Prophets; I mean Enos, Henoch, Noe, and the rest; upon Abraham, Isaac, Jacob. That Joseph had in him the Spirit of God even Pharaoh himself understood. You have often heard of the wondrous works wrought by the Spirit in the days of Moses. That most courageous man Job had this Spirit, and all the saints, though we do not recount all their names. The Spirit was sent in the building of the tabernacle, and filled with wisdom the wise men about Beseleel.

(28) In the power of this Spirit, as we have it in the Book of Judges, Othoniel judged, Gideon grew strong, and Jephte was victorious; Deborah, a woman, waged war; and Samson, while he acted justly and did not vex Him, performed deeds beyond man's powers. We learn clearly in the Book of Kings

---

60 Cf. *ibid.* 29.
61 Deut. 34.9.
62 The latter part of this chapter seems to refer to Confirmation, and the matter treated in *Myst.* 3.

of Samuel and David, how by the Holy Spirit they prophesied and were leaders of the prophets. Samuel in fact was called the Seer. David says plainly: "The spirit of the Lord hath spoken by me";[63] and in the Psalms: "and your holy spirit take not from me";[64] and again: "May your good spirit guide me on level ground."[65] As we read in Paralipomenon, Azaria in the time of King Asa, and Jahaziel in the time of King Josaphat, were inspired by the Holy Spirit, and again another Azaria (Zacharia), who was stoned. Esdras says: "And thou gavest them thy good spirit to teach them."[66] Though we say nothing, it is quite clear that those inspired and wonder-working men, Elia—who was taken up—and Eliseus, were filled with the Holy Spirit.

(29) Whoever scans all the books of the Prophets, both of the Twelve and of the others, will find many testimonies regarding the Holy Spirit. Michea, for example, speaking in the person of God, says: "But as for me, I am filled with power, with the spirit of the Lord";[67] Joel cries: "Then afterward," God says, "I will pour out my spirit upon all mankind."[68] Aggai says: "For I am with you, says the Lord of hosts, and my spirit continues in your midst";[69] and Zacharia in like manner: "But yet receive my words and my decrees, which I entrusted by my spirit to my servants the prophets."[70]

(30) Isaia also, that lofty-voiced herald, says: "The spirit of the Lord shall rest upon him: a spirit of wisdom and of understanding, a spirit of counsel and of strength, a spirit of knowledge and of godliness; and he shall be filled with the spirit of the fear of the Lord";[71] signifying that the Spirit was indeed one and indivisible, but His operations diverse; and

63 2 Kings 23.2.
64 Ps. 50.13.
65 Ps. 142.10.
66 2 Esd. 9.20.
67 Mich. 3.8.
68 Joel 3.1.
69 Agg. 2.4, 5.
70 Zach. 1.6 (Sept.).
71 Isa. 11.2, 3 (Sept.).

again: "Jacob my servant," and subsequently: "upon whom I have put my spirit";[72] again: "I will pour out my spirit upon your offspring";[73] and: "Now the Lord God has sent me, and his spirit";[74] again: "The spirit of the Lord is upon me, because the Lord has anointed me";[75] and in the words against the Jews: "But they rebelled, and grieved his holy spirit";[76] and: "Where is he who put his holy spirit in their midst?"[77] You have also in Ezechiel—if you are not now weary of listening—what has already been quoted: "Then the spirit of the Lord fell upon me, and he told me to say: thus says the Lord."[78] The phrase "fell upon me" must be rightly understood as meaning "lovingly"; as Jacob, upon finding Joseph, "fell on his neck";[79] and as in the Gospel that loving father, when he saw his son returning from his wandering, "was moved with compassion, and ran and fell upon his neck and kissed him."[80] Again in Ezechiel: "And he brought him into Chaldea, to them of the captivity, in vision, by the spirit of God."[81] You have heard other texts also in our discourses on Baptism: "I will sprinkle clean water upon you," . . . "I will give you a new heart and place a new spirit within you";[82] and a little later: "I will put my spirit within you";[83] and "The hand of the Lord came upon me, and he led me out in the spirit of the Lord."[84]

(31) The spirit filled with wisdom the soul of Daniel and made him, though a youth, a judge of elders. The chaste Susanna was condemned as wanton; there was no one to

72 Cf. Isa. 44.1; 42.1.
73 Isa. 44.3.
74 Isa. 48.16.
75 Isa. 61.1.
76 Isa. 63.10 (Sept.).
77 *Ibid.* 11.
78 Ezech. 11.5.
79 Gen. 46.29.
80 Luke 15.20.
81 Cf. Ezech. 11.24.
82 Ezech 36.25, 26.
83 *Ibid.* 27.
84 Ezech. 37.1.

defend her, for who was to deliver her from the rulers? She was being led away to death, and was already in the hands of the executioners. But her Helper stood by, the Advocate, the Spirit who sanctifies every rational nature. "Come hither to me," He says to Daniel; "young though you are, you must convict elders who have defiled themselves with the sign of youth." Scripture says: "The Lord raised up the holy spirit in a young boy."[85] To sum up briefly, that chaste woman was saved by the sentence of Daniel. We present this story merely as a testimony, for this is not the proper time for exposition. Even Nabuchodonosor recognized that the Holy Spirit was in Daniel, for he said to him: "Baltassar, chief of the magicians, I know that the spirit of the holy God is in you."[86] One thing he said was true and one was false. That he had the spirit was true, but he was not the chief of magicians. He was no magician, but he was wise by the Holy Spirit. Before this Daniel had interpreted for Nabuchodonosor the vision of the statue, which the king had seen but did not understand. Tell me, he said, the vision which I who saw do not understand. You see the power of the Holy Spirit; they who had seen the vision do not understand, while they who had not seen it understand and interpret it.

(32) It would be easy to gather many texts from the Old Testament, and speak more in detail about the Holy Spirit; but time is short and we must show regard for moderation in our discourse. Therefore, being content for the present with these testimonies from the Old Testament, we will go on, God willing, in the next lecture to the remaining texts from the New Testament. May the God of peace, through our Lord Jesus Christ, by the charity of the Spirit, deem all of you worthy of spiritual and heavenly blessings. To whom be glory and power forever and ever. Amen.

---

85 Cf. Dan. 13.45.
86 Dan. 4.6.

CATECHESIS XVII

On the Holy Spirit (2)

"To one through the Spirit is given the utterance of wisdom."[1]

(1) In the preceding lecture, dearly beloved, we set forth for your attention as best we could some small portion of the testimonies regarding the Holy Spirit; in the present, God willing, we shall touch upon, as far as possible, those which remain from the New Testament. We observed due measure in our last discourse, and checked our eagerness (for there is no satiety in speaking of the Holy Spirit); now too we shall use but a small fraction of the available material; we frankly confess that our weakness is overwhelmed by the mass of what is written; and we shall not employ human reasoning today, for this is unprofitable, but we shall simply present the evidence from the sacred Scriptures. That is the safest course according to the blessed Apostle Paul, who says: "Those things we also speak, not in words taught by human wisdom, but in the learning of the Spirit, combining spiritual with spiritual."[2] We shall act like travelers and voyagers who have a single goal in a long journey, and hasten on eagerly, yet because of human weakness are wont to stop at various harbors and cities.

(2) Though the discourses on the Holy Spirit are divided, He Himself is undivided, being one and the same. In discoursing on the Father at one time we gave the doctrine on

1 1 Cor. 12.8.
2 1 Cor. 2.13.

His royal sovereignty, and at another how He is Father, or Almighty, and then how He is Creator of all things; yet the division of lectures implied no division of faith, since the object of devotion was and is One; in discoursing on the Only-begotten Son of God also, at one time we taught the doctrine of His Godhead, and at another His Manhood, and though we divided our teaching on our Lord Jesus Christ into many discourses, we preached undivided faith in Him; so too now, though the lectures on the Holy Spirit are divided, we preach undivided faith in Him. For it is One and the Same Spirit, who, "dividing" his gifts "to everyone according as he will,"[3] yet remains Himself undivided. For the Advocate is not different from the Holy Spirit, but one and the same, though called by different names; living, subsisting, speaking and working; and the Sanctifier of all rational beings made by God through Christ, angels as well as men.

(3) To prevent some in ignorance from thinking, because of the different titles of the Holy Spirit, that these are different spirits and not one and the same (and One only), the Catholic Church has provided for your safety in the traditional confession of the faith, which commands us to "believe in one Holy Spirit, the Advocate, who spoke by the prophets"; thus you know that though His titles are many, the Holy Spirit is One. We shall now mention a few of these many titles.

(4) He is called Spirit according to the text just read: "To one through the Spirit is given the utterance of wisdom";[4] He is called the Spirit of truth, in our Savior's words: "But when he, the Spirit of truth, has come";[5] He is also called Advocate by the Lord: "For if I do not go, the Advocate will not come to you";[6] that He is one and the same, though with different titles, is clear from what follows. That the Holy

3 1 Cor. 12.11.
4 *Ibid.* 8.
5 John 16.13.
6 *Ibid.* 7.

Spirit and the Advocate are the same is manifest from the words: "But the Advocate, the Holy Spirit";[7] the identity of the Advocate and the Spirit of truth, from the words: "and I will give you another Advocate to dwell with you forever, the Spirit of truth";[8] and again: "But when the Advocate has come, whom I will send you from the Father, the Spirit of truth."[9] He is called the Spirit of God, in the words: "I saw the Spirit of God descending";[10] and again: "For whoever are led by the Spirit of God, they are the sons of God."[11] He is also called the Spirit of the Father, as the Savior says: "For it is not you who are speaking, but the Spirit of the Father who speaks through you";[12] and Paul: "For this reason I bend my knees to the Father," and subsequently: "that he may grant you to be strengthened through his Spirit."[13] He is called the Spirit of the Lord, as Peter said: "Why have you agreed to tempt the Spirit of the Lord?"[14] He is called the Spirit of God and Christ, as Paul writes: "You, however, are not carnal but spiritual, if indeed the Spirit of God dwells in you. But if anyone does not have the Spirit of Christ, he does not belong to Christ."[15] He is called also the Spirit of the Son of God, as it is said: "And because you are sons, God has sent the Spirit of his Son."[16] He is called also the Spirit of Christ, as it is written: "What time or circumstances the Spirit of Christ in them was signifying";[17] and again: "Thanks to your prayer and the assistance of the Spirit of Jesus Christ."[18]

7 John 14.26.
8 *Ibid.* 16, 17.
9 John 15.26.
10 John 1.32.
11 Rom. 8.14.
12 Matt. 10.20.
13 Eph. 3.14-16.
14 Acts 5.9.
15 Rom. 8.9.
16 Gal. 4.6.
17 1 Peter 1.11.
18 Phil. 1.19.

(5) You will find besides many other titles of the Holy Spirit. For He is called the Spirit of holiness, as it is written: "According to the Spirit of holiness."[19] He is called too the Spirit of adoption, as Paul says: "Now you have not received a spirit of bondage unto fear, but you have received a spirit of adoption as sons, by virtue of which we cry: Abba! Father!"[20] He is called the Spirit of revelation, according to the words, that He "may grant you the spirit of wisdom and revelation in deep knowledge of him."[21] He is called the Spirit of promise, as the same Paul says: "In him you too, when you believed, were sealed with the Holy Spirit of the promise."[22] He is called the Spirit of grace, as when he says: "And has insulted the Spirit of grace."[23] He has many other such titles. You heard clearly in the preceding lecture that in the Psalms at one time He is called the good Spirit and at another the perfect Spirit;[24] and that in Isaia He was called the Spirit of wisdom and of understanding, and of counsel, and of fortitude, and of knowledge, and of godliness and of fear of God. From all these testimonies, mentioned before and now, it is evident that though the titles are different, the Holy Spirit is one and the same; He is living, subsisting, ever present with Father and Son; not spoken or breathed forth from the lips of Father or Son, nor diffused through the air, but really existing, Himself speaking, working, dispensing, sanctifying; as we said before, the dispensation of salvation to us, from Father, Son and Holy Spirit, is undivided, harmonious and one. I wish you to recall our recent discourse, and to realize that there is not one Spirit in the Law and Prophets and another in the Gospels and the Apostles; it is

19 Cf. Rom. 1.4.
20 Cf. Rom. 8.15.
21 Eph. 1.17.
22 *Ibid.* 13.
23 Heb. 10.29.
24 The reference is not found in the preceding catechesis, but the lapse is understandable when one considers the mass of Old Testament testimonies quoted.

one and the same Holy Spirit, the author of the divine Scriptures in the Old and the New Testaments.

(6) This Holy Spirit came upon the holy virgin Mary. Christ, the Only-begotten, was to be born; the power of the most High overshadowed her, and the Holy Spirit, coming upon her, sanctified her to receive Him "through whom all things were made."[25] I need not speak at length to teach you that this generation was immaculate and undefiled, for you know this. Gabriel says to her: "I am the herald of what is to come to pass, but I have no share in it. Though I am an Archangel, I know my place. Though I announce joyful tidings to you, yet how you shall give birth rests on no grace of mine; 'The Holy Spirit shall come upon thee and the power of the most High shall overshadow thee; and therefore the Holy One to be born shall be called the Son of God.' "[26]

(7) This Holy Spirit wrought in Elizabeth. For He acknowledges not only virgins, but lawfully married women as well. "And Elizabeth was filled with the Holy Spirit,"[27] and prophesied; the noble handmaid says of her Lord: "And how have I deserved that the mother of my Lord should come to me?"[28] For Elizabeth deemed herself blessed. Zachary, the father of John, was filled with the same Holy Spirit and prophesied, telling how many blessings the Only-begotten would usher in, and that John would be His forerunner through Baptism. The just man Simeon received an answer from the Holy Spirit that he would not see death before he had seen the Christ of the Lord: in the temple he received Him into his arms and bore manifest testimony concerning Him.

(8) John, filled with the Holy Spirit from his mother's womb, was sanctified for the purpose of baptizing the Lord;

25 John 1.3.
26 Luke 1.35.
27 *Ibid.* 41.
28 *Ibid.* 43.

he himself did not impart the Spirit, but preached the glad tidings of Him who does. He says: "I indeed baptize you with water, for repentance. But he who is coming after me, He will baptize you with the Holy Spirit and with fire."[29] Why "fire"? Because the descent of the Holy Spirit was in fiery tongues. Concerning this the Lord says with joy: "I have come to cast fire upon the earth, and what will I but that it be kindled?"[30]

(9) The Holy Spirit descended when Christ was baptized to make sure that the dignity of Him who was baptized was not hidden, according to the words of John: "But he who sent me to baptize with water said to me, He upon whom thou wilt see the Spirit descending, and abiding upon him, he it is who baptizes with the Holy Spirit."[31] Observe what the Gospel says: "the heavens were opened"—they were opened because of the dignity of Him who descended. "Behold," it says, "the heavens were opened, and he saw the Spirit of God descending as a dove and coming upon him";[32] this descent, clearly, was from voluntary motion of His own.[33] It was fitting, as some have explained it, that the firstfruits and the first gifts of the Holy Spirit, who is imparted to the baptized, should be conferred on the manhood of the Savior, who bestows such grace. Perhaps, as some say, it was to reveal an image that He came down in the likeness of a pure, innocent, simple dove, working with prayers for the sons He begot and for forgiveness of sins;[34] just as in a veiled manner it was foretold that the beauty of Christ's eyes would be mani-

---

29 Matt. 3.11.

30 Luke 12.49.

31 John 1.33.

32 Matt. 3.16.

33 Cyril seems to be emphasizing here the living, subsisting, independent personality of the Holy Spirit (cf. *Cat.* 16.14).

34 The sense is not entirely clear. The suggestion has been made that the Holy Spirit descended in the form of a dove, a pure and innocent bird, to show that He was a sort of mystical dove in His simplicity, and in His love of children, for whose generation and remission of sins at the time of Baptism He cooperates with the prayers of Christ.

fested in this way. For in the Canticles she cries out and says of the bridegroom: "Your eyes are like doves beside running waters."[35]

(10) Some have regarded the dove of Noe as prefiguring this dove.[36] In Noe's time salvation and the beginning of a new generation came to men through wood and water; the dove returned at evening carrying a bough of an olive tree; so the Holy Spirit, they say, descended upon the true Noe, the author of the second birth, who unites the aspirations of all nations, of whom the animals in the ark were a figure. After His coming the spiritual wolves feed with lambs, and His Church pastures calf, ox and lion together; just as we see to this day worldly rulers led and taught by churchmen. He descended then, according to some interpreters, as the spiritual dove at Christ's baptism, to show that He is the same who by the wood of the Cross saves them that believe, and who would in the evening, by His death, grant them salvation.

(11) Concerning these matters perhaps another explanation should be given; we should listen to the words of the Savior Himself regarding the Holy Spirit. For He says: "Unless a man be born of water and the Spirit, he cannot enter into the kingdom of God."[37] Because this grace comes from the Father He says: "How much more will your heavenly Father give the good Spirit to those who ask him."[38] Because we must worship God in spirit He says: "But the hour is coming, and is now here, when the true worshippers will worship the Father in spirit and in truth. For the Father also seeks such to worship him. God is spirit, and they who worship him must worship in spirit and in truth";[39] and again: "But if I cast out devils by the Spirit of God," and subsequently: "There-

35 Cf. Cant. 5.12.
36 It was a common view among the Fathers that the dove of Noe prefigured the descent of the Holy Spirit in the form of a dove at Christ's baptism.
37 John 3.5.
38 Luke 11.13.
39 John 4.23, 24.

fore I say to you, that every kind of sin and blasphemy shall be forgiven to men; but the blasphemy against the Spirit will not be forgiven. And whoever speaks a word against the Son of Man, it shall be forgiven him; but whoever speaks against the Holy Spirit, it will not be forgiven him, either in this world or in the world to come";[40] again He says: "And I will ask the Father and he will give you another Advocate to dwell with you forever, the Spirit of truth whom the world cannot receive, because it neither sees him nor knows him. But you shall know him, because he will dwell with you, and be in you."[41] Further: "These things I have spoken to you, while yet dwelling with you. But the Advocate, the Holy Spirit, whom the Father will send in my name, he will teach you all things, and bring to your mind whatever I have said to you."[42] Also: "But when the Advocate has come, whom I will send you from the Father, the Spirit of truth who proceeds from the Father, he will bear witness concerning me."[43] Again the Savior says: "For if I do not go, the Advocate will not come to you; but if I go I will send him to you. And when he has come, he will convict the world of sin, and of justice, and of judgment":[44] and subsequently: "Many things yet I have to say to you, but you cannot hear them now. But when he, the Spirit of truth, has come, he will teach you all the truth. For he will not speak on his own authority, but whatever he will hear he will speak, and the things that are to come he will declare to you. He will glorify me, because he will receive of what is mine, and declare it to you. All things that the Father has are mine. That is why I have said that he will receive of what is mine, and will declare it to you."[45] I have read the very words of the Only-begotten, and so you need not pay attention to the words of men.

40 Matt. 12.28, 31, 32.
41 John 14.16, 17.
42 *Ibid.* 25, 26.
43 John 15.26.
44 John 16.7, 8.
45 *Ibid.* 12-15.

(12) He imparted the fellowship of this Holy Spirit to the Apostles; for it is written: "When he had said that, he breathed upon them, and said to them, Receive the Holy Spirit; whose sins you shall forgive, they are forgiven them; and whose sins you shall retain, they are retained."[46] This was the second breathing (the first had been impaired by willful sins),[47] to fulfill the Scripture: "He went up breathing upon your face, and delivering you from affliction."[48] He went up from where? From Limbo. For it was after His resurrection, according to the Gospel, that He breathed on them. He gives the grace at this time, and He will lavish it more abundantly; He says to them: I am ready to give it to you even now, but the vessel cannot yet hold it. Accept for the time the grace of which you are capable, but look forward to yet more. "But wait here in the city," of Jerusalem, "until you are clothed with power from on high."[49] Receive it in part now; then you will be clad in its fullness. For he who receives often has the gift only in part; but he who is clothed is entirely covered by his garment. Fear not, He says, the weapons and darts of the devil, for you will possess the power of the Holy Spirit. But be mindful of our recent admonition, that the Holy Spirit is not divided, but only the grace He bestows.

(13) Jesus ascended into heaven and fulfilled the promise he had made to His disciples: "I will ask the Father and he will give you another Advocate."[50] They were sitting, expecting the coming of the Holy Spirit. "And when the days of Pentecost were drawing to a close,"[51] here in this city of Jerusalem (for this honor also is ours; we speak not of the blessings of others, but of those granted to us), when, there-

---

46 John 20.22, 23.

47 Cf. Gen. 2.7. The first breathing for Cyril was the creation of the soul of Adam by God's breathing upon the man formed from the slime of the earth.

48 Nah. 2.1 (Sept.).

49 Luke 24.49.

50 John 14.16.

51 Acts 2.1.

fore, it was Pentecost, they were sitting and the Advocate descended from heaven, the Guardian and Sanctifier of the Church, the Director of souls, the Pilot of the storm-tossed, the Enlightener of the wandering, to preside over the combat and crown the victors.

(14) He came down to clothe with power and to baptize the Apostles. For the Lord says: "You shall be baptized with the Holy Spirit not many days hence."[52] The grace was not partial, but His power in all its fullness. For just as one immersed in the waters in Baptism is completely encompassed by the water, so they too were completely baptized by the Spirit. The water encompasses the body externally, but the Holy Spirit baptizes the soul perfectly within. Why do you wonder? Take an example from matter, a poor and lowly one perhaps, but useful for the simpler folk. If fire, penetrating the mass of iron, sets the whole aflame, and what was cold becomes hot, and what was black becomes bright—if the body of fire penetrates the body of iron, why do you wonder, if the Holy Spirit enters into the inmost parts of the soul?

(15) To prevent the magnitude of the surpassing gift from being unknown, a sort of heavenly trumpet sounded. For "suddenly there came a sound from heaven, as of a violent wind coming";[53] signifying the advent of Him who grants the grace to men to bear away with violence the kingdom of heaven, to see with their eyes the fiery tongues, to hear with their ears the sound. "And it filled the whole house where they were sitting."[54] The house became the receptacle of the spiritual water. The disciples were within and the whole house was filled. Therefore they were completely baptized, according to the promise. They were clothed in body and soul with a divine and saving vesture. "And there appeared to them parted tongues as of fire, which settled upon each of them.

52 Acts 1.5.
53 Acts 2.2.
54 *Ibid.*

And they were all filled with the Holy Spirit."[55] They partook not of burning but of saving fire, which consumes the thorns of sins but renders the soul radiant. This fire will come to you too, to strip away and destroy your thorn-like sins, and to make the precious possession of your souls shine yet more brightly; and He will give you grace, for He gave it then to the Apostles. He sat upon them in the form of fiery tongues, to crown them with new and spiritual diadems (by the fiery tongues on their heads). A flaming sword of old barred the gates of Paradise; a fiery tongue, bringing salvation, restored the grace.

(16) "And they began to speak in foreign tongues, even as the Holy Spirit prompted them to speak."[56] The Galilean Peter and Andrew spoke Persian or Median. John and the other Apostles spoke all the tongues of various nations, for the thronging of multitudes of strangers from all parts is not something new in Jerusalem, but this was true in Apostolic times.[57] What teacher can be found so proficient as to teach men in a moment what they have not learned? So many years are required through grammar and other arts merely to speak Greek well; and all do not speak it equally well. The rhetorician may succeed in speaking it well, the grammarian sometimes less well; and he who is skilled in grammar is ignorant of philosophical studies. But the Holy Spirit taught them at once many languages, which they do not know in a whole lifetime. This is truly lofty wisdom, this is divine power. What a contrast between their long ignorance in the past and this sudden, comprehensive, varied and unaccustomed use of languages.

(17) The multitude of those listening was confounded; it was a second confusion, in contrast to the first evil confusion at Babylon. In that former confusion of tongues there was a

55 *Ibid.* 3, 4.
56 *Ibid.* 4.
57 Before the coming of Christ the Jews flocked to Jerusalem from all Palestine and from other parts of the world; after the coming of Christ Jerusalem became a place of pilgrimage for all Christians.

division of purpose, for the intention was impious; here there was a restoration and union of minds, since the object of their zeal was pious. Through what occasioned the fall came the recovery. They wondered, saying: "How do we hear them speaking [our own tongue]?"[58] There is nothing to wonder at, if you are ignorant. For even Nicodemus was ignorant of the coming of the Spirit, and it was said to him: "The Spirit breatheth where he will; and thou hearest his voice, but thou knowest not whence he cometh, and whither he goeth."[59] If when I hear His voice I know not whence He comes, how can I explain what He is in essence?

(18) "But others said in mockery, They are full of new wine."[60] They spoke the truth indeed but in mockery. For in truth the wine was new, the grace of the New Testament. But this new wine was from a spiritual vine, which already had often borne fruit in the Prophets, and sprouted forth in the New Testament. For just as in the order of nature the vine, remaining ever the same, brings forth new fruit according to the seasons, so too the same Spirit, remaining what He is, having wrought in the Prophets, now manifested something new and marvelous. His grace had indeed been granted to the fathers aforetime, but now it came in superabundance; in their case they received a share of the Holy Spirit, now they were baptized in all fullness.

(19) But Peter, who possessed the Holy Spirit, and knew it, says: "Men of Israel, who preach Joel, but do not know the Scriptures, these men are not drunk, as you suppose.[61] For they are drunk, not as you suppose, but as it is written: 'They have their fill of the prime gifts of your house; from your delightful stream you give them to drink.'[62] They are drunk with a sober drunkenness, deadly to sin, and vivifying to the

58 Cf. Acts 2.8.
59 John 3.8 (Douay).
60 Acts 2.13.
61 *Ibid.* 15.
62 Ps. 35.9.

heart, a drunkenness quite contrary to that of the body. The latter induces forgetfulness of the known, but this imparts knowledge even of the unknown. They are drunk from drinking the wine of the spiritual vine, which says: 'I am the vine, you are the branches.' "[63] If you do not believe me, then understand what has been said from the time of day, for "it is the third hour of the day."[64] For He who, according to Mark, was crucified at the third hour, has now at the third hour sent His grace. For His grace is not one and the Spirit's another, but He who was then crucified and had promised, fulfilled what He had promised. But if you wish also to receive testimony, listen, he says: "But this is what was spoken through the Prophet Joel: 'And it shall come to pass in the last days, says the Lord, that I will pour forth of my Spirit.' "[65] By "pour forth," He signified a copious largess: "For not by measure does God give the Spirit. The Father loves the Son, and has given all things into his hand."[66] He has given Him the power of bestowing the grace of the All-holy Spirit on whom He will. "I will pour forth of my Spirit upon all flesh; and your sons and your daughters shall prophesy"; and subsequently: "And moreover upon my servants and upon my handmaids in those days I will pour forth of my Spirit, and they shall prophesy."[67] The Holy Spirit is no respecter of persons; He seeks not dignities, but devotion of soul. Let neither the rich be puffed up nor the poor be downcast; only let each man prepare himself to receive the heavenly gift.

(20) We have discoursed at length today and perhaps your ears are weary, but more still remains and in truth a third lecture and more would be necessary for the doctrines concerning the Holy Spirit. But we crave your indulgence on both counts. For as the holy feast of Easter is close at hand, we have extended our discourse to you today, and we have

63 John 15.5.
64 Acts 2.15.
65 *Ibid.* 16, 17.
66 John 3.34, 35.
67 Acts 2.18.

not been able to present all the testimonies we should from the New Testament. For there remain many from the Acts of the Apostles, in which the grace of the Holy Spirit wrought in Peter and in all the Apostles together. There remain many also from the Catholic Epistles and from the fourteen Epistles of Paul. From these we shall attempt to cull a few, like flowers from a broad meadow, merely to call them to your minds.

(21) In the power of the Holy Spirit, by the will of Father and Son, "Peter standing up with the eleven and lifting up his voice"[68] (according to the text: "Cry out at the top of your voice, Jerusalem, herald of good news"),[69] captured in the spiritual net of his words about three thousand souls. So strong was the grace working in all the Apostles that of the Jews who had crucified Christ this huge number believed and was baptized in the name of Christ, and remained steadfast in the teachings of the Apostles and in prayer. Again, in the same power of the Holy Spirit Peter and John, as they went into the temple at the ninth hour of prayer, healed at the Gate Beautiful in the name of Jesus a man lame from his mother's womb forty years; thus were fulfilled the words of Scripture: "Then will the lame leap like a stag."[70] They took in the spiritual net of their doctrine five thousand believers at once. They confounded the misguided rulers of the people and the chief priests, not by their own wisdom, for they were unlearned and ignorant men, but by the efficacy of the Spirit; for it is written: "Then Peter, filled with the Holy Spirit, said to them. . ."[71] So lavish was the grace of the Holy Spirit which the twelve Apostles wrought in all believers; thus they came to have but one heart and one soul; and the enjoyment of their goods was common to all, as the possessors piously offered the prices of their possessions, and there was

---

68 Cf. *ibid.* 14.
69 Isa. 40.9.
70 Isa. 35.6. For the Gate Beautiful healing, Acts 3.1-8.
71 Acts 4.8.

no one needy among them; but Ananias and Sapphira, who attempted to lie to the Holy Spirit, suffered their fitting punishment.

(22) "Now by the hands of the Apostles many signs and wonders were done among the people";[72] the spiritual grace that enveloped the Apostles was extraordinary; though they were meek, they were an object of dread ("for of the rest no man dared join himself to them; but the people magnified them"[73]). And "the multitude of men and women who believed in the Lord increased still more";[74] and the streets were filled with the sick, "on beds and pallets so that, when Peter passed, his shadow at least might fall on some of them."[75] "And there came also" to this holy Jerusalem "multitudes from the towns near Jerusalem bringing the sick, and those troubled with unclean spirits, and they were all cured."[76]

(23) Strengthened by the Holy Spirit, the twelve Apostles, cast into prison by the chief priests for preaching Christ, and unexpectedly delivered by an angel at night, when brought from the temple to the tribunal, boldly reproached the priests in speaking of Christ. They said among other things that "God has given the Holy Spirit to all who obey him."[77] And after they had been scourged, they went forth rejoicing and they ceased not to teach and preach Christ.[78]

(24) The grace of the Holy Spirit wrought not only in the twelve Apostles, but also in the first-born of this once barren Church, I mean the seven deacons.[79] They were chosen "full of the Holy Spirit and wisdom,"[80] as Scripture says; of

72 Acts 5.12.
73 *Ibid.* 13.
74 *Ibid.* 14.
75 *Ibid.* 15.
76 *Ibid.* 16.
77 Cf. *ibid.* 32.
78 Cf. *ibid.* 42.
79 Cyril's words seem to refer to the fact that the seven deacons were not chosen by Christ, but by the Apostles after the Ascension. Their names seem to indicate that they were converts from Hellenism.
80 Cf. Acts 6.3.

these he who was well named Stephen, the first fruit of the martyrs, a man full of faith and the Holy Spirit, "was working great wonders and signs among the people,"[81] and overcame those who disputed with him. For "they were not able to withstand the wisdom and the Spirit who spoke";[82] when falsely accused and brought to the tribunal he shone with angelic radiance; for "all that sat in the Sanhedrin, gazing upon him, saw his face as though it were the face of an angel."[83] When by his wise defense he had confounded the Jews, "stiffnecked and uncircumcised in heart and ear, who always oppose the Holy Spirit,"[84] he saw "the heavens opened," and beheld "the Son of Man standing at the right hand of God";[85] he saw Him, not by his own power, but as sacred Scripture says: "But he, being full of the Holy Spirit, looked up to heaven and saw the glory of God, and Jesus standing at the right hand of God."[86]

(25) By this power of the Holy Spirit Philip also, in the city of Samaria, cast out in Christ's name the "unclean spirits, crying with a loud voice";[87] he healed the palsied and the lame, and brought to Christ huge multitudes of believers; when Peter and John came down to Samaria, by prayer and the imposition of hands, they imparted the fellowship of the Holy Spirit, from which Simon Magus alone was justly declared an alien. On another occasion Philip was called by an angel of the Lord along the way, for the sake of that devout Ethiopian eunuch, and heard clearly from the Holy Spirit the words: "Go near, and keep close to this carriage."[88] He instructed the Ethiopian and baptized him and sent him into Ethiopia as a herald of Christ, to fulfill the Scripture: "Let Ethiopia

81 *Ibid.* 8.
82 *Ibid.* 10.
83 *Ibid.* 15.
84 Acts 7.51.
85 *Ibid.* 55.
86 *Ibid.*
87 Acts 8.7.
88 *Ibid.* 29.

extend its hands to the Lord";[89] then, carried away by an angel, Philip preached the gospel to the cities one by one.

(26) After being called by our Lord Jesus Christ, Paul also was filled with the Holy Spirit. We have a witness of this in the person of the pious Ananias, who said to Paul in Damascus: "The Lord has sent me—Jesus, who appeared to thee on thy journey—that thou mayest receive thy sight and be filled with the Holy Spirit."[90] The Holy Spirit wrought immediately, and not only changed Paul's blindness to sight, but also imparted the seal to his soul, making him a vessel of election, to carry the name of the Lord who had appeared to him before kings and the children of Israel; and He fashioned His former persecutor into a herald and a good servant, who "from Jerusalem round about as far as Illyricum completed the gospel of Christ";[91] he instructed imperial Rome and extended the zeal of his preaching even to Spain, sustaining countless conflicts and performing signs and wonders. Of Paul enough for the present.

(27) By the power of the same Holy Spirit Peter also, the chief of the Apostles, and the keeper of the keys of the kingdom of heaven, healed in the name of Christ the paralytic Eneas in Lydda, which is now Diospolis; and in Joppe he raised from the dead the charitable Tabitha. Being in the upper part of the house, in an ecstasy of mind he saw the heavens opened and a vessel let down, like a linen sheet, full of beasts of many forms and kinds, and learned the clear lesson to call no man common or unclean, even though he be Greek. When sent for by Cornelius, he heard from the Holy Spirit the clear words: "Behold three men are looking for thee. Arise, therefore, go down and depart with them without any hesitation, for I have sent them."[92] To make it manifest that even Gentile believers become partakers of the Holy Spirit—

89 Cf. Ps. 67.32.
90 Acts 9.17.
91 Rom. 15.19.
92 Acts 10.19, 20.

when Peter had come to Caesarea and was teaching the doctrines of Christ—the Scripture says of Cornelius and those with him: "While Peter was still speaking these words, the Holy Spirit came upon all who were listening to his message," and so even "the faithful of the circumcision who had come with Peter were amazed," and when they understood, they said: "On the Gentiles also the grace of the Holy Spirit had been poured forth."[93]

(28) Even as far as Antioch, that famous city of Syria, when the teaching of Christ was taking effect, Barnabas was sent to help in the good work, "a good man and full of the Holy Spirit and of faith."[94] Contemplating a rich harvest for the Christian faith he brought Paul from Tarsus to Antioch as his coadjutor. They instructed and brought together multitudes in the Church, "and it was in Antioch that the disciples were first called Christians."[95] The Holy Spirit, I believe, put upon the believers the new name announced beforehand by the Lord. When the grace of the Spirit was poured out by God rather abundantly at Antioch, there arose prophets and teachers, among them Agabus. "And as they were ministering to the Lord and fasting, the Holy Spirit said, 'Set apart for me Saul and Barnabas unto the work to which I have called them.' "[96] After the laying on of hands they were sent forth by the Holy Spirit. It is clear, as we have said, that the Spirit which speaks and sends is living, subsisting and working.

(29) This Holy Spirit, who in union with Father and Son established the New Testament in the Catholic Church, freed us from the grievous burdens of the Law; I mean those concerning things common and unclean, and meats, Sabbaths, new moons, circumcision, sprinklings and sacrifices. These regulations had been given for a time and had "a shadow of the good things to come";[97] but with the coming of truth they

93 *Ibid.* 44, 45.
94 Acts 11.24.
95 *Ibid.* 26.
96 Acts 13.2.
97 Heb. 10.1.

were justly withdrawn. Paul and Barnabas were sent here because of the question raised at Antioch by those who maintained that the faithful must be circumcised and observe the customs of Moses; the Apostles who were here in Jerusalem by a public letter freed the whole world from all legal and typical practices. They did not attribute the authority in such an important matter to themselves, but they sent out a decree to this effect: "For the Holy Spirit and we have decided to lay no further burden upon you but this indispensable one, that you abstain from things sacrificed to idols and from blood and from what is strangled and from immorality."[98] They indicated clearly by what they wrote that though the decree had been written by men who were Apostles, it was from the Holy Spirit, and universal; Barnabas and Paul took this decree and confirmed it to the whole world.

(30) At this point I must crave indulgence from your love, or rather from the Spirit who dwelt in Paul, if I cannot complete my account, owing to my own weakness as well as the weariness of you, my hearers. For when shall I set forth worthily his marvelous deeds wrought in the name of Christ by the operation of the Holy Spirit? those wrought in Cyprus in the case of Elymas the magician, and at Lystra in the cure of the cripple? and in Cilicia and Phrygia, Galatia, Mysia and Macedonia, or his deeds at Philippi? I mean his preaching and the casting out of the pythonical spirit in the name of Christ; and the salvation of his jailer by baptism with all his house after the earthquake; or the events at Thessalonica, and his speech on the Areopagus in the midst of the Athenians; or his teachings at Corinth and in the whole of Achaea? How shall I describe adequately the deeds wrought by the Holy Spirit through Paul at Ephesus? where men who knew Him not came to know Him by the teaching of Paul? After Paul laid hands on them, "the Holy Spirit came upon them, and they began to speak in tongues and prophesy."[99] So strong

98 Acts 15.28, 29.
99 Acts 19.6.

was the grace of the Spirit in Paul that not only was health restored by his touch, but even handkerchiefs and aprons brought from his person cured diseases and drove out the evil spirits; and those "who had practiced magical arts collected their books and burnt them publicly."[100]

(31) I pass over the miracle wrought at Troas in the case of Eutychus, who "went fast asleep and fell down from the third story to the ground and was picked up dead";[101] he was revived by Paul. I pass over the prophecy to the presbyters of Ephesus summoned to Miletus, in which he declared: "Except that in every city the Holy Spirit warns me, saying that. . ."[102] and what follows. By the words "in every city," Paul signified that the marvels performed in each city proceeded from the operation of the Holy Spirit, by the will of God and in the name of Christ, who spoke in him. By the power of the Holy Spirit Paul hastened to this holy city Jerusalem, though Agabus, inspired by the Spirit, prophesied what was to befall him; and he preached the doctrine of Christ with confidence among the people. When he had been brought to Caesarea, amid the judges' benches, at one time before Felix, at another before the governor Festus and before King Agrippa, the grace of the Holy Spirit in Paul was so powerful and of such surpassing wisdom as to cause Agrippa himself, the king of the Jews, to say: "In a short while thou wouldst persuade me to become a Christian."[103] On the island of Malta by the gift of the Holy Spirit, Paul when bitten by a viper suffered no harm, and he effected many cures of the diseased. The Holy Spirit guided him, the former persecutor, even to imperial Rome to be a herald of Christ. Paul persuaded many of the Jews dwelling there to believe in Christ, while to those who spoke against him he declared: "Well did

100 *Ibid.* 19.
101 Acts 20.9.
102 *Ibid.* 23.
103 Acts 26.28.

the Holy Spirit speak through Isaia the prophet to our fathers, saying . . ."[104] and what follows.

(32) To realize that Paul was filled with the Holy Spirit, and like him all the Apostles, and all who after them believe in Father, Son and Holy Spirit, hearken to the clear words of Paul himself: "And my speech and my preaching were not in the persuasive words of wisdom, but in the demonstration of the Spirit and of power";[105] and again: "God who also stamped us with his seal and gave us the Spirit as a pledge";[106] and: "He who raised Jesus Christ from the dead will also bring to life your mortal bodies because of the Spirit who dwells in you";[107] and again, writing to Timothy: "Guard the good trust through the Holy Spirit,"[108] who has been given to us.

(33) That the Holy Spirit subsists, lives, speaks and foretells I have told you repeatedly on former occasions; Paul writes clearly to Timothy: "Now the Spirit expressly says that in after times some will depart from the faith."[109] This we see in the divisions of former times and in our own day; so diverse and multiform are the errors of the heretics. Paul likewise says: "Which in other ages was not known to the sons of men, as now it has been revealed to his holy apostles and prophets in the Spirit";[110] and again: "Therefore, as the Holy Spirit says";[111] and: "Thus also the Holy Spirit testifies unto us":[112] and again he cries to the soldiers of Justice: "And take unto you the helmet of salvation and the sword of the Spirit, that is, the word of God, with all prayer and supplication";[113] and: "And do not be drunk with wine, for in that is de-

104 Acts 28.25, 26.
105 1 Cor. 2.4.
106 2 Cor. 2.4.
107 Rom. 8.11.
108 2 Tim. 1.14.
109 1 Tim. 4.1.
110 Eph. 3.5.
111 Heb. 3.7.
112 Heb. 10.15.
113 Eph. 6.17, 18.

bauchery; but be filled with the Spirit, speaking to one another in psalms and hymns and spiritual songs";[114] and finally: "The grace of our Lord Jesus Christ, and the charity of God, and the fellowship of the Holy Spirit be with you all."[115]

(34) From all these testimonies and from many more unmentioned, the personal, sanctifying and efficacious power of the Holy Spirit is commended to those who understand. Time would fail me if I wished to adduce the testimonies that remain concerning the Holy Spirit from the fourteen Epistles of Paul, wherein he has taught with such variety, fullness and piety. But let it rest with the power of the Holy Spirit to pardon us for our omissions (because the days are few) and to infuse in you more perfectly the knowledge of what still remains; the diligent among you may gain this knowledge from a more frequent reading of the Holy Scriptures; in fact from our present lectures and our former discourses you may have conceived a firmer faith "in One God, the Father Almighty, and in our Lord Jesus Christ, His Only-begotten Son, and in the Holy Spirit, the Paraclete." The word itself and the title of "Spirit" are applied to Them in common in the Holy Scriptures, for it is said of the Father: "God is spirit,"[116] as it is written in the Gospel according to John; and of the Son: "A spirit before our face, Christ the Lord,"[117] as Jeremia the Prophet says; and of the Holy Spirit: "But the Advocate, the Holy Spirit,"[118] as it has been said; yet the order of the Creed, if devoutly understood, excludes the error of Sabellius.[119] Let us return in our discourse to what is of great moment, and profitable to you.

---

114 Eph. 5.18, 19.
115 2 Cor. 13.13.
116 John 4.24.
117 Cf. Lam. 4.20.
118 John 14.26.
119 In the Creed we have the Father, Son and Holy Spirit with the distinct characteristics of each Person clearly indicated to exclude any confusion of Persons.

(35) See that you never, like Simon, approach the ministers of baptism in pretence, while your heart does not seek the truth. It is our task to warn, yours to be on your guard. If you have remained firm in faith, you are blessed; if you have fallen in unbelief, cast away your unbelief from this day on, and be fully confident. For at the time of baptism, when you advance to the bishops, or priests, or deacons—for the grace is everywhere, in towns and in cities, and for the lowly and the noble, for slaves and for free; for this grace is not of men, but the gift of God through men—advance then to the minister of baptism, but as you approach do not consider the face of the man you see, but be mindful of the Holy Spirit of whom we now speak. For He is present, ready to seal your soul; and He shall give you that heavenly and divine seal at which demons tremble, as it is written: "And in him you too, when you believed, were sealed with the Holy Spirit of the promise."[120]

(36) He tests the soul; He does not cast pearls before swine. If you pretend, men will indeed baptize you, but the Spirit will not baptize you; but if you approach with faith, men will minister to you visibly, but the Holy Spirit will bestow on you what is not visible. For you are coming to an important trial, to an important levy in the space of a single hour; if you lose this hour, the ill is irremediable.[121] But if you are counted worthy of the grace, your soul will be enlightened, and you will receive a power you did not possess before. You will receive arms that cause terror to evil spirits; and if you do not cast your arms away, but keep the seal upon your soul, the evil spirit will not approach; he will cower away in fear; for by the Spirit of God devils are cast out.[122]

(37) If you believe, you will not only receive the remission

---

120 Eph. 1.13.

121 Baptism is not repeated, and though the sins may later be remitted by penance, stains remain on the soul. Baptism devoutly received leaves the soul without spot or stain.

122 Cf. Matt. 12.28.

of your sins but you will accomplish deeds beyond the power of man. God grant that you may be worthy of the gift of prophecy! For you will receive a measure of grace according to your capacity, not according to what I say. For I may speak of humble blessings while you receive far richer; since faith is a broad enterprise. Your guardian will abide with you always. He will be concerned for you as His own soldier, for your comings and your goings, and for those plotting against you. He will grant you gifts of grace of every kind, if you do not grieve Him by sin. For it is written: "And do not grieve the Holy Spirit of God, in whom you were sealed for the day of redemption."[123] How then, dearly beloved, preserve the grace? Be prepared to receive the grace, and once you have received it, do not cast it away.

(38) May the Very God of all things, who spoke by the Holy Spirit, through the prophets, and sent Him forth upon the Apostles here in Jerusalem on the day of Pentecost, send Him forth now upon you also, and through Him guard us, imparting His bounty in common to all of us, so as to exhibit always the fruits of the Holy Spirit, charity, joy, peace, patience, benignity, goodness, faith, mildness, chastity, in Christ Jesus our Lord, through whom, and with whom, together with the Holy Spirit, be glory to the Father, now and always and forever and ever. Amen.

123 Eph. 4.30.

CATECHESIS XVIII

On the Words: "And in One Holy Catholic Church: And in the Resurrection of the Flesh, and in Life Everlasting"

"The hand of the Lord came upon me, and he led me out in the spirit of the Lord and set me in the center of the plain, which was now filled with bones."[1]

(1) The root of all well-doing is the hope of the resurrection. The expectation of the recompense strengthens the soul to undertake good works. Every laborer is ready to endure the toils if he foresees the reward of his toils; but when men weary themselves without return, their spirit soon fails along with their body. A soldier who expects rewards is ready for war; but no soldier serving an undiscerning king, who bestows no premiums for toils, is ready to die for him. So every soul believing in the resurrection is naturally solicitous for itself, but the unbelieving soul abandons itself to perdition. He who believes that the body is destined for resurrection is careful of his robe and does not defile it by fornication; but he who does not believe in the resurrection gives way to fornication, abusing his body as though it were not part of himself. Faith in the resurrection of the dead is a central precept and teaching of the holy Catholic Church; it is both central and essential; though denied by many, it is fully confirmed by the truth. Greeks gainsay it, Samaritans disbelieve it, heretics attack it viciously;[2] the denial takes many forms, the truth is uniform.

1 Ezech. 37.1.

2 Of the three classes of enemies here mentioned the Greeks accepted no scripture, the Samaritans only the Pentateuch; the heretics rejected the Old Testament though they used it in an attempt to refute the Catholics or bolster their own views.

(2) Greeks as well as Samaritans pose the following difficulties to us. The dead man, they say, is gone; he has moldered away and become food for worms. Even the worms have died; such is the decay and destruction that have overtaken the body. How is it to be raised? The shipwrecked have been devoured by fish, which in turn have themselves been devoured. Bears and lions have crushed and consumed the very bones of men who have fought with wild beasts; vultures and ravens have fed on the flesh of unburied corpses and flown all over the world. How then is the body to be reassembled? For it may be said that of the birds that have eaten them one has died in India, another in Persia, another in the land of the Goths. Yet other men have been consumed by fire; wind and rain have scattered their ashes; how are their bodies reconstituted?

(3) To you, poor weak man that you are, India is far from the land of the Goths, Spain from Persia. But to God, who holds the whole earth in the hollow of His hand, all things are near. Do not because of your own weakness charge God with impotence; rather consider His power. If the sun, minor work of God though it be, by one flashing of its beams warms the whole world, and the atmosphere which God made encompasses everything in the world, are we to think that God, the Creator of the sun and the atmosphere, is far off from the world? Suppose for example that different seeds of plants have been mixed—for the weak in faith I propose weak examples—and you hold these different seeds in one hand; now is it a difficult or an easy task for you, man though you are, to arrange the contents of your hand, and pick out the seeds according to their individual nature and group them according to their kind? If you can distinguish the contents of your hand, do you think that God cannot separate the things grasped in His hand and restore each to its proper place? Consider whether the answer "no" would not be blasphemous.

(4) Consider also the very principle of justice and reflect

within yourself. You have a variety of servants, let us say, of whom some are good, some bad. You esteem the good and you punish the bad. If you happen to be a judge, you praise the good and chastise the bad. Do you think that while justice is preserved before you, a mortal man, before God, the ever-changeless King of all, there is no just requital? To deny it would be impious. Or consider this. Many murderers have died in their beds, unpunished; where, then, is the justice of God? Oftentimes a murderer, guilty of fifty murders, is beheaded once; how will he pay the penalty for the forty-nine? If after this world there is no justice and retribution, you charge God with injustice.[3] But do not wonder at the delay of the judgment. Everyone who contends for a prize is crowned or put to shame only after the contest is over; never does the presiding judge crown men while they are still contending; he waits until all the contestants have finished, intending afterwards, having sifted them, to award the prizes and the crowns. So God also, while the strife in this world goes on, assists the just only in part; but afterwards he bestows on them their rewards in all fullness.

(5) If you hold there is no resurrection, why do you condemn grave robbers? For if the body perishes completely and there is no hope of resurrection, why does the grave robber undergo punishment? You see that though you deny it with your lips you retain the indelible consciousness of the resurrection.

(6) If a tree that has been cut down blossoms again, will man, when cut down, not blossom again? If what is sown and reaped remains for the threshing floor, will man, when reaped from this world, remain no more for the threshing? The shoots of vine and of other trees, when cut off and transplanted, quicken and bear fruit. Will man, for whom all these exist, when he has fallen to earth, rise no more?

3 Cyril argues for the resurrection from the necessity of a judgment to reward and punish men according to their deserts.

To compare tasks, which is harder, to fashion from the beginning a statue which did not exist, or to recast to the same shape one which has fallen to pieces? Is God, who made us out of nothing, unable to raise us up again when we have perished? But it is because you are a Greek that you disbelieve the Scripture concerning the resurrection. Well, let us take the analogy of physical nature, and consider what happens in the world today. You sow wheat, let us say, or some other kind of grain; the seed, falling into the ground, dies and rots, becoming useless for food. But then it rises again a green herb; and that tiny seed is reborn in beauty. But wheat was made for us, for it was for our use that wheat and all seeds were created, not for their own sake. If creatures made for our service come to life again, shall we, for whom they were created, rise no more after death?

(7) It is wintertime, as you see; the trees stand as though dead; for where are the leaves of the fig tree, where are the grape clusters of the vine? But these, though lifeless in the winter, are green in the spring; and when the time comes, they have a sort of resurrection from the dead. For God, knowing your disbelief, each year effects a resurrection in these visible things, that seeing what occurs in inanimate creatures, you may believe concerning the animate rational beings. Flies and bees are often drowned in water, yet after a time revive; and there is a species of toad, which remaining motionless in the winter, bestirs itself again in the summer—for your simple thoughts simple illustrations are provided. Will not He who so miraculously restores to life irrational and insignificant creatures grant it also to us, for whose sake He made these?

(8) But the Greeks demand a resurrection of the dead still manifest. They object that the creatures mentioned do rise again, but that they had never completely moldered away. They demand an unequivocal precedent of an animal that after total decay has risen again. God knew men's unbelief,

and for this reason provided a bird called the phoenix.[4] The phoenix, as Clement writes and many others record, alone among birds, comes into Egypt every five hundred years, and demonstrates the resurrection; not just in some out-of-the-way spot, for then the prodigy might go unreported, but in a well-known city that there might be observers of what otherwise would be incredible. This bird makes itself a coffin from frankincense, myrrh and other spices, which when the cycle of years is completed, it enters and then in public view dies and molders away. Then from the decayed flesh of the phoenix a worm is generated, which, when it becomes large, is transformed into a bird. (Do not disbelieve this, for you see the young of bees formed in the same way out of worms; and from liquid eggs you yourselves have seen emerge birds' wings, bones and sinews.) Subsequently this transformed phoenix grows wings and becomes a perfect phoenix, just like the original one, and flies up into the air, rising as publicly as it had died. The phoenix is a wonderful bird, but irrational, and it never sang psalms to God. It flies through the air but does not know who is the Only-begotten Son of God. If resurrection from the dead has been granted to this irrational creature that knows not its Maker, will not a resurrection be granted to us, who praise God and keep His commandments?

(9) But since the sign of the phoenix is a remote and rare occurrence, and still men disbelieve, here is a proof from everyday experience. Where were we, all of us, speakers and hearers alike, one or two hundred years ago? Don't we know the original formation of our bodies? Do we not know that it is from weak, formless, simple elements we were

4 It is amazing that the early Christians accepted so readily such a tale as that of the phoenix. Clement tells the story, in his *First Epistle to the Corinthians* 25, and many of the Fathers seem to have believed it (cf. Ambrose, *On his Brother Satyrus* 2.59). Herodotus first tells the legend in detail; Ovid, Pliny, Tacitus and others repeat the ancient account. The "well-known city" is Heliopolis. For references and further discussion, see Sr. Mary Francis McDonald, O.P., in her introduction to Lactantius' poem *The Phoenix* (in this series, Vol. 54, pp. 207-211).

generated, and that living man is formed from what is weak and simple? And that this weak principle, being made flesh, is transformed into strong sinews, bright eyes, sensitive nose, hearing ears, speaking tongue, beating heart, busy hands, running feet, and into members of all kinds? And that weak principle becomes a shipwright, a builder, an architect, a craftsman of every art, a soldier, a ruler a lawgiver, a king. Cannot God, who has made us of imperfect materials, raise us up when we have decayed? Cannot He, who formed the most insignificant thing into a body, raise up the body again when it dies? Will not He, who made what was not, raise up what is, after it has fallen?

(10) There is another manifest proof of the resurrection of the dead to be seen each month in the sky and the celestial bodies. The body of the moon suffers total eclipse, and not even a trace of it is any longer visible; then it is filled out again and restored to what it was before. For a perfect demonstration of our point, the moon, after certain revolutions of years, suffers eclipse and is apparently turned into blood; yet it recovers its luminous body. God has brought this about to prevent you, a man formed of blood, from disbelieving in the resurrection of the dead; rather should you believe of yourself what you see in the moon. Make use of these arguments, therefore, against the Greeks; for with those who do not accept the Scriptures you must contend, not with arms taken from Scripture, but with rational demonstrations only; for they do not know who Moses is, or Isaia, or the Gospels, or Paul.[5]

(11) Come now to the Samaritans, who accept the Law but do not admit the Prophets; thus the passage just read from Ezechiel seems to them of no weight, as they do not accept the Prophets. How can we convince the Samaritans? Let us go to the writings of the Law. Now God says to Moses:

5 The argumentation is naive if not bizarre and belongs in the same category as the story of the phoenix. It is hard to believe that the Greeks would have been impressed.

"I am God of Abraham, Isaac, and Jacob";[6] that is, clearly, of those who live and have substantial being. For if Abraham, Isaac and Jacob have ceased completely to be, then God is God of those who are not. When did a king ever boast of a paper army or any man make a show of nonexistent wealth? Therefore, Abraham, Isaac and Jacob must exist for God to be the God of things that are. For He did not say, "I was their God," but, "I am their God." That there is a judgment is clear from what Abraham says to the Lord: "He who is judge of all the world, shall he not exercise judgment?"[7]

(12) The senseless Samaritans, however, object that it is possible that the souls of Abraham, Isaac and Jacob still survive, but their bodies cannot rise. If of old it was possible for the rod of the just Moses to become a serpent, is it impossible for the bodies of the just to revive and rise again? The transformation of the rod was above nature: will not the just be restored according to nature? The rod of Aaron also, cut off and dead, budded without scent of waters and, though under a roof as it was, blossomed as if in the fields. Though lying in dry places, it brought forth in one night the flowers and fruits of plants like those which have been watered for years. If the rod of Aaron rose, you might say, from the dead, is Aaron himself not to rise again? If God worked a miracle in wood to preserve for him the high priesthood, will He not grant Aaron himself resurrection? A woman too, against the laws of nature, was turned into salt—flesh was transformed into salt—shall not flesh be made flesh again? If Lot's wife was turned into a pillar of salt, will not the wife of Abraham rise again? By what power was the hand of Moses transformed, which in the space of one hour was made as snow and again restored? Surely by the command of God. Is His command, efficacious then, powerless now?

(13) What, you silly Samaritans, was man's first origin? Go

6 Cf. Exod. 3.6.
7 Cf. Gen. 18.25.

to the first book of the Scripture, which even you accept. "God formed man out of the dust of the ground."[8] What? Is dust transformed into flesh, but flesh not made flesh again? We must ask you also, whence arose the heavens, the earth and the seas? Whence came the sun, the moon and the stars? How did things that fly and swim come from the waters? How did all the beasts come from the earth, of whom so many thousands were brought from nothingness into being? Shall we men, who bear God's image, not be raised again? Surely such a stand manifests complete unbelief, and broad condemnation falls upon the unbelievers: when Abraham calls upon God as "the judge of all the earth" and the learners of the Law disbelieve it; and when it is written that man is of earth, and the readers disbelieve it.

(14) These arguments, then, are for unbelievers, but those from the Prophets are for us who believe. But since even some who make use of the Prophets do not believe what is written and cite against us the text, "The wicked shall not rise again to be judged,"[9] and also, "He who goes down to the nether world shall come up no more,"[10] and "The dead shall not praise thee, O Lord"[11] (for they pervert what is well written), it would be best to answer them in passing, so far as it is now possible. For if it is said, "The wicked shall not rise to be judged," the meaning is that they shall rise, though not to be judged, but to be sentenced. For God needs no lengthy scrutiny, but as soon as the wicked rise again, their punishment forthwith follows. If it is said, "The dead shall not praise thee, O Lord," this indicates that since in this life only is the appointed time for repentance and pardon, for which those who enjoy it "shall praise thee," it is no longer possible for those who have died in sin to offer praise, as having been blessed, but only to grieve for themselves; for

8 Gen. 2.7.
9 Cf. Ps. 1.5.
10 Job 7.9.
11 Ps. 113.17 (Douay).

praise belongs to those who give thanks, but lamentation to those who are punished. Therefore, while the just will then offer praise, those who have died in sin will have no further season for confessing God's goodness.[12]

(15) As regards the text, "He who goes down to the nether world shall come up no more," notice how it goes on: "He shall come up no more. He shall not again return to his house."[13] Since the whole world is to pass away and every house to be destroyed, how will he return to his house when another world has come into being? They ought to hear Job saying: "For a tree there is hope, if it be cut down, that it will sprout again and that its tender shoots will not cease. Even though its root grow old in the earth, and its stump die in the dust, yet at the first whiff of water it may flourish and put forth branches like a young plant. But man when he shall be dead, is gone; but when mortal man is fallen, is he no more?"[14] He is almost reproaching or censuring (for the words "is he no more" should be read thus as a question). Since a tree falls and rises again, he says, shall not man, for whom the trees were made, rise again? To prevent your thinking that I am forcing the passage, read what follows. After saying by way of question, "but when mortal man is fallen, is he no more?" it says: "For if a man die, he shall live again,"[15] and immediately adds: "I wait until I shall be made again";[16] and again elsewhere: "Who shall raise upon the earth my skin, which endures these things?"[17] And the Prophet Isaia says: "But your dead shall live, their corpses shall rise."[18] But the Prophet Ezechiel, now before us, is explicit: "I will open your graves and have you rise from

12 Cf. note 2; in this chapter and the next Cyril is arguing against heretics.
13 Job 7.10.
14 Job 14.7-10 (Sept.).
15 *Ibid.* 14.
16 *Ibid.* (Sept.).
17 Job 19.25, 26 (Sept.).
18 Isa. 26.19.

them."[19] So Daniel says: "Many of those who sleep in the dust of the earth shall wake; some shall live forever, others shall be an everlasting disgrace."[20]

(16) Many Scriptures bear witness to the resurrection of the dead; for there are many further statements about it. Now, however, just as a reminder, we mention in passing the raising of Lazarus after four days, and merely refer, for brevity's sake, to the raising of the widow's son. Let me mention in passing also the ruler's daughter, and how the rocks were rent, the graves were opened, and many bodies of the saints who had fallen asleep arose. But above all let it be remembered that Christ arose from the dead. I have passed over Elia and the widow's son whom he raised, and Eliseus, who twice raised from the dead, once while he was living and once after his death. When alive, he wrought the resurrection through his soul. But not only to honor the souls of the just, but also to instill faith in the power inherent in the bodies of the just, when the corpse cast into the sepulchre of Eliseus touched the dead body of the Prophet, it came back to life. The dead body of the Prophet performed the function of the soul, and his buried corpse quickened the dead, itself, after imparting life, remaining among the dead. Why? Because if Eliseus had arisen, the deed would have been ascribed to his soul alone, and to show that even in the absence of the soul there is a mysterious power in the body of the saints, because of the just soul which dwelt in it so many years and used its ministry. Let us not foolishly disbelieve, as though this had not happened; for if the application to the sick of handkerchiefs and aprons, mere appurtenances of the body, raised them up, how much more should the Prophet's actual body raise the dead.

(17) On this subject we might speak at length, describing in detail each of the miracles. Because of your having come to today's lecture already tired from the prolonged fast of

19 Ezech. 37.12.
20 Cf. Dan. 12.2.

preparation and from the vigils,[21] let this cursory mention suffice for the present; we have sown, we may say, a few seeds; may you receive them like rich soil, and increase and bring forth fruit. Remember that the Apostles also raised the dead; Peter raised Tabitha at Joppe, and Paul raised Eutychus at Troas; so did all the rest of the Apostles, though not all the wonders wrought by each have been recorded. Be mindful too of the whole argument of the First Epistle to the Corinthians, which Paul wrote against those who said: "How do the dead rise? or with what kind of body do they come?"[22] Paul says: "If the dead do not rise, neither has Christ risen";[23] and he called them senseless who did not believe. Remember all his teaching there concerning the resurrection of the dead; and how he wrote to the Thessalonians: "And we would not, brethren, have you ignorant concerning those who are asleep, lest you grieve, even as others who have no hope," and all that follows, especially the words: "And the dead in Christ will rise up first."[24]

(18) Note particularly how Paul, all but pointing the finger, says: "For this corruptible body must put on incorruption, and this mortal body must put on immortality."[25] For this body shall be raised, not in its present weakness; it shall be raised the very same body, but by putting on incorruption, it shall be transformed, just as iron becomes fire when combined with fire, or rather as the Lord, who raises us, knows. This body, therefore, shall rise, but it will not abide in its present condition, but as an eternal body. No longer will it, as now, need nourishment for life, nor stairs for its ascent, for it will become spiritual, a marvelous thing, beggaring description. "Then shall the just," it is said, "shine forth like the sun and the moon, and like the splendor of the

21 The prolonged fast would last at least two days, probably longer.
22 1 Cor. 15.35.
23 *Ibid.* 16.
24 1 Thess. 4.13, 17.
25 1 Cor. 15.53.

firmament."[26] God, foreknowing men's unbelief, has given to the smallest worms to emit from their bodies beams of light in the summer, that natural fluorescence might be a parable of what we expect. For He who gives in part can also give wholly; and He who makes the worm shine luminously will much more illumine the just man.

(19) Therefore we shall rise again, all with eternal bodies, though not all with like bodies. A just man will receive a heavenly body, to dwell worthily with the angels, whereas the sinner will receive an eternal body, and so never be consumed, though it burn eternally in fire. Justly does God make this dispensation of both classes, for nothing is done without the body. We blaspheme with the mouth, with the mouth we pray. We commit fornication through the body, and through the body we preserve our purity. We rob by the hand, by the hand we give alms, and so forth. Since the body has ministered to us in everything, it will share our lot hereafter.

(20) Therefore, brethren, let us be careful of our bodies, and not abuse them as though they were not our own. Let us not say, like the heretics, that the vesture of the body does not belong to us, but let us be concerned for it as our very own. For we must render an account to God of everything we have done through the body. Do not say "No one sees me," or think that there is no witness of your deeds; for though there is no human witness, He who fashioned us, an infallible witness, remains faithful in heaven and sees what is done. Moreover the stains of sin remain in the body. For just as when a wound has pierced the body, and though some healing is applied the scar remains, so also sin wounds both soul and body, traces of the scars remaining in both, only to be removed by the reception of Baptism. God heals the past wounds of soul and body by Baptism; but against future wounds let us all henceforth secure ourselves, and so keep

26 Cyril combines Matt. 13.43 and Daniel 12.3 and adds something of his own.

pure the vesture of the body. Let us not by fornication, wantonness or any other sins of short duration lose the salvation of heaven, that we may inherit the eternal kingdom of God, which may He, by His grace, vouchsafe to all of you.

(21) Let these remarks suffice for the proof of the resurrection of the dead. And now, as I repeat for you the profession of faith, pronounce the words carefully, and commit it to memory.[27]

* * * * * *

(22) The Creed which we repeat contains in order the following: "And in one Baptism of repentance unto the remission of sins; and in one Holy Catholic Church; and in the resurrection of the flesh; and in life everlasting." Of Baptism and repentance we have spoken in earlier lectures; our present discourse concerning the resurrection of the dead treats of the article, "In the resurrection of the flesh." Let me complete what remains to be said, dealing with the article, "And in one Holy Catholic Church," regarding which, though there is much to be said, we will discourse but briefly.

(23) The Church is called Catholic because it is spread throughout the world, from end to end of the earth; also because it teaches universally and completely all the doctrines which man should know concerning things visible and invisible, heavenly and earthly; and because it subjects to right worship all mankind, rulers and ruled, lettered and unlettered; further because it treats and heals universally every sort of sin committed by soul and body, and it possesses in itself every conceivable virtue, whether in deeds, words or in spiritual gifts of every kind.

(24) Well is the Church named *Ecclesia* [assembly], because it calls forth and assembles all men, as the Lord says in Leviticus: "Then assemble the whole community at the en-

---

27 At the end of chapter 21 Cyril presumably recited the whole creed and the candidates for Baptism repeated it.

trance of the Meeting Tent."[28] It is worthy of note that this world "assemble" is used in the Scriptures for the first time in the passage when the Lord established Aaron in the high priesthood. In Deuteronomy God says to Moses: "Assemble the people for me; I will have them hear my words, that they may learn to fear me."[29] He mentions the name of the Church again when He says of the tablets: "And on them were inscribed all the words that the Lord spoke to you on the mountain from the midst of the fire on the day of the assembly";[30] as if He would say more plainly, "on the day on which you were called and gathered together." And the Psalmist says: "I will give you thanks in a great church [*ecclesia*], in the mighty throng I will praise you."[31]

(25) The Psalmist of old had sung: "In the churches bless God; bless the Lord, you of Israel's wellspring."[32] But since the Jews for their plots against the Savior were cast down from grace, the Savior built out of the Gentiles a second holy Church, the Church of us Christians, concerning which He said to Peter: "And upon this rock I will build my Church, and the gates of hell shall not prevail against it."[33] Prophesying of both these Churches, David said plainly of the first, which was rejected: "I hate the assembly of the evildoers";[34] and of the second, which is built up, he says in the same psalm: "O Lord, I have loved the beauty of your house";[35] and immediately thereafter: "In the assemblies I will bless thee, O Lord."[36] For after the rejection of the first Church in Judea, the Churches of Christ are multiplied throughout

28 Lev. 8.3. The word used for church in Latin and Greek is *ecclesia*, which etymologically means a calling out, and suggests the idea of people summoned to a public assembly. An ordinary translation for *ecclesia* is "assembly."

29 Deut. 4.10.

30 Cf. Deut. 9.10.

31 Cf. Ps. 34.18.

32 Cf. Ps. 67.27.

33 Matt. 16.18.

34 Ps. 25.5.

35 *Ibid.* 8.

36 *Ibid.* 12.

the whole world, and of them it is said in the Psalms: "Sing to the Lord a new song of praise in the assembly of the faithful."[37] In keeping with this the Prophet also said to the Jews: "I have no pleasure in you, says the Lord of hosts," and he immediately adds: "For from the rising of the sun, even to its setting, my name is great among the nations."[38] It is of this holy Catholic Church that Paul writes to Timothy: "That thou mayest know how to conduct thyself in the house of God, which is the Church of the living God, the pillar and mainstay of the truth."[39]

(26) But the word *Ecclesia* [Church, assembly] has several different applications—for example, to the multitude in the theatre of the Ephesians, "And with these words he dismissed the assembly";[40] and one might properly and truly say that there is a "church [assembly] of the malignant" (I mean the meetings of the heretics, the Marcionists, the Manichaeans and the rest). For this reason the Faith has delivered to you for your security the article, "And in one holy Catholic Church," to teach you to avoid their abominable meetings, and hold fast always to the holy Catholic Church, in which you were reborn. If ever you sojourn in the cities, do not ask simply where the Lord's house is (for the sects of the impious also dare to call their haunts houses of the Lord) nor merely where the Church is, but where the Catholic Church is. For this is the distinctive name of this holy Church, the mother of us all, and the spouse of our Lord Jesus Christ, the Only-begotten Son of God (for it is written: "As Christ also loved the Church, and delivered himself up for her,"[41] and all that follows); and it is the figure and copy of the Jerusalem above, which is free and the mother of us all; barren before, it now has many children.[42]

37 Ps. 149.1.
38 Mal. 1.10, 11.
39 1 Tim. 3.15.
40 Acts 19.40.
41 Eph. 5.25.
42 Cf. Gal. 4.26, 27.

(27) After the rejection of the first Church, in the second, the Catholic Church, God, as Paul says, "has placed first apostles, secondly prophets, thirdly teachers; after that miracles, then gifts of healing, services of help, power of administration, and the speaking of various tongues,"[43] and every kind of excellence, such as wisdom and understanding, temperance and justice, mercy and loving-kindness, and invincible patience in persecutions. And she, "with the armor of justice on the right hand and on the left, in honor and dishonor,"[44] in former times in persecutions and afflictions crowned the holy martyrs with divers flowery diadems of endurance; but now in times of peace, by the grace of God, she receives honors from kings and dignitaries, and from every rank and race. While kings of the various nations have limits to their power, the holy Catholic Church alone has unlimited power throughout the whole world. For God has placed peace as her border, as it is written.[45] If I wished to speak fully concerning her, my discourse would require many more hours.

(28) Instructed in this holy Catholic Church and conducting ourselves rightly, we shall gain the kingdom of heaven and inherit life everlasting; it is to receive this from the Lord that we endure all things. For it is no trifling goal we strive for, but eternal life. Therefore, in the Creed, after the article, "and in the resurrection of the flesh," that is, of the dead, of which we have discoursed, we are taught to believe, "and in life everlasting," the prize of the Christian contest.

(29) The real and true life, then, is the Father, who through the Son in the Holy Spirit pours forth upon all as from a fountain His heavenly gifts; and of His love towards men He promises to us also the blessings of eternal life. We should not think that this is impossible, but rather believe, looking not to our own weakness, but to His power, for "with God all

---

43 1 Cor. 12.28.
44 2 Cor. 6.7, 8.
45 Cf. Ps. 147.14.

things are possible."[46] That it is possible, and that we may look for eternal life, Daniel confirms, saying: "And of the many just, like the stars forever."[47] And Paul says: "And so we shall ever be with the Lord";[48] for the words, "ever be with the Lord" signify life everlasting. The Savior also says plainly in the Gospels: "And these will go into everlasting punishment, but the just into everlasting life."[49]

(30) There are many proofs of life everlasting. For us who desire to possess it, the Sacred Scriptures propose the ways to achieve it. Of these we shall now adduce only a few testimonies because of the length of our discourse; the rest we shall leave for the diligent to discover. The Scriptures say that at times life everlasting is gained by faith, for it is written: "He who believes in the Son has everlasting life,"[50] and again He Himself says: "Amen, amen, I say to you, he who hears my word, and believes him who sent me, has life everlasting."[51] At another time it is by the preaching of the Gospel, for He says: "And he who reaps receives a wage, and gathers fruit unto life everlasting."[52] At another time it is by martyrdom and confession of Christ, for He says: "And he who hates his life in this world, keeps it unto life everlasting."[53] And it is by putting Christ above riches and kindred: "And everyone who has left brothers, or sisters," and what follows, "shall possess life everlasting."[54] It is also by the observance of the commandments, "Thou shalt not commit adultery, thou shalt not kill,"[55] and so forth, as He answered the man who came to Him, saying: "Good Master, what shall I do to gain eternal

46 Matt. 10.26.
47 Dan. 12.3 (Sept.).
48 1 Thess. 4.17.
49 Matt. 25.46.
50 John 3.36.
51 John 5.24.
52 John 4.36.
53 John 12.25.
54 Matt. 19.29.
55 *Ibid.* 18.

life?"[56] Further, it is by shunning wicked deeds and serving God for the future, for Paul says: "But now set free from sin and become slaves to God, you have your fruit unto sanctification, and as your end, life everlasting."[57]

(31) There are many other ways, too numerous to mention, of finding life everlasting. For God in his loving-kindness has opened up not one, or two, but many doors that lead into life everlasting, to enable all, so far as it rests with Him, to enjoy it without hindrance. We have said enough for the present about life everlasting; it is the last doctrine we profess in the Creed, and its conclusion. God grant that all of us, both teachers and hearers, may enjoy it.

* * * * * *

(32) My final words, beloved brethren, in this instruction, will be words of exhortation, urging all of you to prepare your souls for the reception of the heavenly gifts. On the holy and Apostolic Faith handed down to you to profess, we have by the grace of God delivered as many lectures as possible in these past days of Lent; not that we have said all that might be said, for much has been omitted; and perhaps it has been more logically developed by better teachers. But when the holy day of Easter dawns, and your love of Christ is enlightened by the water of regeneration, you will, God willing, receive the further necessary instruction.[58] I mean with what devotion and order you must come forward when summoned; for what purpose each of the holy mysteries of Baptism is performed; with what reverence and order you must proceed from Baptism to God's holy altar, and there enjoy its spiritual and heavenly mysteries; so your soul, enlightened beforehand

56 *Ibid.* 16.

57 Rom. 6.22.

58 In this chapter and the next there are references to supplementary lectures. In the catechetical lectures before baptism it would have been forbidden to reveal the mysteries to the candidates for baptism, and besides they were not prepared for them.

by instructive discourse, may discover in detail the magnitude of the gifts imparted to you by God.

(33) After Easter's holy day of salvation, you will come every day, starting Monday, immediately after the assembly into the holy place of the Resurrection, where, God willing, you will hear other lectures. In these you will be instructed again in the reasons for everything that has been done, reasons warranted by proofs from the Old and the New Testaments; first concerning what is done immediately before Baptism; then how you were cleansed by the Lord "in the bath of water by means of the word";[59] how like priests you have become partakers of the name of Christ; and how the seal of the fellowship of the Holy Spirit has been given to you. You will be instructed concerning the mysteries at the altar of the New Testament, those mysteries first instituted here in Jerusalem. You will hear what the Sacred Scriptures have delivered to us, and of the efficacy of these mysteries; how you must approach them, when and how to receive them; and last of all, how you must behave in word and deed worthily of the grace received, that all of you may be able to enjoy life everlasting. These points will, God willing, be the burden of our talks.

(34) "For the rest, my brethren, rejoice in the Lord always; again I say, rejoice,"[60] "because your redemption is at hand,"[61] and the heavenly host of the angels is looking forward to your salvation. Already you can hear "the voice of one crying in the desert, Make ready the way of the Lord."[62] The Prophet cries: "All you who are thirsty, come to the water!" and then: "Heed me, and you shall eat well, you shall delight in rich fare."[63] Soon you will hear read that fine passage: "Be enlightened, be enlightened, O new Jerusalem! Your light has come."[64] It is of this Jerusalem that the Prophet said: "After

59 Eph. 5.26.
60 Phil. 3.4; 4.4.
61 Luke 21.28.
62 Matt. 3.3.
63 Isa. 55.1.
64 Cf. Isa. 60.1.

that you shall be called city of justice, faithful city, Sion,"[65] "for from Sion shall go forth instruction, and the word of the Lord from Jerusalem";[66] from here it poured out like rain upon the whole world. To Jerusalem the Prophet speaks of you: "Lift up your eyes round about, and see your children gathered together";[67] and she answers, saying: "Who are these that fly as clouds, and as doves with their young over me?"[68] She says "clouds," because of their spiritual nature, and "doves," because of their innocence. Again: "Who ever heard of such a thing, or saw the like? Can a country be brought forth in one day, or a nation be born in a single moment? Yet Sion is scarcely in labor when she gives birth to her children."[69] All things shall be filled with ineffable joy, because of the Lord who said: "I will rejoice in Jerusalem and exult in my people."[70]

(35) Of you also may it be said in that hour: "Sing out, O heavens, rejoice, O earth," "for the Lord comforts his people, and shows mercy to his afflicted."[71] All this will come to pass through the loving-kindness of God, who says to you: "I have brushed away your offenses like a cloud, your sins like a mist."[72] You have been accounted worthy of the name of faithful—of whom it is written: "My servants shall be called by a new name, which shall be blessed upon the earth"[73]—and you will say with gladness: "Blessed be the God and Father of our Lord Jesus Christ, who has blessed us with every spiritual blessing on high in Christ. In him we have redemption through his blood, the remission of sins, according to the riches of his grace. This grace has abounded beyond

65 Cf. Isa. 1.26, 27.
66 Isa. 2.3.
67 Cf. Isa. 49.18.
68 Cf. Isa. 60.8 (Sept.).
69 Isa. 66.8.
70 Isa. 65.18.
71 Cf. Isa. 49.13.
72 Isa. 44.22.
73 Isa. 65.15, 16 (Sept.).

measure in us";[74] and again: "But God, who is rich in mercy, by reason of his very great love wherewith he has loved us even when we were dead by reason of our sins, brought us to life together with Christ."[75] In this strain praise the Lord, the Author of blessings, saying: "But when the goodness and kindness of God our Savior appeared, then not by reason of good works that we did ourselves, but according to his mercy, he saved us through the bath of regeneration and renewal by the Holy Spirit; whom he has abundantly poured out upon us through Jesus Christ our Savior, in order that, justified by his grace, we may be heirs in the hope of life everlasting."[76] May God Himself and Father of our Lord Jesus Christ, the Father of glory, "grant you the spirit of wisdom and revelation in deep knowledge of him: the eyes of your mind being enlightened";[77] and may He keep you ever in good works and words and thoughts; to whom be glory, honor, and power through our Lord Jesus Christ, with Holy Spirit, now and ever, and all the infinite ages of eternity. Amen.

74 Eph. 1.3, 7, 8.
75 Eph. 2.4, 5.
76 Titus 3.4-7.
77 Eph. 1.17, 18.

THE MYSTAGOGICAL LECTURES

(*Katēchēseis mystagōgikai*)

Translated by

ANTHONY A. STEPHENSON

University of Exeter
England

INTRODUCTION

Authorship and Text

THE FIVE MYSTAGOGICAL (OR EASTER) LECTURES were delivered in Jerusalem, in the Church of the Resurrection *(Myst.* 2.4, 7), during Easter Week *(Cat.* 18.33; *Peregrinatio* 47).[1]

Authorship[2]

Before W. J. Swaans's article in *Le Muséon* in 1942 the Cyrilline authorship of the Easter Lectures was in this century rarely challenged. It had not, however, always been so, and the case for Cyril's authorship has always rested on thin ice. In the sixteenth and seventeenth centuries the Cyrilline authorship was strongly contested by E. Aubertin and others. What later encouraged the belief in Cyril's authorship was the (unforeseen) result of Touttée's new departure (1720) in numbering the two series of *Catecheses* consecutively 1-23. This

1 However, for the fragility of the arguments that connect these lectures with Jerusalem, see Supplementary Note below, p. 150.—*Peregrinatio sive Itinerarium Egeriae,* ed. E. Franceschini and R. Weber, *Corpus christianorum: Series latina* 175 (Turnhout 1965) 88f.

2 F. L. Cross, pp. xxxvi-xxxix; W. Telfer, pp. 39-40; T. Schermann, reviewing J. P. Bock, *Die Brotbitte,* in *Theologische Revue* 10 (1911) 575-579; reply by S. Salaville, "Une question de critique littéraire: Les Catéchèses Mystagogiques de S. Cyrille," *Echos d'Orient* 17 (1915) 531-537; W. J. Swaans, "A propos des 'Catéchèses Mystagogiques' attribuées à S. Cyrille de Jérusalem," *Le Muséon* 55 (1942) 1-43; E. Bihain, "Une vie arménienne de S. Cyrille de Jérusalem," *Le Muséon* 76 (1963) 319-348, esp. 340 n. 73; A. Piédagnel, pp. 18-40; A. A. Touttée, PG 33.136-142 (Diss. 2, ch. 3). G. Garitte, I believe, pioneered the research in the Armenian field. A. Renoux, "Les Catéchèses Mystagogiques dans l'organization liturgique Hiérosolymitaine du IVe et Ve siècle," *Le Muséon* 78 (1964) 355-359.

gave the impression that the two series were a single work, and since the first series of eighteen was clearly Cyril's, it seemed that the second series must be his too. Actually, however, in all the manuscripts the numbering begins anew with the Mystagogical Lectures. This changes the picture; the *independent* evidence, manuscript and other, for the Cyrilline authorship of the *Mystagogiae* is weak. Again, the significance of the alleged cross-references between the two series and of the promise in *Cat.* 18.33 of six *(sic)* Easter Lectures is altered when it is appreciated that the general pattern of catechizing at Jerusalem was to some extent constant and survived Cyril, so that both series of lectures continued to be given by someone every year.

Several liturgical elements in the Fifth Lecture probably suggest a date in the period 380-410. Here, however, the separation of the *Mystagogiae* from the Lenten Lectures favours Cyril, who could then have delivered these Easter Lectures any year in the period 350-386. A more important objection to the Cyrilline authorship is the marked differences between the two series' expositions of Baptism and Chrismation (Confirmation), discussed below, though the last sentence of *Cat.* 16.26 provides a bridge between them in one important point. Again (cf. the advertisement "To the Reader," with note 47, vol. 1, pp. 84-85), the *Mystagogiae* would not have been available to *phōtizomenoi.*

But the nearly decisive evidence is that of the manuscripts. In his recent valuable discussion of the question, Auguste Piédagnel, who cannot decide between Cyril and John (see below), puts the case sympathetically towards Cyril when he observes[3] that only one Greek manuscript, *Monac. gr.* 394, ascribes the *Mystagogiae* to John alone, and of the four manuscripts (*Vatic. Ottob.* 86 and 446, *Monac. gr.* 278 and *Vaticanus gr.* 602) which ascribe them to "Cyril and John," the last three depend upon *Ottob.* 86. The decisive facts, however, are the

3 P. 37.

following.[4] In by no means all of the manuscripts are the Lenten Lectures followed by the *Mystagogiae,* and often, where they are so followed, the latter have no author assigned; identity of authorship has simply been assumed by modern scholars. Of the seven Greek manuscripts earlier than 1200 in which the *Mystagogiae* are included, the tenth-century *Monac. gr.* 394 twice attributes them to John (i.e., presumably Cyril's successor, John II, bishop of Jerusalem 387-417), in *Ottob.* 86 Cyril's name has been inserted before that of John, and the other five do not name the author of the *Mystagogiae.* Since the names of famous ancient theologians act like a magnet upon works of unknown authorship (catechetical lectures and works of a Jerusalem provenance naturally gravitating towards Cyril), it seems pretty clear what has happened: Cyril's name was first joined to John's and then supplanted it. Again, the Arabic codex *Sinait.* 309, which Bihain has dated to 909 (Piédagnel, however, thinks it is related to *Monac.* 394), attributes the *Mystagogiae* to John alone. The Syro-Palestinian version of the Lenten Lectures apparently knows nothing of Cyrilline *Mystagogiae.* The only works of Cyril known to the intelligent monk Alexander, who wrote of Cyril's life before 614,[5] were the Lenten Lectures and the Letter to Constantius. Neither the Armenian version of the Lenten Lectures nor the tradition of the Armenian Church shows any knowledge of Cyrilline *Mystagogiae,* even though, as we know from the Old Armenian Lectionary, the Armenian Church had a program of Easter mystagogical lecturing. Also significant is the comparatively late external attribution of the *Mystagogiae* to Cyril, the earliest witness being Eustratius *ca.* 600.

The internal evidence is, taken as a whole, hardly less decisive against identity of authorship. All scholars have recognized a difference in style between the two series. The

4 Bihain *(loc. cit. supra,* n. 2).
5 Alexander's notice of Cyril may be read in PG 87.3 (Paris 1860) 4069; on this valuable text see Bihain 321 and n. 6.

jejune style of the Easter Lectures might be due to their subject matter and to a tradition of brevity in the Easter teaching after the rigours of Lent. But it is hard to believe that the theological expositions, always pedestrian and often threadbare, of the *Mystagogiae* are the product of the same mind as the Lenten Lectures, whose theological texture is commonly quite rich and whose often moving piety intermittently blazes into something like poetry.

While in sacramental theology the two series have much in common, notably the dualism of thing and sign, and while the conclusions about the relative importance of Baptism and Chrism probably do not greatly differ, yet the typology here is markedly different. In *Cat.* 3.14 and 17.9 (where the Greek is unambiguous) the dualism of Our Lord's baptism is that of simultaneous sign (water) and reality (descent of the Spirit), whereas in the *Mystagogiae* the descent of the Spirit is a subsequent event, to which Chrism answers. (See notes and appended notes below.) Again, in *Cat.* 17.13-15 Pentecost is the Apostles' Baptism and the Pentecostal fire is "the intelligible *(noētou)* water" (but contrast 16.26), whereas in the *Mystagogiae* there is not a word about Pentecost. Similarly St. John the Baptist, so prominent in the third Lenten Lecture (see also 4.11; 10.19; 14.19), appears only briefly in the *Mystagogiae* (2.6).

It is, indeed, logically possible that between the Lenten Lectures and the *Mystagogiae* Cyril met an *Ur*-Dix and his theology of Baptism *vis-à-vis* Confirmation underwent an agonizing reappraisal—there are perhaps signs of this in (later strata of?) the Lenten Lectures—but in that case he would probably have constructed a new synthesis.

Again, the *Mystagogiae,* both as a theological and a literary work, seem unworthy of Cyril. Compared with the praises of Baptism in the Lenten Lectures, set in a rich context of biblical theology, the *Mystagogiae* seem somewhat jejune and lame, as well as obscure. Awe and exclamations of pious wonder have taken the place of understanding. Cyril, on the other hand, commanded considerable biblical and theological resources, to which corresponded a notable mastery of language, a quite rich vocabulary and some imagination. The diction of the *Mystagogiae* is, by comparison, poverty-stricken; I have deliberately, in my translation, left some of its infelicities unimproved.

Such judgments, however, are liable to subjectivity. The circumstances, subjects, and perhaps also the method of reporting differed in the two series.[6] These differences would have led to some difference in style. If the difference between the Lenten Lectures and the *Mystagogiae* is as great as that between patristic and post-patristic literature, this is partly because the *Mystagogiae,* like the comparable works of Chrysostom and Ambrose, are a new literary *genre.* It does not in itself exclude Cyrilline authorship of the *Mystagogiae,* since their piecemeal, analytic, fragmented method was imposed by the artificial necessity of explaining the symbolism of the successive parts of the rite *seriatim.* For the main scope of the *Mystagogiae* was limited to the explanation of the symbolism. The case for John's authorship is less strong than the case against Cyril's. For John seems to have been a cultured Origenist of some renown, and the *Mystagogiae* do not seem to be very markedly Origenist.

Only this paucity of Origenisms in the *Mystagogiae* prompts reservations in ascribing them to John. In any case the double ascription may contain an element of truth. John is likely to have used the work of his predecessor. Catechizing is the responsibility of the bishop, so that there may well have been something like a diocesan script, subject to continuing revision.

6 There is even perhaps an outside chance that the text of the *Mystagogiae* derives from a Syriac original; we know from Aetheria (*loc. cit. supra,* n. 1) that there was a simultaneous translation of the Easter Lectures into Palestinian Syriac. This might explain the plethora of genitives in 3.3; since in Semitic thought "the Spirit" and the "divine Presence" were synonymous, two or three of the Greek genitives might be alternative renderings of a single Syriac word.

Liturgical documents are often traditional and conservative; they are an especially notable group in stratified "evolved" or "snowball" literature; they may be the work of several hands; several "new and revised" editions may appear; they are almost certain to be highly stratified, many-layered. On the other hand, when it is appreciated that John's (?) *Mystagogiae* date from towards the end of the fourth century (they may be later than St. Ambrose's *De mysteriis* and *De sacramentis),* one sees that they belong to a period of liturgical experiment and innovation. For all its alleged conservatism, liturgy appears in history as developing considerably; *e pur si muove.*

The Blessed John, as he is styled in the Jerusalem calendar reproduced *ca.* 440 in the Old Armenian Lectionary, was Bishop of Jerusalem 387-417 and is a personage fairly well known, principally from the correspondence of St. Jerome. Here it is relevant to mention only two episodes. In the famous Origenist controversy of 393-398 Jerome (who stigmatized St. Cyril as an Arian) bitterly disapproved of the shelter and friendship extended by John to such champions of Origen as Rufinus and savagely attacked him as an "Origenist" in his open letter to Pammachius.[7] Later the famous English heresiarch, the lay monk Pelagius,[8] came to Palestine and resided for some time in Jerusalem, where his voluntarist and anti-predestinarian teaching quickly became a live and divisive issue. Opposition to him was organized by Jerome and Augustine, who had recently condemned Pelagian teaching; and in 415 Pelagius was twice personally examined in Palestine about his views, first at a diocesan council at Jerusalem presided over by John, July 28. When Pelagius's opponents appealed to the authority of Augustine of Hippo as

7 A long letter (an apologia) of John is extensively reproduced by St. Jerome in his reply to it addressed "To Pammachius, Against John of Jerusalem" (the *Contra Ioannem Hier.):* PL 23.371-412 *(al.* 355-396).

8 Cf. J. Ferguson, *Pelagius* (Cambridge 1956), ch. 6; J. Brochet, *S. Jérôme et ses ennemis* (Paris 1905).

decisive, John said: "I am Augustine here." Pelagius was again examined at a provincial council held at Diospolis (Lydda) towards the end of December. John was present, but the president was Eulogius, bishop of Caesarea, the metropolitan see. At both synods Pelagius was acquitted after a rather superficial theological debate. For Pelagian tendencies in the Cyrilline *corpus* see the notes to the Sermon on the Paralytic.

Text

Auguste Piédagnel has done a notable service to scholarship by providing a considerably improved text and a vastly improved apparatus. Only thrice, I think, have I departed from this text; twice (1.1, end, and 3.3) Piédagnel himself in his translation (a revision of that of P. Paris) follows the old text. Although the first draft of my translation dated from the pre-Piédagnel era, I hope I have, in revising it, caught all the textual changes. The text looks irrecoverably corrupt at some points; even the new text presents some difficulties to the translator. For greater precision in text citations, I will sometimes speak of the chapters of both series of the Catecheses, together with the *Procatechesis,* as if divided into five approximately equal parts, A-E, although these subdivisions are not indicated in either the Piédagnel text or this translation.

Fr. Piédagnel has (pp. 51, 58, 80) classified the important manuscripts into three families α, β, γ. But this nomenclature (adopted in my notes) does not imply a grading of the manuscripts into a first, second, and third class. For, while Piédagnel judges α the best family, both β and γ are of ancient lineage, β's *Bodl. Roe* 25 being probably and γ's *Ottob.* 86 certainly pre-Conquest.

SUPPLEMENTARY NOTE

(See above, p. 143, opening sentence.)

The general view, at least, is that the *Mystagogiae* were delivered in Jerusalem, in the Church of the Resurrection. The link with Jerusalem, however, provided by the internal evidence is a slender thread. In 2.7 the Mystagogue is developing St. Paul's argument (Rom. 6.1-6) that Christians are baptized into Christ's *death* and so become "fellows" (partakers) of His passion. The Mystagogue proceeds, first quoting Rom. 6.5 and taking "planted" as a metaphor for burial (symbolized by the immersion in the baptismal pool): " 'For if we were planted along with him by this symbolic enactment of his death, we shall also share his resurrection.' 'Planted along with' is apt. For since it was here *(entautha)* that the true Vine was planted, we, by partaking, through baptism, in His death, have been 'planted along with' Him." So the manuscripts and the received text; the candidates were planted or buried "along with" Christ because the Jerusalem baptistery adjoined the Holy Sepulchre. A nice pastoral thought. Yet what a trivialization of the great theme in sacramental theology, elsewhere (in 2.6-7) expounded at so high a level of serious exegesis: that baptism is a mystical enactment of the heart and climax of the Christ event. Instead of reaching a climax, the development of this theme is here sacrificed to an essentially silly conceit. Moreover the conceit is left uncompleted in the apodosis, and, by contrast with the Lenten Lectures in such passages as 16.4, nowhere in the *Myst.* do we meet the note of pride in the singular glories of the church of Jerusalem. In our sentence in 2.7 what theology and context alike require is not "Since it was here . . .," but "Since it was *in death* (or *by dying*) that the true Vine was planted . . ."—cf. John 12.24; then the sentence continues naturally, "We by partaking of this death/baptism have become 'one planting' with Him." Since for the Vine death was only a planting, when it buds again, it includes all the baptized. The original Greek, therefore, was not *entautha,* but *en tōi tha, tha* being an abbreviation for *thanatōi;* for a comparable abbreviation, *anon* for (anarthrous) *anthrōpon,* in an Athanasian manuscript, cf. F. L. Cross, in *Journ. Theol. Stud.* 49 (1948) 94. Abbreviations, however, seem to be normally marked by a line above them.

This emendation is confirmed by 2.4, where *entautha* seems again to be a mistake for *en tōi thanatōi,* "in dying." Here, in a passage of central theological importance—for the Mystagogue is explaining the symbolism of the actual baptismal immersion—the received text gives: "You made the saving confession and immersed yourselves three times in the water and rose up again, *also herein (kai entautha)* hinting by a symbol at Christ's three days in the grave." But the "herein" is redundant, and the "also" has no possible reference. Moreover baptism then symbolizes, not death and burial, but only burial; the candidates are apparently buried alive. If, however, we substitute *en tōi tha(natōi)* for *entautha,* we get: "in your symbolic dying, hinting *also* at Christ's three days' burial"—i.e., by the *tripleness* of the immersion, to which the burial symbolism is confined. For the *candidates,* the water is a grave only in the sense that they die in it. Yet, while the rest of 2.4 as well as 2.5-7 favours our emendation here, the first sentence of 2.4 tells against it and suggests that the candidates perhaps "died" when they "stripped off the old man" in 2.2.

The other link with Jerusalem (*Myst.* 2.4) is also tenuous: "as Christ was carried from the Cross to the tomb which lies in your view *(prokeimenon).*" This link would be severed if *prokeimenon* meant "which lay in view of the Cross," or "prescribed" ("predicted"?), or "above-mentioned"; or if the true reading were *prokeimenōn,* meaning simply "tomb," or (since *prokeimenon* would be a familiar word to copyists of liturgical texts, both in reference to the eucharistic *oblata* and to the "proper" antiphon) *proskeimenon,* "the adjacent, or nearby, tomb."

FIRST LECTURE ON THE MYSTERIES

The First Part of the Baptismal Ceremony (The Rites of the Outer Chamber: Renunciation of Satan, Profession of Faith) With a Lesson from Peter's First Catholic Epistle, Beginning, "Be sober, be watchful," to the End[1] By the same Cyril and Bishop John

(1) It has long been my wish, true-born and long-desired children of the Church, to discourse to you upon these spiritual, heavenly mysteries. On the principle, however, that seeing is believing, I delayed until the present occasion, calculating that after what you saw on that night I should find you a readier audience now when I am to be your guide to the brighter and more fragrant[2] meadows of this second Eden. In particular, you are now capable of understanding the diviner mysteries of divine, life-giving baptism. The time being now come to spread for you the board of more perfect instruction, let me explain the significance of what was done for you[3] on that evening of your Baptism.

(2) First you entered the antechamber of the baptistery and faced towards the west. On the command to stretch out your hand, you renounced Satan as though he were there in person.

1 1 Peter 5.8ff.

2 Note the comparatives. The imagery continues and *develops* that of the exordium of the *Procatechesis,* which is a point in favour of identity of authorship. For further paradisal imagery cf. *Procat.* 16; *Myst.* 1.4 (end), 9; 2.2 (end). Christians, therefore, live in the East, the fiends (the "opposite Powers") in the West.

3 Here I follow a neat emendation suggested by Touttée, and my translation agrees with Piédagnel's—though not with his text!

This moment, you should know, is prefigured in ancient history. When that tyrannous and cruel despot, Pharaoh, was oppressing the noble, free-spirited Hebrew nation, God sent Moses to deliver them from the hard slavery imposed upon them by the Egyptians. The doorposts were anointed with the blood of a lamb that the destroyer might pass over the houses signed with the blood; so the Jews were miraculously liberated. After their liberation the enemy gave chase, and, on seeing the sea part miraculously before them, still continued in hot pursuit, only to be instantaneously overwhelmed and engulfed in the Red Sea.

(3) Pass, pray, from the old to the new, from the figure to the reality. There Moses sent by God to Egypt; here Christ sent from the Father into the world. Moses' mission was to lead out from Egypt a persecuted people; Christ's, to rescue all the people of the world who were under the tyranny of sin. There the blood of a lamb was the charm against the destroyer; here, the blood of the unspotted Lamb, Jesus Christ, is appointed your inviolable sanctuary against demons. Pharaoh pursued that people of old right into the sea; this outrageous spirit, the impudent author of all evil, followed you, each one, up to the very verge of the saving streams. That other tyrant is engulfed and drowned in the Red Sea; this one is destroyed in the saving water.[4]

4 Baptism is the new Exodus; sometimes (e.g., in the Odes of Solomon) it is the crossing of Jordan and the entry into the Promised Land that is prominent. John 1.17 ("The Law . . .") represents Christ as the new Moses, and from as early as the Epistle of Barnabas the Church is represented by Christian writers as the true Israel. For baptism and the Red Sea, cf. 1 Cor. 10.1, 2 on which cf. Origen, *In Exod., Hom.* 5.5 (GCS, Origen, 6.190), where the baptizand escapes (like the stag) by entering the water, in which the Egyptians then drown. Cf. *In Lib. Iesu Nave, Hom.* 26.2 (GCS, Orig., 7.459), where Israel's travels in the desert symbolize the baptismal renunciation, and the emergence from the Red Sea represents the baptismal grace; also Ephraem Syrus, *Hymni in Fest. Epiph.* 1.6 (Lamy, 1.7): "Israel passed over the sea and was unbelieving; the Gentiles, plunged in the baptismal waters, believed and received the Holy Spirit." D. Daube (*The New Testament and Rabbinic Judaism* 106-140) says that a convert to Judaism in N.T. times, regenerated by proselyte baptism, was

(4) You are told, however, to address him as personally present, and with arm outstretched to say: "I renounce you, Satan."[5] Allow me to explain the reason of your facing west, for you should know it. Because the west is the region of visible darkness,[6] Satan, who is himself darkness, has his empire in darkness—that is the significance of your looking steadily towards the west while you renounce that gloomy Prince of night.

What was it that each of you said, standing there? "I renounce you, Satan, you wicked and cruel tyrant; I no longer" (you said in effect) "fear your power. For Christ broke that power by sharing flesh and blood with me, planning through

---

thought of as passing through the experience of ancient Israel (Exodus, etc.). And 1 Cor. 10.1-2 shows that the baptism of the desert generation of Israelites was a model for Christian baptism also.

5 For the renunciation of Satan cf. 1 Thess. 1.9-10: ". . . how you turned from Idols to be the servants of the living and true God, and to wait expectantly . . . the deliverer from the terrors of judgment to come."

6 The Light-Darkness antithesis, so common in the Bible from Gen. 1 to the Apoc., perhaps originated in Babylonia or Persia. In Gnosticism it has an intellectual, in Christianity an ethical slant, though implying also a (nonradical or at least optimistic) cosmic dualism. Darkness is evil and falsehood, irrationality and unreality. Darkness reigned for three hours during the Crucifixion, but then Christ rose like the Sun on the first day of the week. The ethical dualism of Zoroastrianism taught a cosmic conflict between Ormuzd, god of light and good, and Ahriman, god of darkness and evil. The Fourth Gospel uses similar imagery and the War Scroll from Qumran speaks of the war between the Sons of Light and the Sons of Darkness. The opening chapters of the *Didache* (A.D. *ca.* 110?) speak of the Two Ways, of Life and Death, while the corresponding closing chapters of (the Alexandrian?) Pseudo-Barnabas speak of the Two Ways of Light and Darkness. Both derive from an earlier, probably, pre-Christian Jewish moral catechism. Inevitably there is some overlap between religions in their symbolism and ethical teaching. The Jerusalem word for Baptism was "enlightenment" and the candidates were "those being enlightened" (*phōtizomenoi*); we know from the *Peregrinatio* of Aetheria that the Jerusalem Church of the Resurrection, where the candidates were initiated, was brilliantly illuminated by a thousand lamps on Holy Saturday night.

The West as Satan's abode: Porphyry (*The Nymphs' Cave in the Odyssey* 29) connects mortal and servile beings with the north, semidivine beings with the south, gods with the east and demons with the west. Proclus (*Comm. in Platonis Timaeum* 24D) places the hylic demons in the west, "since the west, as the Egyptians said, is the place of the lowest demons."

their assumption to break, by His death, the power of Death, to save me from subjection to perpetual bondage.[7] I renounce you, crafty scoundrel of a serpent; I renounce you, traitor, perpetrator of every crime, who inspired our first parents to revolt. I renounce you, Satan, agent and abettor of all wickedness."

(5) Then in a second phrase you are taught to say, "and all your works." All sin is "the works of Satan"; and sin, too, you must renounce, since he who has escaped from a tyrant has also cast off the tyrant's livery. Sin in all its forms, then, is included in the works of the Devil. Only let me tell you this: all your words, particularly those spoken at that awful hour, are recorded in the book of God. Whenever, therefore, you are caught in conduct contrary to your profession, you will be tried as a renegade. Renounce, then, the works of Satan, that is, every irrational[8] deed and thought.

(6) Next you say, "and all his pomp."[9] The pomp of the Devil is the craze for the theatre, the horse races in the circus, the wild-beast hunts, and all such vanity, from which the saint prays to God to be delivered in the words, "Turn away mine eyes that they may not behold vanity."[10] Avoid an addiction to the theatre, with its spectacle of the licentiousness, the lewd and unseemly antics of actors and the frantic dancing of degenerates. Not for you, either, the folly of those who, to gratify their miserable appetite, expose themselves to wild beasts in the combats in the amphitheatre. They pamper their belly at the cost of becoming themselves, in the event, food for the maw of savage beasts; of these gladiators it is fair to say that in the service of the belly which is their God they

7 Cf. Heb. 2.14-15.

8 *Para logon:* J. Bouvet and Piédagnel prefer: "contrary to your baptismal promise."

9 This phrase is not found in all, even later, liturgies. The ApTrad (21.9) has simply: "I renounce thee, Satan, and all thy service and all thy works."

10 Ps. 118.37.

court death in the arena.[11] Shun also the bedlam of the races, a spectacle in which souls as well as riders come to grief. All these follies are the pomp of the Devil.

(7) The food, also, which is sometimes hung up in pagan temples and at festivals—meat, bread, and so forth—since it is defiled by the invocation of abominable demons, may be included in "the pomp of the Devil." For as the bread and wine of the Eucharist before the holy invocation of the adorable Trinity were ordinary bread and wine, while after the invocation the bread becomes the Body of Christ, and the wine his Blood, so these foods of the pomp of Satan, though of their own nature ordinary food, become profane through the invocation of evil spirits.[12]

(8) After this you say, "and all your service." The service of the Devil is prayer in the temples of idols, the honoring of lifeless images, the lighting of lamps or the burning of incense by springs or streams; there have been cases of persons who, deceived by dreams or by evil spirits, have gone to this length in the hope of being rewarded by the cure of even bodily

11 ApTrad, ch. 16, lists among the trades and professions forbidden to Christians, idolatry, the circus and the amphitheatre. While Cyril emphasizes gluttony as the motive of the gladiator or *bestiarius,* the attractiveness of such professions is otherwise explained by S. Dill (*Roman Society from Nero to Marcus Aurelius,* 2d ed. [London 1905, reprinted 1925] 238-244). The "stars" of this dangerous and glamorous profession commanded salaries comparable to those of a successful footballer or bull-fighter in modern times. While they were fed like fighting cocks, they were subject to harsh discipline. What is the explanation of Cyril's emphasis? A sentence in Tert. *Apol.* 42 suggests the possibility that the *bestiarii* sometimes were banqueted before the combat. Botte, cited by Piédagnel, suggests that Cyril misunderstood an obsolete prohibition. I assume, against Piédagnel, that *kynēgesion,* like *venatio,* can, and here does, mean, not "hunting," but "combats with wild beasts" in the arena. Circus shows were denounced by Hippolytus and Tertullian (*Apol.* 38-42 *passim; Spec.* 10 [theatre], 16-17). They were connected with the worship of the pagan gods of Greece and Rome and, on festivals, were inaugurated by a religious procession (*pompē*). When Hadrian rebuilt Jerusalem as Aelia Capitolina in 135, he included a theatre; there were theatrical performances in Jerusalem in Cyril's time (Sozomen, *Hist. eccl.* 4.25.3-4).

12 Cf. *Cat.* 3.3; *Myst.* 3.3; 1 Cor. 10.20. For the omission, in some versions of ApTrad, of one or other forbidden crafts as they became irrelevant, see ApTrad, p. 25, n. 10.

ailments. Have nothing to do with these practices. The observation of birds, divination, omens, charms and amulets, magic and similar chicanery—all such practices are the cult of the Devil. Shun them. For if you should succumb to such practices after renouncing Satan and transferring your allegiance to Christ,[13] you will find the usurper[14] more cruel than ever. For if formerly, treating you as a familiar, he abated the rigors of your slavery, now he will be furiously exasperated against you. So you will lose Christ and taste Satan's tyranny.

Have you not heard the old story which recounts the fate of Lot and his daughters? Was not Lot himself saved together with his daughters after gaining the mountain, while his wife was turned into a pillar of salt,[15] a monumental warning and a memorial of her wicked choice (her looking back)? So be on your guard: do not turn back to "what is behind,"[16] first "putting your hand to the plow"[17] and then "turning back" to the bitter savor of the things of this world. No; flee to the mountain, to Jesus Christ, the "stone hewn without hands"[18] that has filled the world.

(9) When you renounce Satan, trampling underfoot every covenant with him, then you annul that ancient "league with Hell,"[19] and God's paradise opens before you, that Eden, planted in the east, from which for his transgression our first father was banished. Symbolic of this is your facing about from the west to the east, the place of light. It was at this point that

13 Cf. (besides baptism itself) the turning to the east and the declaratory Creed in ch. 9. A fourth-century (T) version of the ApTrad, 10a, interpolates, after the Renunciation and first Unction, a declaration of adherence to the Blessed Trinity. The K text (*ca.* 500) interpolates, slightly later (11a), a more elaborate form.

14 At baptism rebels and traitors return to their true allegiance.

15 Clement of Rome (1 Clem. 11.2) speaks of this pillar of salt "standing to this day" (A.D. *ca.* 97). Josephus (*Antiq.* 1.203) had seen it. This (Sodom) area abounds in pillars of salt, and medieval and later travellers (or their guides) have delighted to identify one or another with *the* pillar.

16 Phil. 3.13.

17 Cf. Luke 9.62.

18 Cf. Dan. 2.45.

19 Cf. Isa. 28.15.

you were told to say: "I believe in the Father, and in the Son, and in the Holy Spirit, and in one Baptism of repentance."[20] But these subjects have been treated at large, as God's grace allowed, in the previous discourses.

(10) In the security, then, of this formula of faith, "be sober." For "our adversary, the devil," in the words just read, "as a roaring lion, goes about seeking whom he may devour."[21] Yet if in former times Death was mighty and devoured, now, in the time of the holy laver of regeneration, "the Lord God hath wiped away all tears from every face."[22] No more shall you mourn, now that you have "put off the old man,"[23] but you shall ever keep high festival, clad in Jesus Christ as in a garment of salvation.

(11) That was what was done in the outer chamber. When we enter, God willing, in the succeeding discourses on the mysteries, into the Holy of Holies, we shall receive the key to the rites performed there. Now to God,[24] with the Son and the Holy Spirit, be glory, power and majesty forever and ever. Amen.

---

20 Quite likely Cyril summarizes here, and the candidates recited the whole of the Jerusalem creed. The closely parallel passage in ApCo 7.41 suggests that, turning to the east after the renunciation *(apotassomai),* the candidates prefaced the Creed with a "consociation" *(syntassomai)* with Christ. See note 13 above.

21 1 Peter 5.8, 9.

22 Cf. Isa. 25.8 and Apoc. 7.17.

23 Cf. Eph. 4.22.

24 The use of the word "God" as a designation of the Father is, in a document of this date, rather striking: archaic? traditionalist? Origenist?

PREFATORY REMARK TO THE SECOND AND THIRD LECTURES ON THE MYSTERIES

The B Theory and the C Theory

Mystagogical Lectures 2 and 3 are relevant to an important continuing debate about the relative importance of Baptism and Confirmation, and especially about the answer to the question, "In which sacrament is the Holy Spirit given?" For convenience I shall refer to the theory which exalts Baptism (the theory to which I provisionally subscribe) as the B theory, and to the other as the C (Chrism or Confirmation) theory. The B theory holds that the Spirit, being inseparable from other graces incontestably given in Baptism (dying and rising with Christ, regeneration, adoptive sonship, sanctifying grace, new creation), is Himself given in Baptism. Thus (as the Lenten Lectures hold) Baptism is the sacrament of the Death and Resurrection of the Lord and also corresponds to Pentecost, the primal creation of the Church through the Spirit; so Peter after Pentecost says (Acts 2.38): "Be baptized . . . and you will receive the gift of the Holy Spirit"; cf. John 3.5. On this view Confirmation, whether by imposition of hands or by chrismation (anointing), though primitive, is a subsidiary rite; it rounded off the rite (though sometimes it preceded Baptism) and gave a high sacramental grace (of variable interpretation) but was not strictly essential. The bishop's role is safeguarded in this theory by the fact that the whole initiation rite is under his control and direction.

The C theory holds that Pentecost corresponds to Confirmation (Chrism) and that it is in Chrism that the Spirit is given. Among the texts to which it appeals are Acts 8.14-17 (Peter and John in Samaria), 19.5, and the problematic 1 John 2.20, 27 ("You have an anointing, *chrisma. . .*"). It holds that quite often in the New Testament "baptism" refers not simply to water-baptism but to a larger rite of which this was only a part. It interprets the "born again of water and the Spirit" of John 3.3-5 as referring to two baptisms, water-baptism and baptism of Spirit by chrismation. Similarly in the Gospel narratives of Our Lord's baptism by John it finds two successive events (the exemplars of Baptism and Confirmation) instead of the dualism of a single event in which one element (the Dove and the Voice) is but the visibilization[1] of the spiritual grace conferred in the other (the baptism in Jordan). Emphasizing that "Christ" means "anointed," it holds that Chrism christens.

While in the notes to Mystagogical Lectures 2 and 3 I have occasionally criticized the theological assumptions and implications of the C theory, I nowhere discuss the earlier evidence, on which the answer to the question depends.

1 I owe this useful term "visibilization" to the Revd G. G. Harrop (Hamilton, Ontario).

SECOND LECTURE ON THE MYSTERIES

Baptism: The Rites of the Inner Chamber

"Do you not know that all we who have been baptized into Christ Jesus have been baptized into his death? . . . since you are not under law but under grace."[1]

(1) The daily initiatory expositions, with their new teaching telling of new realities, are profitable to you, especially to those of you who have just been renewed from oldness to newness. I shall, therefore, resuming from yesterday, expound the bare essentials of our next topic, explaining the symbolical meaning of what you did in the inner chamber.[2]

(2) Immediately, then, upon entering, you removed your tunics. This was a figure of the "stripping off of the old man with his deeds."[3] Having stripped, you were naked,[4] in this also imitating Christ, who was naked on the cross, by His nakedness "throwing off the cosmic powers and authorities like a garment and publicly upon the cross leading them in his triumphal procession."[5] For as the forces of the enemy

1 Rom. 6.3-14. No further references are given to this passage.

2 This sentence seems to support Piédagnel's translation against his text in the last sentence of 1.1.

3 Col. 3.9.

4 The tunic *(chitōn)* was the garment worn by both sexes next to the skin. The candidates would already have removed their shoes and outer garments for the Renunciation in *Myst.* 1. Cf. Thomas Bingham, *Antiquities of the Christian Church* 11.11.1: All "persons were baptized naked, either in imitation of Adam in Paradise, or our Saviour upon the cross, or to signify their putting off . . . the old man. . . ."

5 Col. 2.15. So Cyril, against Blass-Debrunner and Arndt-Gingrich, who take *apekdyomai* as = "disarm" the principalities and powers. Well E. H. Gifford (LPNF): "Christ . . ., clothed with the likeness of sinful flesh during His life on earth, submitted therein to the assaults

made their lair in our members, you may no longer wear the old garment. I do not, of course, refer to this visible garment, but to "the old man which, deluded by its lusts, is sinking towards death."[6] May the soul that has once put off that old self never again put it on, but say with the Bride of Christ in the Canticle of Canticles: "I have put off my garment: how shall I put it on?"[7] Marvelous! You were naked in the sight of all and were not ashamed! Truly you bore the image of the first-formed Adam, who was naked in the garden and "was not ashamed."[8]

(3) Then, when stripped, you were anointed with exorcised olive oil from the topmost hairs of your head to the soles of your feet,[9] and became partakers of the good olive tree, Jesus Christ. Cuttings from the wild olive tree, you were grafted into the good olive tree and became partakers of the fatness of the true olive tree.[10] The exorcised olive oil, therefore,

---

of the powers of evil, but on the Cross threw off from Himself both it and them."

6 Eph. 4.22.

7 Cant. 5.3. This chapter shows that at Jerusalem as elsewhere the newly baptized donned white garments (the color of the Resurrection).

8 Gen. 2.25.

9 Scandalized by this total unction, Grodecq, an early commentator, wished, impossibly, to translate "from the top to the bottom of their hair."

The *Didascalia Apostolorum* (ed. R. H. Connolly, xlix-li) shows that the early N. Syrian Church required, before the bath, an anointing on the head by the bishop, with imposition of hands, the anointing of the body being completed by deacon or deaconess; and this was the only unction. T. W. Manson ("Entry into Membership of the Early Church," *Journal of Theological Studies* 48 [1947] 25-33) argued that this was the (or a) primitive usage; he pointed to Cornelius (Acts 10), St. Paul's initiation (Acts 9.17-19) and 1 John 5.7. ApCo 7.22 makes this first anointing confer the *koinōnia* (participation) of the Holy Ghost; the water signifies death, and the post-baptismal unction is a confirmatory seal of the baptismal covenant—the earlier N. Syrian use? ApCo 7.22 continues: "But if there be neither oil nor ointment (Chrism), water is sufficient both for the unction and the seal and the confession of Him with Whom we have died." See also *Did.* (Cop. and ApCo texts only) 10.8.

10 Cf. Rom. 11.17-24 and Irenaeus, *Adv. Haer.* 5.10. In the *Myst.* the second, post-baptismal anointing is clearly regarded as the important one. The first anointing is with previously exorcised olive oil *(elaion)*, the second with chrism *(myron)*. The threat from Chrismation or

symbolized the partaking of the richness of Christ; its effect is to disperse every concentration of the cosmic forces arrayed against us. For as the breath of the saints[11] upon you, with the invocation of the name of God, burns the devils like fierce fire and expels them, so this exorcised olive oil receives, through prayer and the invocation of God, power so great as not only to burn and purge away the traces of sin but also to put to rout all the invisible forces of the Evil One.

(4) After this you were conducted to the sacred pool of divine Baptism, as Christ passed from the cross to the sep-

---

Confirmation to the primacy of Baptism in the initiatory rite arose from the feeling that "christening," incorporation into Christ (lit. "the Anointed One"), was more appropriately symbolized by anointing or chris-mation, which was originally (I take it) a secondary ceremony. Then the sacramental (so to say) "dualism" of the Gospel account of the baptism of Jesus was re-interpreted. Following Matthew or Luke rather than Mark, one could argue that the descent of the Dove and the heavenly Voice proclaiming the Messiahship of Jesus were not related to the actual baptism simply as its *interpretation* (the proclamation through Dove and Voice being the mere visibilization of what had actually happened at the baptism), but as a second, subsequent event on the same plane; so that the Christian sacraments of Baptism and Confirmation could be regarded as corresponding to two successive events in the life of Jesus. The second sacrament, conveying the Spirit, would then be the greater. On the other (earlier?) view, Mark would provide the exemplar, and the two events would be simultaneous, the descent of the Spirit being but the visibilization of the spiritual reality granted to Our Lord as man *in* his baptism in Jordan.

The present passage, connecting the anointing with olive oil with Rom. 11.17ff., suggests, when compared with *Myst.* 3.5, that the two anointings form a doublet. Since not uncommonly in Syria the anointing preceded Baptism, this anointing with olive oil may be the original. But in our Jerusalem rite this first anointing is no more than a preparatory purification. It first appears in apocryphal literature: Acts of Thomas, Testament of Levi, Acts of Xanthippus. See PGL, *s.v. elaion,* C.

In *Cat.* 3.11-13, it is in the baptismal waters that Death and the Dragon are defeated.

Who are the ministers of this total unction? For the men, no doubt, priests, deacons and the lower clergy. But for the women? Epiphanius mentions deaconesses in connection with baptism, and ApCo 3.15-16 says that the deaconesses completed the anointing after a deacon had begun it on the forehead. It seems likely that this was the general practice.

11 The candidates had themselves been exorcised every morning during Lent (*Procat.* 9).

ulchre you see before you.[12] You were asked, one by one, whether you believed in the name of the Father and of the Son and of the Holy Spirit; you made that saving confession, and then you dipped[13] thrice under the water and thrice rose up again, therein mystically signifying Christ's three days' burial. For as our Savior passed three days and three nights in the bowels of the earth, so you by your first rising out of the water represented Christ's first day in the earth, and by your descent the night. For as in the night one no longer sees, while by day one is in the light, so you during your immersion, as in a night, saw nothing, but on coming up found

12 This passage does not point necessarily to Jerusalem and the Church of the Resurrection; see above, p. 150, Suppl. Note.—Even after the early days, when Baptism was in pools or rivers (Justin, 1 *Apol.* 61; Tertullian, *Bapt.* 4; *Didache* 7, though here it could be from a basin), not all churches had baptisteries. But the Bordeaux Pilgrim, who visited Jerusalem A.D. 333-4, tells us (CSEL 39.23): "There on the orders of Constantine a church was built . . . with a reservoir at the side and at the rear a bath where the infants are washed," i.e., where the candidates receive the laver.

13 Who is the minister of the sacrament? About the minister of Baptism in Hippolytus, Dix (TCB 15-16) asks: "Is it the Presbyter . . . who asks the questions? Or . . . the Deacon . . . who lays a hand on his head? Or is it conceivably the candidate himself?" Hippolytus (21.12) does mention a minister, the deacon, who probably pushed the candidates under. But the *Myst.* mention no minister; the candidates seem to duck down or submerge themselves.

There was no need to explain to the newly baptized who the ministers were. Unlike the ApTrad, the *Myst.* are not a Church Order. But certainly in the *Myst.* no one baptizes in the later sense of pouring the water and saying "I baptize thee." The candidates themselves seem to be mainly responsible both for the "proximate matter" (descending into and under the water, as at John's baptism) and the "form" (in making the threefold credal confession in response to the Trinitarian interrogation). But *Cat.* 17.35 provides important evidence here. There Cyril (*ca.* 350) speaks of a baptizer and says that he may be bishop, presbyter or deacon since in any case it is the Holy Spirit who seals the soul. The ancient 49th Apostolic Canon speaks of "Bishop or Presbyter." Clearly everything was done under the authority of the Bishop (who may also have previously consecrated the elements: oil, water, chrism), and the clergy presided, organized and directed proceedings, besides performing the anointing.

yourselves in the day. In the same moment you were dying and being born, and that saving water was at once your grave and your mother. What Solomon said in another context is applicable to you: "A time for giving birth, a time for dying";[14] although for you, contrariwise, it is a case of "a time for dying and a time for being born." One time brought both, and your death coincided with your birth.

(5) The strange, the extraordinary, thing is that we did not really die, nor were really buried or really crucified; nor did we really rise again: this was figurative and symbolic; yet our salvation was real. Christ's crucifixion was real, His burial was real, and His resurrection was real; and all these He has freely made ours, that by sharing His sufferings in a symbolic enactment we may really and truly gain salvation. Oh, too generous love! Christ received the nails in His immaculate hands and feet; Christ felt the pain: and on me without pain or labor, through the fellowship of His pain, He freely bestows salvation.

(6) Let no one imagine, then, that Baptism wins only the grace of remission of sins plus adoption, as John's baptism conferred only the remission of sins.[15] No; we know full well that Baptism not only washes away our sins and procures for

14 Eccles. 3.2. So the traditional translation. But does not Cyril/John make Eccles. say, "The time of (giving) birth is also the time of dying"? If so, reinterpret the sequel accordingly.

15 It is rather surprising that so staunch a disciple of Origen as John of Jerusalem should attribute the forgiveness of sins to John's baptism when Origen *(Comm. in Ioh.* 6.33, PG 14.257B) denied regeneration to it. Pseudo-Hippolytus (*Theoph.* 3, PG 10.853D) takes exactly the same view as the text here: remission of sins but not adoption. Cyril also glorifies John the Baptist against Origen; contrast the first sentence of *Cat.* 3.6 with Origen's statement (*Comm. in Rom.* 5.8, PG 14.1039B) that John's baptism was *not* the beginning of the New Dispensation. But Cyril regarded John as one of the patron saints of Jerusalem; to glorify him was to glorify Jerusalem, cf. *Cat.* 3.7 *init.* Yet Origen, *In Ioh.* 1.13 (Preuschen; PG 14.48AB), closely approximates Cyril, *Cat.* 3.6.

us the gift of the Holy Spirit,[16] but is also the antitype[17] of the Passion of Christ. That is why Paul just now proclaimed: "Do you not know that all we who have been baptized into Christ Jesus have been baptized into His death? For through Baptism we were buried along with Him." Perhaps this was directed against those who supposed that Baptism procures

16 What is "the gift (*dōrea,* cf. Acts 2.38) of the Spirit," and when is it conferred: at Baptism or Confirmation? Here we meet the great controversy between Stone and Lampe, etc., *versus* the Dix-Mason line, which glorifies Confirmation ("Spirit-Baptism"), the former saying that *the* gift of the Spirit, i.e., the Spirit Himself, is given in Baptism, while the latter say "in Confirmation." The Lenten Lectures, on the whole, strongly support the former view (though not in its terms), while the Mystagogical support the latter, though in its terms only, not in its emphasis or its interpretation of the relative importance of the terms.

Three times in this chapter participation in Christ's Passion is contrasted with a pair of other graces of Baptism; twice this pair is forgiveness and the adoptive sonship; once it is forgiveness and the "gift of the Spirit." Therefore "the gift of the Spirit" is, here, adoption.

But it does not *immediately* follow that in the *Myst.* the gift of the Spirit is mediated by Baptism, since in 3.3 the Chrism brings an advent or presence (*parousia*) of the Spirit and here (2.6) adoption is not explicitly correlated with any ceremony. It is arguable, therefore, that, as Touttée suggested, "Baptism" is here used in a *broad* sense that includes Chrismation. Moreover it is possible to read 3.1 (*init.*) as meaning that the putting on of Christ at Baptism prepares for the Adoption which follows (in Chrism). Yet it is certain that "the gift of the Spirit" (as = Adoption) is, in the *Myst.,* given in Baptism. For (1) presumably the preacher is keeping to the order of events; to depart from it without warning would be unpardonably confusing in a programmatic work like the *Myst.* (2) The terminology of 5.1 (formally canonized in the Code of Justinian) exhibits "baptism" as the regular word for water-baptism. Elsewhere the *Myst.* seem to adhere to this usage; see 2.4; 3.2, 4 (twice); (3.1?). (3) Once "the gift of the Spirit" is identified as Adoption, it must be given in Baptism; and, further, Adoption is inseparable from "the gift of the Spirit" in the strong sense (defining genitive) (Rom. 8.14-17, Gal. 4.6, 7). The gift, or descent, of the Spirit in *Myst.* 3.3, therefore, must be some special supplementary grace, "confirming" and topping off what has been done. (4) Otherwise Baptism would not differ from John's baptism. This is decisive.

17 A representation or (sacramental) sign of a spiritual original. Cf. 3.1 (twice); 4.3; 5.20. See note 8 on 3.1.

only the remission of sins and the adoption of sons and does not, beyond this, really make us imitatively partakers of the sufferings of Christ.

(7) To teach us, then, that all that Christ endured "for us and for our salvation," He suffered in actual fact and not in mere seeming, and that we have fellowship in His Passion, Paul cries aloud in unequivocal language: "For if we have become one planting with him by the likeness of His death, we shall be one with him by the likeness of His Resurrection also." "One planting" is apt, for since the true Vine was planted here,[18] we, by partaking in the Baptism of His death, have become "one planting" with Him. Mark closely the words of the Apostle: he did not say: "for if we have become one planting by His death," but "by the likeness of His death." For in the case of Christ death was real, His soul being really separated from his Body. His burial, too, was real, for His sacred Body was wrapped in clean linen. In His case it all really happened. But in your case there was only a likeness of death and suffering, whereas of salvation there was no likeness, but the reality.[19]

(8) That should be sufficient instruction on these points. I urge you to keep it in your memory that I too, though unworthy, may be able to say of you: "I love you because at all times you keep me in mind and maintain the tradition I handed on to you."[20] God, "who has presented you as those who have come alive from the dead," is able to grant to you to "walk in newness of life," because His is the glory and the power, now and forever. Amen.

---

18 But for the text here see above, p. 150, Suppl. Note.

19 The "reality" here is the same as the *res*, i.e., the benefit or grace of the sacrament, in later theology. But the reality or original of the "antitype" or sign is a person or event of sacred history, and this ambiguity, perhaps, sometimes led to confusion in later theology.

20 Cf. 1 Cor. 11.2.

THIRD LECTURE ON THE MYSTERIES

The Holy Chrism

"But you have an anointing from God and you know all things, etc. . . . that we may have confidence and may not shrink ashamed from him at his coming."[1]

(1) "Baptized into Christ" and "clothed with Christ,"[2] you have been shaped to the likeness of the Son of God.[3] For God, in "predestining us to be adopted as his sons,"[4] has "conformed us to the body of the glory"[5] of Christ. As "partakers[6] of Christ," therefore, you are rightly called "Christs," i.e., "anointed ones": it was of you that God said: "Touch not my Christs."[7] Now, you became Christs by receiving the antitype[8] of the Holy Spirit; everything has been wrought in you

---

1 1 John 2.20-28.
2 Gal. 3.27.
3 Cf. Rom. 8.29.
4 Cf. Eph. 1.5.
5 Phil. 3.21.
6 Heb. 3.14; or "partners" or "fellows."
7 Ps. 104.15, Sept.
8 Counterpart, sign, sacramental element; cf. below, 3.1; 2.6; 4.3 ("type"); 5.20. The idea of Greek type and antitype is that of the die or "engraved stamp for coining, striking medal, embossing paper, etc." *(Concise Oxford Dictionary, s.v.* die). Thus in theology the antitype is the earthly copy of the heavenly reality and model (Heb. 9.24) *or,* as in 1 Peter 3.21 (saving Baptism as the antitype of the Deluge) and in *Myst.,* the sacrament which, without being identical with the heavenly realities or the saving events, mediates their benefits. Thus in 2.6 Baptism confers the *benefits* of Christ's Passion and perhaps a mystical identification with it, yet "you did not really die"; it was the salvation that was "in truth" (2.5; cf. 2.7 end). Similarly here the antitype is contrasted with the Spirit *"ousiōdēs,"* and "all is done imagewise." On the other hand, compared with the Old Testament figures (types, 3.6), the sacrament is the fulfillment and reality.

"likewise" because you are likenesses of Christ.[9]

He bathed in the river Jordan and, after imparting the fragrance of His Godhead to the waters, came up from them. Him the Holy Spirit visited in essential presence, like resting[10] upon like.[11] Similarly for you, after you had ascended from the sacred streams, there was an anointing with chrism, the antitype of that with which Christ was anointed,[12] that is, of the Holy Spirit. Concerning this Spirit the blessed Isaia, in the prophetical book which bears his name, said, speaking in the person of the Lord: "The Spirit of the Lord is upon me because he hath anointed me. He hath sent me to preach glad tidings to the poor."[13]

(2) For Christ was not anointed by men with material oil or balsam; His Father, appointing Him Savior of the whole world, anointed Him with the Holy Spirit as Peter says: "Jesus

---

Gifford's gloss, "figure," therefore is too weak; but Touttée goes too far in saying that the antitype may be simply identical with its heavenly original. Even in the Eucharist *(Myst.* 5.20) "the antitype of the Body" seems not simply to identify the heavenly Body of Christ and its sacramental sign; the Presence is sacramental. For Irenaeus's usage, see *Adv. haer.* 4.17.5, 4.18.1-5, and fragment 13.

9 The chapter glides elusively from Baptism to Chrism. As partakers of Christ, they are "christs," but, since "Christ" is "anointed," they became christs not at Baptism but at Chrism. Yet in the pre-baptismal anointing (2.3) they became "partakers of Christ and His richness" and at Baptism (2.4, 5) they imitated and partook of His death, burial and resurrection. The author has, indeed, one more card to play; he can say (3.1, 2, 4) that, while at Baptism they imitated Christ's baptism, it is only in Chrismation that they received the "counterpart" ("antitype") of the Holy Spirit's subsequent descent upon Him. But since the descent of the Spirit manifested Christ's Messianic Sonship, and the candidates had already in Baptism (2.6) received adoptive sonship, it is a weak card; it involves separating adoption from the Spirit. So already in 3.1 the author begins to emphasize the *verbal* connection between christ-ening and chrism (anointing). Compare 3.5.

"Likewise": i.e., "iconically," i.e., as "images" of Christ, following in the footsteps of the leader and trail-blazer *(archēgos,* 3.7): the master theme of *Myst.* 2 and 3.

10 *Epanapauomenou,* found not at John 1.33, but at Luke 10.6 and Num. 11.25, 26.

11 Cf. Sir. 13.16.

12 Cf. Clem. Alex, *Paed.* 1.6.25.

13 Isa. 61.1.

of Nazareth, whom God anointed with the Holy Spirit."[14] The prophet David also made proclamation: "Thy throne, O God, is forever and ever: the sceptre of thy kingdom is a sceptre of uprightness. Thou hast loved justice, and hated iniquity: therefore God, thy God, hath anointed thee with the oil of gladness above thy fellows."[15]

As Christ was really crucified and buried and rose again, and you at Baptism are privileged to be crucified, buried, and raised along with Him in a likeness, so also with the chrism. Christ was anointed with a mystical oil of gladness; that is, with the Holy Spirit, called "oil of gladness" because He is the cause of spiritual gladness; so you, being anointed with ointment, have become partakers and fellows of Christ.

(3) Beware of supposing that this ointment is mere ointment. Just as after the invocation of the Holy Spirit the eucharistic bread is no longer ordinary bread, but the Body of Christ, so this holy oil, in conjunction with the invocation,[16] is no longer simple or common oil, but becomes the gracious gift of Christ and the Holy Spirit, producing the advent [presence?] of His deity.[17] With this ointment your forehead

---

14 Cf. Acts 10.38.

15 Ps. 44 (45).7, 8: the anointing of the Messianic King; cf. 3.5 below.

16 The "with" (not "after") perhaps implies that the "invocation" *(epiklēsis)* is the accompanying prayer (the "form") and that the chrism does not owe its supernatural efficacity to a previous consecration by the Bishop. But one cannot be sure; see ApTrad 21.6-10, 19; 22.1-4. Note the analogy (not necessarily exact) drawn here (3.3) between the chrism and the Eucharistic elements.

17 See *Myst.* 2, n. 16. The text, translation and meaning of this very important sentence have been hotly debated. I read *parousias, "of* His advent/presence," following Piédagnel's text and the practically unanimous MS tradition. But this gives a rather difficult text (a plethora of genitives), so much so that the best earlier editors and interpreters (Milles, Touttée, Reischl-Rupp, F. L. Cross, supported by Dean Church, E. H. Gifford, Pusey, and Piédagnel in his translation) emended to *parousiāi* (dative), "by His advent producing His deity." But the MS text (genitive) gives the better sense; while a sacrament cannot produce a divine person or his deity, it can bring his advent/presence. The MS text could also be translated: "gift of Christ, working the advent of the Holy Ghost (of His deity)," and the rhythm favours this. My criterion was the reader's convenience; my translation gives a better indication of the various possible meanings of the sentence.

and sense organs are sacramentally anointed, in such wise that while your body is anointed with the visible oil, your soul is sanctified by the holy, quickening Spirit.[18]

(4) You are anointed first upon the forehead[19] to rid you of the shame which the first human transgressor bore about with him everywhere; so you may "reflect as in a glass the

---

(See further the interesting but unreliable reading of MS *Monac.* 394.)

Gifford, reading *parousiāi,* translates: "and imparts (*Christ's*) divine nature by the advent of the Holy Ghost." This *interpretation* has something to be said for it. It explains "of His deity," since Christ has two natures. It is, moreover, supported by the Prayer for the consecration of the Chrism in ApCo 7.44: "Grant that this ointment may be made effectual to the baptized one, that the sweet savour of Christ (cf. *Myst.* 3.4) may remain in him and that, having died in Him, he may rise again and live with Him." Cf. also *Myst.* 3.2, end. It fits also the quite strong doctrine of Baptism in *Myst.* 2. Thus here (Gifford): "Chrism confirms the work of Baptism"—while indicating, we may add, the Eastern doctrine of post-baptismal progressive "divinization."

This may well have been the original import of the passage. But in the *Myst.* we are dealing with stratified literature of a date, presumably, when the enhanced prestige of the Holy Ghost, whose deity and consubstantiality were being emphasized, combined with the (late?) idea that it is chris-mation which christens, threw the earlier doctrine of initiation into confusion or seemed to put it in question. We may, therefore, have here a C doctrine superimposed on earlier formulas. Certainly Gifford's interpretation hardly does full justice to the context, in which the "parousia" of the Holy Ghost—"of His Deity" (an interpolation? the superimposed interpretation, exalting this Coming over "the gift of the Holy Ghost = Adoption" in 2.6—*not* a theologically possible distinction; see Appended note A)—is itself the main thing.

On this interpretation the intention of *Myst.* 3, esp. 3.3, is to exalt Chrism over Baptism. This is to attempt the impossible, even within the context of the *Myst.,* in view of all that is ascribed to Baptism in *Myst.* 2 and 3.5 and the denial (3.1) that in Chrism the Spirit visits the baptized *ousiōdēs.* (Nor can the Chrism, as Gifford suggests, impart Christ's divine nature, since this was given in Adoption.)

If this sentence, therefore, is to be harmonized with the rest of the *Myst.,* the gift of 3.3, however lofty, is but accessory and confirmatory of Baptism. The question also arises whether the graces listed in 3.4-7 are additional minor graces or whether they define the great grace mentioned in the problematic sentence. The immediate sequel of this sentence suggests the latter.

18 Cf. Tert., *Bapt.* 6.

19 With the sign of the Cross (the Western episcopal "consignatio"?), cf. Ps.-Dionysius, *Hier. eccl.* 2.2.7. In *Didasc. Ap.* and (women only) ApCo 3.15 the bishop anoints the head or forehead only, showing

splendor of the Lord."[20] Then upon the ears, to receive ears quick to hear the divine mysteries, the ears of which Isaia said: "The Lord gave me also an ear to hear,"[21] and the Lord Jesus in the Gospels: "He who has ears to hear, let him hear."[22] Then upon the nostrils, that, scenting the divine oil, you may say: "We are the incense offered by Christ to God, in the case of those who are on the way to salvation."[23] Then on the breast, that "putting on the breastplate of justice you may be able to withstand the wiles of the Devil."[24] For as Christ after His Baptism and the visitation of the Holy Spirit went forth and overthrew the adversary, so must you after holy Baptism and the mystical Chrism, clad in the armor of the Holy Spirit, stand firm against the forces of the Enemy and overthrow them, saying: "I can do all things in the Christ who strengthens me."[25]

(5) Once privileged to receive the holy Chrism, you are called Christians and have a name that bespeaks your new birth.[26] Before admission to Baptism and the grace of the Holy Spirit you were not strictly entitled to this name but were like people on the way towards being Christians.

(6) You must know that this Chrism is prefigured in the Old Testament. When Moses, conferring on his brother the divine appointment, was ordering him high priest, he anointed him after he had bathed in water, and thenceforward he was

---

its special importance. In *Myst.* it reverses the sign of Cain (Gen. 4.15).

20 2 Cor. 3.18.

21 Cf. Isa. 50.4.

22 Matt. 11.15.

23 2 Cor. 2.15.

24 Eph. 6.14, 11.

25 Phil. 4.13 in the version of, among others, Origen. The Chrism theory may have come to Antioch from Alexandria. Both Clement and Origen were strong on Chrism, and cf. the "Ointment" addition in Coptic *Did.* 10.8.

26 Did this verbal correspondence cause Chrismation to be originally chosen as the medium of the conveyance of the Spirit or only later suggest the connection of the Spirit with Chrismation and so confuse theology? In the next sentence "and" is missing in γ.

called "christ"[27] ["anointed"], clearly after the figurative[28] Chrism. Again, the high priest, when installing Solomon as king, anointed him after he had bathed in Gihon.[29] But what was done to them in figure was done to you, not in figure but in truth, because your salvation began from Him who was anointed by the Holy Spirit in truth. Christ is the beginning of your salvation, since He is truly the "first handful" of dough and you "the whole lump":[30] and if the first handful be holy, plainly its holiness will permeate the lump.

(7) Keep this Chrism unsullied; for it shall teach you all things if it abide in you, as you heard the blessed John declaring just now as he expatiated upon the Chrism.[31] For this holy thing is both a heavenly protection of the body and salvation for the soul. It was of this anointing that in ancient times the blessed Isaia prophesied saying: "And the Lord shall make unto all people in this mountain" (elsewhere also he calls the Church a mountain, as when he says: "And in the last days the mountain of the Lord shall be manifest")[32] ". . . and they shall drink wine, they shall drink gladness, they shall anoint themselves with ointment."[33] To alert you to the mystical meaning of "ointment" here, he says: "All this deliver to the nations: for the counsel of the Lord is upon all the nations."[34]

Anointed, then, with this holy oil, keep it in you unsullied, without blame, making progress through good works and becoming well-pleasing to "the trail-blazer of our salvation,"[35] Christ Jesus, to whom be glory forever and ever. Amen.[36]

27 Lev. 8.5, 12; cf. 4.5.
28 Gk.: "typical."
29 1 (3) Kings 1.38, 39.
30 Cf. Rom. 11.16.
31 In the text lesson, 1 John 2.27.
32 Isa. 2.2. Such interrupted quotations occur in the Lenten Lectures.
33 Isa. 5.6, Sept.
34 Isa. 25.7, Sept.
35 Heb. 2.10; 2 Cor. 5.9.
36 *Myst.* 3 mentions neither Pentecost nor imposition of hands; *Cat.* 16.26 (end) suggests that the chrismation of the (fore)head (consignation) was equivalently a laying on of the hand.

TWO APPENDED NOTES ON BAPTISM AND CHRISM (CONFIRMATION) AT JERUSALEM

Appended Note A

Myst. 3.3: When is the Holy Spirit Given?

With *Myst.* 3.3 compare Tert., *Bapt.* 7-8: " (After the Bath) we are anointed thoroughly with a blessed unction according to the ancient rule . . . The unction *runs bodily over us, but profits spiritually.* Next the hand is laid upon us, through the blessing calling upon and inviting the Holy Spirit." B. Neunheuser remarks *(Baptism and Confirmation* 89) that if Tertullian really means what he says (cf. ch. 6), that the Holy Spirit is not given in *Baptism,* he stands in opposition to the universal early tradition.

St. Cyprian says several times that it is by the post-baptismal laying on of hands that the Holy Ghost is given. Besides *Ep.* 73 (72).6 and 21, we read *(Ep.* 74[73].7) : "A person is not *born* through the laying on of hands, when he receives the Holy Spirit, but in *Baptism,* that, born, he may *then* receive the Holy Spirit. Compare the case of the first man, Adam; God first formed him, and then breathed into his nostrils the breath of life (Gen. 2.7). For before the spirit can be received there must be something there to receive it." There could hardly be a stronger statement of the C theory (see above, p. 160), for Cyprian here implies that the New Creation produced by Baptism is not quickened—has no supernatural life—until a further sacrament follows. (Certainly it is the Spirit who quickens, but He does so in Baptism.) Yet in *Ep.* 73 (72).12 Cyprian can say that Baptism confers the remission of sins, that remission of sins entails sanctification, and "if he was sanctified, he was made the temple of God"—without receiving the Holy Spirit? The context excludes the possibility that Cyprian was using the word "Baptism" in the broad sense. When Cyprian reserves the gift of the Spirit to imposition of hands, one often feels that he is accepting, for argument's sake, premisses which are not quite his own (and perhaps not Stephen's either).

Ca. 252 Cornelius of Rome (Eusebius, *Hist. eccl.* 6.43.14) complained that the anti-Pope Fabian had not received the Spirit because, after a clinical Baptism, he had not bothered to receive the ordinary additional ceremonies, especially the sealing by the bishop. Apparently against this position Cyprian *(Ep.* 69[75].13-14) asserts that clinical Baptism *bestows the Holy Spirit in the same fullness* that ordinary Baptism does. And his whole position, asserting against St. Stephen of Rome the invalidity of heretical schismatic Baptism, is based on his emphasis upon the intimate association of the Holy Spirit with Baptism as at least its agent. M. J. Rouët de Journel, *Enchiridion patristicum* (20th ed. Freiburg im B. etc. 1958) 795 (under the thesis "Confirmatio est verum sacramentum"), is, I think, right in his judgment that Cyprian held that Confirmation is a sacrament (a vague word in Cyprian) but did not hold that it is necessary to salvation. This is still the Roman position (Canon 787). The explanation of Cyprian's contradictions is probably that, though misled in such passages as *Ep.* 74 (73).7 (above) by the phrase "the gift of the Spirit," which sounds like a greater grace than any of the Spirit's gifts or graces, yet in his deepest thinking he knew that the grace of Baptism was greater than that of Confirmation. So in *Ep.* 74 (73).5, arguing against Pope Stephen, who refused to rebaptize those who came to the Church after receiving heretical Baptism but only imposed hands to bestow the Spirit, he writes (again, incidentally, implying that Baptism makes one a temple of God) : "*If* a man born (i.e., baptized) outside the Church can become God's temple, why cannot further the Holy Spirit be poured out upon the temple? For when sanctified . . . and spiritually recreated a new man, a person is fitted for the reception of the Spirit . . . If a person baptized among heretics can put on Christ, *much more* can he receive the Spirit whom Christ sent. Otherwise he who is sent will be greater than he who sends. . . As if it were possible either for Christ to be put on without the Spirit or for the Spirit to be separated from Christ." That is, the position attacked implies an Ebionite Christology.

The *De rebaptismate* (A.D. *ca.* 256) defended the validity of schismatic Baptism "by a very peculiar and unfortunate distinction between Baptism of water and Baptism of the Spirit to be conferred by the bishop's imposition of hands" (Quasten, *Patrology* II 368).

Let us now return to *Myst.* 3.3, careful to distinguish the questions what is the right answer to this problem and what is the teaching of the *Mystagogiae* The author of the *Mystagogiae* is forced by his chosen typology here unduly to exalt Chrism against Baptism (see *Myst.* 2 n. 10). Where he ought (*I* think) to say that Christ's washing in Jordan corresponds to the sacrament of Baptism, that the descent of the Spirit corresponds to the grace of Baptism (forgiveness of sins and Sonship) and that the Voice and the Dove are but the visibilization of this grace, he has chosen to regard the washing in Jordan and the descent of the Spirit as two successive historical events on the same plane. If they are to be correlated with Baptism and Chrism/Confirmation, the only solution seems to be to say that Baptism gives forgiveness of sins, while Chrism gives the Spirit, or (like the *De rebaptismate)* to correlate the two events with Baptism of water and Baptism of the Spirit (and reinterpret John 3.5 accordingly). *Myst.* 3 avoids such a drastic solution. Still it must say that at Chrism the Holy Spirit descends; He "is given." But we saw (*Myst.* 2 n. 16) that at 2.6 *Baptism* bestowed "the gift of the Spirit (=Adoption)." Still perhaps "upon this gift (of Adoption) *by* the Spirit now comes the gift *of* the Spirit in Chrismation"? In a sense. But, first, this distinction is bogus. Whenever the Holy Spirit gives any grace, He does so by descending, by coming; He can do no other. Second, the Spirit is never, strictly, "given" to us; we do not possess Him, but He us; and He possesses us through the grace of Adoption. Third, we need to correct our semantic or lexical values: "the gift of the Spirit" in the New Testament is not, commonly, a stronger phrase than such descriptions of the benefits of Baptism as regeneration, adoption of sons, new creation, etc. On the contrary, the "giving of the Spirit" often denotes such inessential graces as charismata, speaking with tongues, working miracles, etc.; see Acts *passim.* This seems to be the regular usage of Cyril's Lenten Lectures. The Mystagogical Lectures seem to agree. Not only do the *Mystagogiae* (2.6) ascribe to Baptism the supreme gifts of regeneration, the putting on of Christ and Adoption, but in 3.1 they three times sharply distinguish the grace of Chrism from the Spirit's descent *ousiōdēs* upon Christ, twice by saying that the candidates received only the antitype of the Holy Ghost, and further by the phrase "in likeness" *(eikonikōs).*

Similarly there is a sense in which Chrism *does* give "the fullness" of the Spirit; probably *Myst.* 3.3 has in mind the permanent "indwelling" of the Spirit in us (cf. "resting" in 3.1). Naturally (Basil, *Hom. in Ps. 44.* PG 29.405A), since Chrism follows Baptism, it must mark some advance upon it. But this is compatible with giving the essential and supreme gift in Baptism. Chrism completes, confirms and tops off what has been done, like a dash of an additive in the fuel tank. To improve Cyprian's regrettable analogy with Adam: you must have a car, and a tank with fuel in it before there is any point in introducing the additive; or we may say that Confirmation gives a (permanent) "overdrive."

But the Chrism of *Myst.* gives rather more than this. Apart from (or included in) the important grace (*Myst.* 3.3) which we have tried to assess, it is almost certainly in Chrism (4.7; cf. 2 Cor. 1.22?) that the Seal is given (contrast *Cat.* 3.4), though the word used in 4.7 is *elaion.* The "Seal," however, is a variable quantity. It may mean the great eschatological seal, or a writer may mean that the document (covenant) is not valid until the seal has been affixed, or this may be thought of as a desirable but not essential formality, or the Seal may be thought of merely as the securing of the sanctified soul against unlawful entry by the powers of evil.

Again, the Chrism sanctifies the senses (3.4), makes us incontestably Christians, enables us to do battle with the Enemy (3.5), and confers (3.6) "lay ordination," participation in Christ's royal priesthood, so important in Eastern Christendom (N. Zernov, *Eastern Christendom* [New York 1961] 250).

Appended Note B

The Doctrine of Baptism in the Lenten Lectures

On the whole, the Lectures on the Mysteries teach the B theory (see above, p. 160). For, while they correlate Chrism certainly with the descent of the Spirit, almost certainly with the Seal, and probably with the indwelling of the Spirit, yet they do not seem to regard any of these as privileged categories and therefore they do not seem to exalt Chrism over against Baptism. The Seal is mentioned casually only in *Myst.* 4.7. To Baptism they ascribe forgiveness of sins, the putting on of Christ, regeneration (3.5), participation in Christ's Passion, and "the gift of the Spirit" in the sense of adoptive sonship (2.6).

The opening lectures in the Lenten series teach a very decided B theory, but there are a few passages in the later lectures which perhaps require a (drastic?) modification of the impression left by the early lectures. In the opening lectures it is clear that practically everything is mediated by "the water," and if St. Cyril ever here has any other ceremony in mind, he clearly regards it as supplementary and secondary. But while the two series are thus not very far apart in doctrine, they differ markedly in their biblical exegesis and typology or, as we perhaps may here more appropriately call it, christ-iconology.

For the most part the Lenten Lectures know no distinction between the Spirit as gift and His sanctifying, transforming and recreating activity. When in some later passages such a distinction is implied, the gift of the Spirit (objective, defining genitive) seems to be a *weaker* phrase than the gift (=grace) of the Spirit. In *Procat.* 2A and 4E the Spirit acts through the water. (For the use of the letters A, B, C, D, E, see above, p. 149.) "The reception *of* the Holy Ghost" in *Cat.* 3.2B is clearly the same thing as acceptance *by* the Holy Ghost in *Procat.* 4E and the "reception of the grace" in *Cat.* 3.7E. The "grace" or "gift" (usually *charis,* less often *charisma;* in *Cat.* 1.4E *dōrea)* is the commonest and apparently all-inclusive term (especially) in these opening lectures. It is normally thought of as the gift or grace of the Spirit as agent but with no hint of a contrast with the Spirit Himself as gift. And it is clear that this gift is mediated by water. Sometimes this is said explicitly or unmistakably implied (e.g., *Procat.* 2A, 15C; *Cat.* 3.3D, 4C), and it is consistently implied by the very frequent references to "the water" or "the laver." Note especially

3.3-5, with the praise of water in 3.5; also the passages about Simon Magus's baptism, invalid from the first through lack of proper intention (*Procat.* 2A, 4E; cf. *Cat.* 3.7D; 17.35-36; in 17.35 the Spirit seals the soul even, apparently, when a deacon baptizes). Again, water is mentioned in the more or less immediate vicinity of all the great gifts of Baptism: adoption, new birth, new life, union with Christ, the Seal etc.

In the Lenten Lectures (contrast *Myst.* 4.7), the Seal is certainly given through the water. *Cat.* 1.2C, 3D; and 3.3B are most naturally read in this sense, and it is actually said twice in 3.4, once equivalently: "As the water purifies the body, so the Spirit seals the soul," where the two actions are clearly parallel and the dualism is that of inner and outer, of sacramental sign and spiritual grace; once explicitly: "the seal (conveyed) by water." *Cat.* 5.6D, though not strictly explicit, is equally clear. The Lenten Lectures (4.17A) connect the Seal with the credal profession and so with the baptismal contract or covenant.

Another, equally important and significant, difference from the Mystagogical Lectures is the fact that, while the Mystagogical Lectures (3.1CD, cf. 4E) regard the descent of the Spirit upon Our Lord by the Jordan as an event different from and subsequent to His baptism, and as typifying a different sacrament (Chrism), in the parallel passages in the Lenten Lectures the Holy Spirit descends upon Jesus *while* John is baptizing Him. For in *Cat.* 17.9A the Greek has two present participles: "This Holy Ghost came down while the Lord was being baptized, that the dignity of Him who was being baptized might not pass unnoticed"; and the context shows that "baptism" is water-baptism. So also probably 3.14C: "that John, who *was baptizing* Him *(ho baptizōn)* might see (the Spirit in the form of a dove)." (Incidentally, such passages as 3.6A, 7A, 11A, 14; 17.9A, establishing a close connection between John's Baptism and Christian Baptism, show that St. Cyril regarded the physical rite in the two baptisms as the same, and therefore prove that "Baptism" in the Lenten Lectures regularly means water-baptism.) Thus, whereas in the *Mystagogiae* (3.4DE) Jesus, and Christians after Him, give battle to Satan, not immediately after Baptism, but only after the descent of the Spirit regarded as a second event (=Chrism), in the Lenten Lectures (3.11-13, cf. *Procat.* 10, 16BE) Jesus overcomes the Dragon and binds "the Strong One" *in the water* and preaches immediately afterwards, while the candidates likewise receive their armour from the pre-baptismal teaching and from Baptism, after which they fight and preach (*Procat.* 10; *Cat.* 1.4; 3.13-14).

Another striking difference between the typology of the Mystagogical and the Lenten Lectures is that, while the *Mystagogiae* are as enigmatically silent about Pentecost as they are about

John the Baptist and John 3.3-5, in the Lenten Lectures Pentecost is the fulfillment and realization of the promise implicit in John's baptism and is the Baptism of the Apostles. See *Cat.* 3.9 (cf. 3.15D) and the fine account (17.13-15, 19) where the Pentecostal baptismal flames which enveloped the Apostles are interpreted as "spiritual" *(noētou)* water and are compared with the waters which encompassed and whelmed the candidates when they "submerged" in the font. The fire/water burns away sin and "further" *(eti)* burnishes the soul and imparts to it *charis* (grace, beauty).

A comparable difference between the two series concerns the Aaronic priesthood. In *Myst.* 3.6 Aaron and Solomon together are the prefiguring type of the royal priesthood which is bestowed on the candidates by the chrismation. Both Aaron and Solomon are said to have first bathed and then been anointed respectively priest and king. In the Lenten Lectures, by contrast, Solomon appears only as an example of a penitent (2.13), and "Aaron was first washed, then became high priest" (3.5E)—no anointing. Moreover in the Lenten Lectures Aaron is a type of Christ's high priesthood in which the ordinary faithful do not partake. For in 3.5E the High Priest "prays for the rest" (cf. Our Lord's intercessory priesthood in Hebrews). So in 10.11, the Lord "is called Christ (anointed), because He is a Priest. . . For Christ is a High Priest like Aaron" (cf. Eus., *Hist. eccl.* 1.3). If there is any reference to the New Covenant in 10.11, 14 and 11.1, it is apparently the ordained ministers of the Church who partake, imperfectly, of Christ's priesthood after ordination by anointing. Apart from 18.33, the Lenten Lectures apparently know nothing of a "priesthood of all believers" bestowed by Chrismation; believers are Christians not Christs. Perhaps *Cat.* 10.16 changes this picture. There all believers have the "new name"; i.e., they are called "Christians" after "Christ" meaning priest king. As, however, it is not inferred that Christians share in the priestly rulership of their Lord, this may be a transitional passage. In *Procat.* 6 the divine name bestowed in Baptism is "faithful" *(pistos).*

Finally, John 3.3-5 and Acts 2.38 are always interpreted in the Lenten Lectures in the B sense. And normally the Lenten Lectures associate together as inseparable all the great graces of Baptism and connect them with the water. For example, in *Cat* 1.1-2 the cleansing by water seems inseparable from the new birth, adoption, the mystical Seal, the opening of the gates of Paradise and the singing of the bridal song. Similarly in 3.1-3 the washing clean from sin in the laver seems inseparable from "the reception of the Holy Ghost," introduction into the bridal chamber of the King and the bestowal of the Seal.

Now, however, we must consider briefly a few passages of a very different tenor towards the end of the Lenten Lectures. According to *Cat.* 14.25E (after mention of Elia and Eliseus), Christ bestowed the Spirit upon His disciples (the Apostles?) in such fullness as to enable them "by the laying on of their *hands* to impart the fellowship of It to believers." In 17.25 we are told of the visit of Peter and John to Samaria and how they imparted the fellowship of the Holy Ghost "with prayer and the imposition of hands" to Philip's new converts (cf. Acts 8.14-17). Nothing, however, is made of the fact that Philip was a mere deacon, nor is Baptism explicitly mentioned.

But the crucial passage is *Cat.* 16.26E, for in the above passages the candidates are not brought into the picture. After a discussion of the Seventy Elders (with Eldad and Medad) (Num. 11.24-30), a reference to Deut. 34.9 and the statement that Num. 11.29 was "fulfilled" at Pentecost, we read:

> Thou seest the same figure everywhere in the Old and New Testaments. In the time of Moses the Spirit was given by the laying on of hands *(cheirothesia),* and by the laying on of hands Peter also gives the Spirit [Acts 8.17]. Upon thee also, the baptizand, soon shall the grace come. But just how, I am not telling you now, for I won't anticipate "the proper season."

It looks as if the baptizand will receive the Spirit by some form of imposition of hands (chrismation? consignation?). *Cheirothesia* in ApCo 2.32.3 is consignation; in 3.16.3 it confers the royal priesthood as in *Myst.* 3.6; in 7.44.3 it distinguishes Christian from Jewish baptism; but see also Serapion, *Euchologion* 15, title.

Do these texts transform the whole picture sketched above? They would if that picture had relied on silence instead of on positive texts. Is interpolation at 16.26E a possibility? It has apparently occurred in the "consubstantial" insertion in some manuscripts at 16.24C. And note the repetition (16.26C, 27A) of "Abraham, Isaac and Jacob." *Cat.* 16.27 could follow naturally on 16.25. Again, 16.11-12 strongly suggests that the Holy Ghost is given through water, and 16.12C seems to mean that the candidates are prepared by their Lenten repentance for the Holy Spirit whom they will receive in the water.

But probably the Lenten Lectures are "stratified"; i.e., they contain some additions by Cyril, or possibly by another hand. Another example may be the *hieratikōs* ("like priests") in 18.33C; 18.33 looks rather like a later doublet of 18.32, the latter representing a period when there was no Easter Week catechizing.

FOURTH LECTURE ON THE MYSTERIES

The Eucharist (I): The Body and Blood of Christ

"For I myself received from the Lord the traditions which in turn I passed on to you. . . ."[1]

(1) The teaching of the blessed Paul is of itself sufficient to give you full assurance about the divine mysteries by admission to which you have become one body and blood with Christ. For Paul just now proclaimed "that on the night in which he was betrayed our Lord Jesus Christ took bread and, after giving thanks, broke it and gave it to his disciples saying, 'Take, eat: this is my body'; then, taking the cup, he gave thanks and said, 'Take, drink: this is my blood.' "[2] When the Master himself has explicitly said of the bread, "This is my body," will anyone still dare to doubt? When He is Himself our warranty, saying, "This is my blood," who will ever waver and say it is not His Blood?

(2) Once at Cana in Galilee He changed water into wine[3] by His sovereign will; is it not credible, then, that He changed wine into blood? If as a guest at a physical marriage He performed this stupendous miracle, shall He not far more readily be confessed to have bestowed on "the friends of the bridegroom"[4] the fruition of His own Body and Blood?

(3) With perfect confidence, then, we partake as of the Body and Blood of Christ. For in the figure[5] of bread His

1 1 Cor. 11.23ff.
2 Cf. 1 Cor. 11.23-25; Matt. 26.26.
3 Cf. John 2.1-11.
4 Matt. 9.15 (paraphrase).
5 *Typos:* but a sacramental figure (sign) makes present according to context its corresponding heavenly reality or its saving power. Cf.

Body is given to you, and in the figure of wine His Blood, that by partaking of the Body and Blood of Christ you may become of one body and blood with Him. For when His Body and Blood become the tissue of our members, we become Christ-bearers and as the blessed Peter said, "partakers of the divine nature."[6]

(4) Once, speaking to the Jews, Christ said: "Unless you eat my flesh and drink my blood, you can have no life in you." Not understanding His words spiritually, they "were shocked and drew back," imagining that He was proposing the eating of human flesh.[7]

(5) The Old Covenant had its loaves of proposition,[8] but they, as belonging to the Covenant, have come to an end. The New Covenant has its heavenly bread and cup of salvation, to sanctify both body and soul. For as the bread is for the body, the Word suits the soul.[9]

"figuratively" and "figurative chrism" in 3.6; but those are Old Covenant signs. In the New Covenant figure or sacramental sign its correlative reality is conveyed ("given").

6 2 Peter 1.4.

7 *Sarkophagia:* "cannibalism"? Cf. John 6.53, 60, 66.

8 Cf. Lev. 24.5-9, etc.

9 *Either* (a) with Touttée: the "word" *(logos)* is the eternal Word which feeds the soul. But (i) there is no expressed contextual background for this. (ii) Where, then, do the Body and Blood come in (though, granted, in 4.3 these sanctify our members)? (iii) In 5.15 the "essential" or "superessential" Bread is "appointed for the soul." (iv) The Thomistic doctrine of the presence of the Word by concomitance, though perhaps vaguely assumed, is not mentioned. *Or* (b): While the data are too sparse to permit a confident solution, probably the "word" is the word of the preaching correlative to faith and contemplation, together with the consecratory word of the Invocation. This is the ordinary dualism of both the Lenten and the Mystagogical Lectures. Compare *Procat.* 2; *Cat.* 3.3, 4, 12A; *Myst.* 1.7; 3.3; 4.3; 5.7. In the Greek Fathers, especially in those of the Alexandrian tradition, it is knowledge, contemplation, instruction which are the true food, the food of the soul. This *suggests* the Word (which is not excluded), but it is the Body itself that is in the foreground and is the heavenly Bread, feeding the soul. The bread is made the heavenly Bread by the word of Invocation. Cf. Iren. *Adv. haer.* 4.18.5: "For as the bread from the earth, after receiving the Invocation, is no longer common bread (cf. *Myst.* 4.6), but the Eucharist, consisting of two realities *(pragmata)*, an earthly and a heavenly. . . ." Cf. the Prayer in the Liturgy of St. James (Dix 192)

(6) Do not then think of the elements as bare bread and wine; they are, according to the Lord's declaration, the Body and Blood of Christ. Though sense suggests the contrary, let faith be your stay. Instead of judging the matter by taste, let faith give you an unwavering confidence that you have been privileged to receive the Body and Blood of Christ.

(7) The blessed David is hinting to you the meaning[10] of these rites when he says, "You have prepared a table before me, against those who oppress me."[11] What he means is this: "Before your coming the devils prepared a table for mankind, a table defiled and polluted, impregnated with diabolical power; but since your coming, Lord, you have prepared a table in my presence." When man says to God, "You have prepared a table before me," what else does he refer to but the mystical and spiritual table which God has prepared for us "over against," meaning "arrayed against and opposed to,"

---

that the consecrated bread and cup may be "unto the hallowing of souls and bodies." Cf. Justin, *1 Apol.* 66. Compare (and contrast) perhaps the nearest parallel, Clem. Alex., *Paed.* 2.1-2: "The blood of the Lord is twofold . . . The mixture of . . . the water and the word (Word?) is called Eucharist . . . They who by faith partake of it are sanctified both in body and in soul"; cf. *ibid.* 2.1: "The divine food is the contemplation of true reality." It is because the soul is incorporeal and *rational (logikos)* that it is fed by the word *(logos)*, while bodies are composed of the four elements and consequently are fed by bread; cf. Nemesius of Emesa, *The Nature of Man* 2 (Eng. trans., Telfer, p. 228); 12 (Telfer, p. 264): "The soul's nourishment is learning." Cf. Clem. Alex., *Strom.* 6.14, *ad fin.:* ". . . regarding nothing bad but ignorance and action contrary to right reason *(logos)*," and 5.10, end, where "the meat of the full-grown" is "mystic contemplation, for this is the flesh and blood of the Word, that is, the comprehension of the divine power and essence. 'Taste and see. . .' (cf. *Myst.* 5.20)"; in those who eat spiritually "the soul now nourishes itself." But it is easier to say what such language originally meant than what it actually means in the jejune (emasculated? mutilated?) form in which it appears in *Myst.* 4.5. In any case the two interpretations (a) and (b) are complementary, since in Alexandrian theology the apprehension of the Logos through teaching and contemplation was not unrelated to sacramental communion, but provided its wider context.

10 Or "efficacy," "virtue."

11 Ps. 22 (23).5, Sept.

the evil spirits? And very aptly: for that table gave communion with devils, while this gives communion with God.

"You have anointed my head with oil."[12] He has anointed your head with oil upon your forehead, meaning the seal which you have of God, that you may be made "the engraving of the signet,"[13] that is, the sanctuary of God.

"Your chalice, also, which inebriates me, how goodly is it!"[14] You see here spoken of the chalice which Jesus took in His hands and of which, after giving thanks, he said: "This is my blood shed for many for the forgiveness of sins."[15]

(8) For this reason Solomon also, in Ecclesiastes, covertly alluding to this grace, says: "Come hither, eat your bread with joy,"[16] that is, the mystical bread. "Come hither," he calls: a saving, beatific call. "And drink your wine with a merry heart": that is, the mystical wine. "And let oil be poured out upon your head": you see how he hints also of the mystical chrism. "And at all times let your garments be white, because the Lord approves what you do."[17] It is now that the Lord approves what you do; for before you came to the grace your doings were "vanity of vanities."[18]

Now that you have put off your old garments and put on those which are spiritually white, you must go clad in white all your days.[19] I do not, of course, mean that your ordinary clothes must always be white, but that you must be clad in those true, spiritual garments which are white and shining. Then you will be able to say with the blessed Isaia: "Let my soul rejoice in the Lord; for he has dressed me in the gar-

12 *Ibid.*
13 Cf. Exod. 28.36, Sept.; Sir. 45.12.
14 Ps. 22 (23).5, Sept.
15 Matt. 26.28.
16 Eccles. 9.7-8.
17 Cf. *ibid.*
18 Eccles. 1.2.
19 After Baptism the candidates put on new, white garments, symbolizing the putting on of the New Man, and wore them throughout Easter Week. Cf. 1.10.

ments of salvation, and with the robe of gladness he has clothed me."[20]

(9) In this knowledge, and in the firm conviction that the bread which is seen is not bread,[21] though it is bread to the

20 Isa. 61.10.

21 *(Ho phainomenos artos)* Rather than "what seems bread" or "the seeming bread." The *Myst.* unequivocally teach the Real Presence, but they are vague about the mode of the presence and the way in which it is brought about (e.g., by transubstantiation). One cannot press *either* the analogies with the merely qualitative change effected by the *epiklēsis* (invocation) in the baptismal water, the chrism or food offered to idols *(Cat.* 3.3; *Myst.* 1.7; 2.3; 3.3, cf. 5.7) *or* the analogy with Cana (4.3), especially as the miracle there was not a case of "transubstantiation," since the appearance ("accidents"), as well as the substance of the water, was changed. The mark of transubstantiation is that the substance of the bread, instead of remaining as the sacramental mediating sign of the Body of Christ, ceases to exist, being changed into that Body. *Phainomenos artos* (4.9) *could* mean "what seems bread," but consider the other relevant passages—the repeated denial that the bread (and water and oil) is "mere, bare, common or ordinary *(litos, psilos, koinos)* bread" (1.7; 3.3, 6) (which implies it is bread), and the description of the bread as the "antitypical Body" (5.20; cf. note 17 on "antitype" at 2.6). Again at 4.3, "in the figure of bread is given to thee His Body," Touttée's transubstantiationist thesis leads him into the absurdity of arguing that "figure" *(typos)* means "semblance" (Diss. 3, cap. 11, n. 83: PG 33.265-266). But obviously the genitive is defining; the bread *is* the figure, the figure of the Body of Christ. Similarly what is meant here (4.9) is that "the bread that is seen with the eyes of the body" is not *"really"* bread by comparison with the true, heavenly Bread which it signifies and makes sacramentally present; it is not denied that it is, at its own lowly level, bread. The thought-category is that of the early Platonic doctrine of ideas or forms, in which earthly, sensible things are mere imperfect copies of the archetypal heavenly realities; it is these latter that are "really real." So, too, the Fathers say that the baptized, or monks, are "not men, but angels." Certainly this ("visible, sensible") is the usual meaning of *phainomenos* in Cyril. Cp. "the visibly lame" in *Cat.* 10.13. The *Sermon* provides some remarkable analogies. There (9) the paralytic is addressed: "Why await the *visible (ph.)* motion of the waters? . . . Glimpsing God visible in the flesh, attend not to the *visible* (man) but to the God who works through the *visible* man." Similarly (5) Cyril equivalently says that it was not the two blind men but the Pharisees who were "really" blind. So (6) immediately after telling the paralytic that he has Christ, he tells him that he "has no man" and continues: "God you have . . ., One who is both God and man under different aspects (*kata ti . . . kata ti*)." Probably in this last phrase—and cf. Cyril's statement (*Cat.* 4.9) that "Christ was twofold (*diplous*)" and 15.1, "All things are twofold in . . . Christ"—we have the clue to the Eucharistic theology of the *Myst.* Its model is christological: either as

taste, but the Body of Christ, and that the visible wine is not wine, though taste will have it so, but the Blood of Christ; and that it was of this that David sang of old: "Bread strengthens the heart of man, soon his face glistens joyously with oil,"[22] strengthen your heart, partaking of this Bread as spiritual, and make cheerful the face of your soul. God grant that, your soul's face unveiled with a clear conscience, you may "reflecting as in a glass the glory of the Lord," go "from glory to glory"[23] in Christ Jesus our Lord, whose is the glory forever and ever. Amen.

Appended Note C

The Doctrine in the Mystagogical Lectures on the Eucharistic Presence

Two early Reformed theologians, Aubertin and Rivetus, interpreted the Eucharistic teaching of the Mystagogical Lectures in a way which, though inadequate, will reward the attention of the student. I shall therefore first summarize their interpretation as presented by Touttée and then make the necessary adjustments in a Catholic sense. Their interpretation is as follows.

While the Mystagogical Lectures recognize a real, spiritual (but not substantial) presence of Christ in the Eucharistic action, they

---

the Word "became" flesh without ceasing to be the Word or (better) the mysterious coexistence, co-presence of two natures, a lower and a more exalted, in Christ. This interpretation accords well with the "dualism" of sacramental sign (water, oil, bread) and spiritual, supernatural reality which pervades the sacramental teaching of both the Lenten and the Mystagogical Lectures. Their viewpoint is pre-Scholastic: somewhat fluid and imprecise. Much earlier St. Irenaeus *(Adv. haer.* 4.18.5) stated this simple "dualism" of earthly and heavenly: "For as the bread from the earth, after receiving the invocation of God, is no longer common bread, but the Eucharist, consisting of two realities, an earthly and a heavenly. . . ." That the model of the *Myst.* is christological is made practically certain by the parallel language in the Lenten Lectures, where Cyril repeatedly emphasizes (12.1; 13.2, 3, 33) that Christ is "not a mere *(psilos)* man." Cf. also the "*phainomenos* darkness" of *Myst.* 1.4.

22 Ps. 103 (104).15, Sept.

23 Cf. 2 Cor. 3.18.

view this presence dynamically and in terms of the benefit (spiritual effect) of the sacrament: that is, the devout believer's spiritual communion with Christ and, through his continued eating, his ever-deepening mystical union with Him. References to the Bread and Wine being and becoming the Body and Blood of Christ are only symbolic, the language of signs and symbols which is appropriate to sacraments. The Mystagogical Lectures apply to the sacramental signs language strictly appropriate only to the reality (the spiritual benefit) which they signify and convey. In Holy Communion we spiritually partake of the Lord's Body and Blood in the sense that we gain the benefits of His Body broken and His Blood shed for us and are vouchsafed fellowship with God. Thus the consecrated Bread is the symbol or sacrament of the Body of Christ, or is the mystical Body of Christ; it become the efficacious figure of Christ's Body insofar as it mediates the grace of His Passion. Lest the illustration from the miracle at Cana should mislead the audience, they are immediately warned (4.4) that they do not literally eat Christ's flesh *(sarkophagia)* but that the eating spoken of is spiritual, that (4.7) it is a mystical and spiritual Table to which they are invited, and (4.9) that they must "partake thereof as spiritual." In spite of some rhetorical flights the *Mystagogiae* have no serious doctrine of a "res et sacramentum." In all three sacraments the *Mystagogiae* know only two things: the sacramental sign and the grace-effect of the sacrament. It is true that they speak of the bread as being "changed," but not every change is substantial. In 5.7 it is said that *"everything* that the Holy Spirit touches is sanctified and changed." That "changed" is here defined more precisely by "sanctified" is clear from the numerous passages (*Cat.* 3.3-4; *Myst.* 1.7; 3.3) implying that the changes effected by the consecration in the baptismal water, the chrism, and the eucharistic bread and wine are all of the same kind. It is a qualitative, not substantial, change and is compared to the change effected in meat when offered to idols. The illustration from Cana, therefore, is only intended to prove that He who changed the water substantially and sensibly can also change the wine sacramentally. Again, the warning in *Myst.* 4.6 not to regard the consecrated eucharistic elements as "bare" is exactly parallel to the warning in 3.3 not to regard the consecrated ointment as "bare." In no case is the change effected by the consecration substantial or "physical"; the sacramental elements are "changed" only in the sense that the consecration makes them God's instruments and imparts to them a spiritual or mystic power through which they impart to us the precious gifts promised by the Gospel. It is true that 4.9 says that the Bread is not bread, except to the taste; yet six times *Myst.* 4 calls it bread, and, after the statements in 3.3 that it is "not plain bread" or "bare bread," the 4.9 passage is clearly a metaphor or hyperbole. The comparison with the consecrated ointment in 3.3

is clearly the decisive passage, especially when taken in conjunction with the other parallels. The *Mystagogiae* speak indeed (4.3 and 5; 5.15) of the Body of Christ being "distributed through" or "assimilated into" our members and sanctifying not only our soul but our body, but they speak of the baptismal water and the chrism in exactly the same way: in *Cat.* 3.3-4 Cyril speaks of the water as purifying the body and enabling "the body also to partake of the Grace," while *Myst.* 3.4 and 7 describe the chrism as "a spiritual preservative of the body" and use of it language applicable only to the Holy Spirit whom it conveys.

The lectures are, indeed, somewhat inconsistent, but they are consistently inconsistent. To cite a parallel, the *Mystagogiae* (3.2) speak of the chrism as mere material ointment and as being only the "antitype" of the Holy Ghost, with whom Christ was anointed, and yet they go on (3.3, 4, 7) to identify it with the Holy Ghost, or at least to attribute to it sanctifying power, and even say (3.6) that the newly baptized were, after all, "truly anointed by the Holy Ghost." Similarly, *Cat.* 3.3-4 speaks of the baptismal water as a material element affecting only the body and yet also speaks of it as sanctifying and sealing the soul. In just the same way the *Mystagogiae* speak of the eucharistic Bread as the Body of Christ and yet also speak of it (4.5) as a material element affecting only our body: "for as bread answers to the body, so is the Word appropriate to the soul." In each case the material element sacramentally mediates a divine grace which sanctifies the soul. Such "strong" passages, therefore, as 4.3 and 6 about the eucharistic Bread are entirely analogous (1) to what is said in *Cat.* 3.3-4 about the baptismal water: "Regard not the Bath as simple water, but rather regard the spiritual grace that is given with the water. . . . For since man is body and soul . . . the water cleanses the body and the Spirit seals the soul. . . When going down, therefore, into the water, regard not the bare element. . ."; and (2) to what is said in *Myst.* 3.3 about the Chrism: "But beware of supposing this to be plain ointment. For as the bread. . ., (so the ointment after the invocation becomes Christ's divinizing grace)," for "while your body is anointed with visible ointment, your soul is sanctified by the holy, life-giving Spirit." Again, there is the use of the word "antitype." *Myst.* 5.20 speaks of the Bread and Wine as "the antitype of the (or "the antitypical") Body and Blood of Christ." Now, only thrice elsewhere do the Mystagogical Lectures use the word "antitype": in 2.6 and twice in 3.1: and always in contrast with the archetype or original, though with reference to the spiritual grace conveyed through the sacramental symbol. Baptism (2.4-7) is the antitype of Christ's Passion, because our sacramental imitation of His death and resurrection mediates for us the fruits of the Redemption. Then in 3.1 the Chrism is twice called the antitype of the Holy Spirit, and is *contrasted* with Him; and yet in 3.7 it is identified with the Holy Spirit: "It shall teach you all things if It abides in you." Finally, there is the absurdity that if we take *Myst.* 4 literally, then we must, in logic, take literally the statement in 5.10 that in the Eucharist "we offer Christ slain in sacrifice," where the perfect participle suggests that "slain" represents a present state; then Holy Communion would indeed be a gruesome banquet (but see n. 33 there).

Now let us make the necessary adjustments. It is clear that the *Mystagogiae* conceive the Presence, not as merely virtual or dynamic, but in the traditional Catholic sense. For (a) neither the Lenten nor the Mystagogical Lectures ever say that the baptismal water actually becomes or is "the grace" which it imparts. (b) There is a closer analogy with Chrism. The Holy Spirit does seem to be conceived as actually "arriving" in person in His "antitype." (c) The parallels drawn between the Bread and the water and ointment show (i) an analogy in the mode of consecration (by invocation) and (ii) that in each case the element is changed. But it remains to inquire into the nature of the change in each case. And the *Mystagogiae* speak of the Bread in a way which contrasts with its language about the water and the Chrism; they say repeatedly and with the utmost emphasis that it becomes and is the Body of Christ. Moreover (4.3) *"in* the figure (the Bread) the Body *is given* to thee." (d) Finally the denial (4.6) that the bread is *psilos* (mere, bare bread) both proves the real Presence and shows how the *Mystagogiae* conceive it. The Lenten Lectures provide the key. In *Cat.* 4.9 Cyril says that "Christ is double" (cf. 15.1) and in 12.1; in 13.2, 3, 33 he says that Christ is not a mere *(psilos)* man, since He is also God. Thus the model of the Jerusalem doctrine of the Eucharistic presence is christological. This, while excluding transubstantiation (for the bread is then as real as the sacred Manhood), safeguards the objective and substantial Presence. The emphasis, however, is upon the action and the eating. Finally, Cyril confined both doctrine and theological speculation to a minimum. He had no theory of *how* the divinity and humanity co-existed in Christ, though he may have thought of this co-presence as the *Mystagogiae* thought of the co-presence in the Eucharist (*Myst.* 4.7: "the mystic, intelligible [*noētēn*] Table") on the model of the indwelling of a Platonic "sensible" (earthly reality) by a *noēton* (the corresponding spiritual, heavenly reality) or as the soul permeates the body, "tota in toto et tota in qualibet parte" (cf. the Logos-Sarx Christology). Cyril does not tell us how he conceived the "conversion" of the bread into the Body of Christ; probably he would have accepted the other christological analogy, that of the incarnation of the Word; this is the analogy suggested by Theophilus of Alexandria—as the Word became flesh without ceasing to be the Word *(menōn ho ēn)*. Other Fathers, however, from *ca.* 380 use language hardly if at all distinguishable from that of transubstantiation: transelement, *metousioun, metastoicheioun, metarrhythmizein* suggesting a change in what we would call the invisible atomic or nuclear structure of the bread—a regrettable concession, one may think, to the literalist piety of the simpler faithful.

FIFTH LECTURE ON THE MYSTERIES

The Eucharist (II): The Liturgy[1]

"Laying aside, then, all malice, deceit and slander" etc.[2]

(1) By the mercy of God you have in our former assemblies received sufficient instruction about Baptism, Chrism, and the partaking [communion] of the Body and Blood of Christ.[3] We must now pass on to the next subject, intending today to crown the work of your spiritual edification.

The Hand-Washing

(2) You saw the deacon[4] who offers the water for the washing of hands to the celebrant and to the presbyters who

1 This lecture is not a liturgical *text,* but a commentary, with short quotations, upon the Jerusalem rite, which resembled the rather Semitic and partly archaic "Addai and Mari" (Dix 178-180). It is often closely paralleled by Theodore and ApCo 8.11-15 and was probably the nucleus of the Liturgy of St. James (A.D. 450–). For an interesting commentary on *Myst.* 5 see Dix, esp. 187-203; but, *pace* Dix, *Myst.* 5 is unlikely to antedate 390.

2 Cf. 1 Peter 2.1ff.

3 Note the three distinct sacraments co-ordinated; but among the manuscripts the group *a* family lacks "Chrism."

4 Entirely omitting the Proanaphora, with which the newly baptized would be familiar (and which was no doubt in any case omitted—cf. ApTrad—in the Easter Mass), the commentary starts with the Lavabo, whose origins presumably lie in the Jewish grace with meals or the ablution preceding the cultic *berakah* (benediction, = Greek "eucharist" or *eulogia).* The people's offerings of bread and wine have just been set upon the altar by the deacons. Cf. ApTrad 4.2: "[To the Bishop] let the Deacons bring the oblation, and he with all the Presbyters laying his hand on the oblation shall say giving thanks [eucharistizing] thus . . ." (Dialogue and Preface follow).

encircle the altar of God.[5] Not that he offered this water on account of any bodily uncleanness: of course not; for we did not originally enter the church unwashed. No; the ablution is a symbolic action, a symbol of our obligation to be clean from all sins and transgressions. The hands symbolize action; so by washing them we signify evidently the purity and blamelessness of our conduct. Did you not hear the blessed David supplying the key to this ceremony in the divine mysteries when he says: "I will wash my hands among the innocent: and will circle thy altar, O Lord"?[6] The hand-washing, then, is a symbol of innocence.

The Kiss

(3) Next the deacon cries:[7] "Welcome one another," and "Let us kiss one another."[8] You must not suppose that this kiss is the kiss customarily exchanged in the streets by ordinary friends. This kiss is different, effecting, as it does, a commingling of souls and mutually pledging unreserved forgiveness. The kiss, then, is a sign of a true union of hearts, banish-

---

5 In Syria the altar sometimes stood against the rear wall of the apse (J. Lassus, *Sanctuaires chrétiens de Syrie* [Paris 1947]; art. "Syrie," *Dictionnaire d'archéologie chrétienne et de liturgie* 15.2 [1953] 1855-1941); alternatively it was placed on the chord of the apse (e.g., Gerasa, St. Peter and St. Paul); in N. Africa it sometimes stood in the nave near the chancel steps (cf., e.g., the Tabarka [Thabraca] mosaic); and sometimes it stood in a central position in the nave (e.g., Sabratha, Forum Basilica) [M. Moreton].

6 Ps. 25 (26).6, Sept. Possibly the whole of this psalm was chanted.

7 Bishop, deacons and the holy people (laity) had each their proper "liturgy" in the common action (cf. 1 Clem. 40.5-41.3). The deacon presented the offerings (bread and wine) brought to church by the people and in later times, when in the East the celebrant was secluded first by the veil, then by the solid screen, he acted as the link between priest and people, who gradually became passive spectators. But there are already some late elements in *Myst.* 5. Note the people's responses in the *Myst.*

8 The liturgical kiss of peace (origin in Jewish nonliturgical practice?) is a token of that "unity of spirit in the bond of peace" which for St. Paul was the foundation of the "one Body" (1 Cor. 10.17). Syrian *Didascalia* (cf. Ethiopic) 2.45 tells of private Christian courts for the peaceful settling of disputes.

ing every grudge. It was this that Christ had in view when He said: "If, when you are bringing your gift to the altar, you suddenly remember that your brother has a grievance against you, leave your offering by the altar; first go and make your peace with your brother, and then come back and offer your gift."[9] The kiss, then, is a reconciliation and therefore holy, as the blessed Paul said somewhere when he commanded us to "salute one another with a holy kiss";[10] and Peter: "Salute one another with a kiss of charity."[11]

The Dialogue

(4) Then the celebrant cries: "Lift up your hearts."[12] For truly it is right in that most awful[13] hour to have one's heart on high with God, not below, occupied with earth and the things of earth. In effect, then, the bishop[14] commands everyone to banish worldly thoughts and workaday cares and to have their hearts in heaven with the good God.

Assenting, you answer, "We have them lifted up to the Lord." Let no one present be so disposed that while his lips

9 Matt. 5.23, 24; cf. *Didache* 14.1-2.

10 1 Cor. 16.20.

11 1 Peter 5.14.

12 This part of the Dialogue is apparently of purely Christian origin and early, cf. ApTrad 4.3. The real action of the liturgy takes place beyond time "in the Age to Come." That is, the Eucharist is eschatological: Christ is Host at the Messianic Banquet, already realized by anticipation (Dix p. 127).

13 This awe and fear of the sacrament was apparently a late fourth-century Syrian development and something of a revolution. Not so much earlier, Dix (p. 480) remarks, Christians had been accustomed to communicate themselves at home with the reserved Sacrament. Jungmann (J. A. Jungmann, *Die Stellung Christi im liturgischen Gebet* [Liturgiegeschichtliche Forschungen 7/8; Münster in W. 1925] 217) also thinks that it marks *Myst.* 5 as late (380-400). Even *ca.* 374, "All the solitaries in the desert, where there is no priest, communicate themselves, keeping the communion at home. And at Alexandria and in Egypt the laity commonly keep the communion in their houses, each communicating when he likes" (St. Basil the Great, Letter 93).

14 Literally "priest," but the title is reserved for the bishop, priests (cf. 5.2) being styled "presbyters"; so in the Latin Fathers "sacerdos" and "presbyter."

form the words, "We have them lifted up to the Lord," in his mind his attention is engaged by worldly thoughts. At all times we should commemorate[15] God, but at least, if this is not possible to human weakness, we must aspire to it in that hour.

(5) Then the priest says: "Let us give thanks [make eucharist] to the Lord."[16] Indeed we ought to give thanks to

15 The Eucharist is an *anamnēsis* ("commemoration" in a pregnant sense) and, if Dix and P. Audet are right, is modelled, as a literary form, upon the Jewish cultic *berakah* which had three basic elements: (i) a benediction or brief invitation to praise God; (ii) the motive, i.e., the wonderful works of God in creation and, especially, in salvation history; in recalling *(anamnēsis)* these, the people also recalls, and anew identifies itself with, its own past history, which, as salvation history, is a history with God; (iii) a doxology; in ch. 6 the Sanctus (Trisagion) is called a "doxology." M's use of the word *mnēmoneuteon* ("mention, commemorate, make anamnesis") at this point, therefore, is probably not accidental; cf. Exod. 20.4: "In every place where I cause my name to be remembered, I will come to you and bless you."

16 The great puzzle of *Myst.* 5 is the absence, in the Eucharistic Prayer, of any reference to the Mystery of Salvation, Christ's historic redemptive work (incarnation, passion, resurrection). But since the Great Prayer (I take it) begins here (*eucharistēsōmen*), the triple *hoti* (giving thanks "because of" or "for" three things) is highly significant. Here "ought" implies "is." Even allowing for the possibility that the reference is to the ground of the obligation rather than to the expressed content of the thanks and is, directly, to the baptismal grace, nevertheless this passage points to the commemoration of Christ's work. The solution cannot be (F. E. Brightman, *Liturgies Eastern and Western* I [Oxford 1896] 469) that the Mystagogue "skips" and "is only expounding the salient points of the rite," for the repeated "next" and "after that" show continuity and, while the "great gap" occurs between chaps. 6 and 7, chap. 7 (the Epiclesis) clearly follows immediately upon 6 (the Trisagion, Sanctus); moreover the *anamnesis* of Christ, the very heart of the Eucharist, is surely a "salient point." The explanation probably is that what is being expounded is that part of the service which the congregation were allowed to hear and see, as distinct from the prayers recited by the celebrant in a low voice and perhaps behind a curtain (veil, screen). The prominence, in *Myst.* 5, of awe and dread shows that this document is not prior to the great liturgical revolution of the late fourth century which transformed the primitive Christian Eucharist: "The Eucharist, at the beginning a simple Lord's Supper in the private homes of the Christians, takes the form more and more of a court ceremonial" (Quasten, *Patrology* III 4-5). This "byzantinizing" of the Eucharist involved chanting and, very soon, performance of the most sacred parts by the celebrant privately. Since, except for extensive additions, the great Eastern liturgies have remained stationary since the fifth cen-

the Lord for calling us, when we were unworthy, to so great a grace, for reconciling us when we were enemies, and for vouchsafing to us the spirit of adoption.

Then you say: "It is meet and just." In giving thanks we do indeed a meet thing and a just; but He did, not a just thing, but one that went beyond justice, in deigning to bestow on us such marvellous blessings.

Memorial of Creation: Sanctus

(6) After that we commemorate the heavens,[17] the earth and the sea; the sun and moon, the stars, the whole rational and irrational creation, both visible and invisible: Angels and Archangels; Virtues, Dominions, Principalities, Powers, Thrones and the many-faced Cherubim: equivalently saying with David, "O magnify ye the Lord with me."[18] We commemorate also the Seraphim whom Isaia in the Holy Spirit

---

tury, we have probably the clue to *Myst.* 5 in the relatively modern form of, e.g., the Armenian liturgy as given by Brightman, pp. 412-57. There the parts performed aloud before the screen are precisely those commented upon in *Myst.* 5—the Hand-washing with Ps. 25.6, the Kiss, the Dialogue introducing the Eucharistic Prayer, and the Sanctus —while the Eucharistic Prayer itself is recited secretly, the clerks meanwhile prolonging the Sanctus with angelic hymns up to the Epiclesis. J. A. Jungmann noted an exactly parallel phenomenon in medieval and later times in the West, where the celebrant had reached the words of institution by the time the choir had finished singing the Sanctus (*Missarum Sollemnia* I [Vienna 1958] 172-73). From the people's point of view, then, the Epiclesis (or words of institution) *did* follow immediately upon the Sanctus. Thus the Jerusalem liturgy very probably had a rich christological *anamnesis,* including, as *Myst.* 4 suggests, the institution narrative. But both Preface and Anaphora may have been still variable in length and content. The *Peregrinatio* of Aetheria/Egeria, while very reticent about the Mass, is compatible with the hypothesis that it was quite simple in Jerusalem *ca.* 395 and that, so thorough was the preaching about the Lord's life, much could be taken for granted.

17 *(Mnēmoneuomen)* Or "make mention of"; but "commemorate" brings out the literary structure; creation, redemption, the Institution-narrative, the Saints of the time of the Church (5.9) are all contents of the same one Eucharist or Anamnesis; the Last Supper takes its place, a central place, in salvation history. And cf. "commemorate God" in 5.4E.

18 Ps. 33.4.

saw encircling the throne of God, "with two wings veiling their faces[19] and with twain their feet, while with twain they did fly,"[20] as they chanted: "Holy, Holy, Holy, Lord of Hosts."[21] It is to mingle our voices in the hymns of the heavenly armies that we recite this doxology which descends to us from the Seraphim.[22]

Epiclesis (Invocation) and Consecration

(7) Next,[23] after sanctifying ourselves by these spiritual songs, we implore the merciful God[24] to send forth His Holy Spirit upon the offering to make the bread the Body of Christ and the wine the Blood of Christ.[25] For whatever the Holy Spirit touches is hallowed[26] and changed.

19 Gk. *prosōpon,* singular. Dix (197) interprets "His face"; cf. Origen, *Peri archōn* 4.3.14. *Myst.* 5.6, however, envisages not two, but a considerable number of Seraphim, and as they "surround" God, it is not clear how all of them could veil His face.

20 Really "treading air," as they are apparently stationary.

21 Cf. Isa. 6.2-3, Sept.

22 Apparently explaining the "with me" above. The liturgy takes place in the heavenly courts; cf. ch. 4. I read *touto* with the γ family instead of the untranslatable *to.*

23 Here, since the exposition clearly goes straight from the Sanctus to the Epiclesis, comes the alleged "great gap." But see n. 16 above.

24 For the phrasing compare "the invocation of the Holy Spirit," *Myst.* 3.3, and "the invocation of the adorable Trinity," 1.7.

25 So it is the Invocation which consecrates and changes the elements. Compare 3.3; 4.3 and Greg. Nyss., *In bapt. Chr.* (PG 46.581): "The bread [after the consecration] is called, and becomes, the Body of Christ. So also the mystic oil, so the wine: of little worth before the blessing, they both after the consecration of the Spirit have a new efficacy." Now too there is a clear "moment of consecration"; in Chrysostom, *Hom.* 2 *de proditione Iudae* 6, this moment is when the Words of Institution are pronounced: " 'This is my body,' [Christ] says. This word transforms the oblation." There is an Epiclesis in ApTrad (4.12) *after* the Words of Institution; there, however, it is not a petition for the action of the Holy Spirit upon the oblation itself, but upon the minds and hearts of the communicants (R. H. Connolly, "The Eucharistic Prayer of Hippolytus," *Journ. Theol. Stud.* 39 [1938] 367). There is a remarkably close parallel in (spurious?) Irenaeus, frag. 37 (ANF vol. 1, p. 574); see also frag. 13. Note that in *Myst.* 1.7 the Eucharistic Epiclesis is an invocation of "the adorable Trinity."

26 Or "consecrated."

The Intercession

(8) Next, when the spiritual sacrifice, the bloodless worship, has been completed,[27] over that sacrifice of propitiation we beseech God[28] for the public peace of the Churches, for the good estate of the world, for the Emperors,[29] for the armed forces and our allies,[30] for those in sickness, for the distressed: for all, in a word, who need help, we all pray and offer this sacrifice.

(9) Then we commemorate also those who have fallen asleep:[31] first of all, the patriarchs, prophets, apostles, and martyrs, that God through their intercessory prayers may accept our supplication. Next we pray also for the holy Fathers and Bishops who have fallen asleep, and generally for all who have gone before us, believing that this will be of the greatest benefit to the souls of those on whose behalf our supplication is offered in the presence of the holy, the most dread Sacrifice.

---

27 *(apartisthēnai)* One could translate "has found its completion in that sacrifice of propitiation"; but the latter will still be the spiritual and unbloody sacrifice. The text perhaps implies that the *Myst.* here skips, in its exposition, part of the liturgy, possibly the *anamnesis* of Christ's work. Compare Chrys. *De prod. Iud.* 1.6, where the Words of Institution "complete" *(apērtismenēn)* the sacrifice. To the objection that as in *De prod. Iud.* the Words of Institution effect both the Presence and the Sacrifice, so that the *Myst.* may understand the Epiclesis as effecting both, it may be replied that (1) unlike the Words of Institution, the typical Epiclesis does not signify the Sacrifice, and (2) the *Myst.* seem to view the Epiclesis as effecting only the Presence. If the liturgy commented on in the *Myst.* did include an Institution-narrative, we must revise Dix's remark (pp. 278, 280) that in *Myst.* 5 Christ plays a purely passive role, especially as in *De prod. Iud.* Christ is Priest as well as Victim. Not that a Eucharist without an Institution-narrative is unthinkable; "Addai and Mari" probably had none, and there is none in what is probably a Eucharist, *Didache* 9-10.

28 The intercessions in this liturgy are unusually developed and prominent (Dix 201).

29 Plural: Theodosius and Gratian?

30 Cl. Beukers, S.J., "For our Emperors, Soldiers and Allies," *Vigiliae Christianae* 15 (1961) 177-84, argues learnedly and persuasively that the reference can only be to the convert Visigoths planted in Moesia and, 3 October 382, granted the status of *socii* by Theodosius.

31 "Cemetery," a Christian word, is the Greek form of Latin "dormitory."

(10) Let me use an illustration for an argument. For I know that many of you say:[32] "What does it avail a soul departing this world, whether with or without sins, to be remembered at the Sacrifice?" Well, suppose a king banished persons who had offended him, and then their relatives wove a garland and presented it to him on behalf of those undergoing punishment, would he not mitigate their sentence? In the same way, offering our supplications to Him for those who have fallen asleep, even though they be sinners, we, though we weave no garland, offer Christ slain for our sins,[33] propitiating the merciful God on both their and our own behalf.

The Lord's Prayer

(11) Then, after this, we recite that prayer which the Savior delivered to His own disciples, with a clear conscience designating God as our Father, saying: "Our Father who art

32 Was the teaching, then, a novelty that met resistance? In the time of Cyprian (*Ep.* 39.3) "sacrifices were offered for" martyrs at their annual commemoration in the liturgy; but Cyprian speaks of their "crowns," and their passion was linked with Our Lord's. Presumably Tertullian (*Cor. mil.* 3) referred to the same custom. Martyrs are commemorated much earlier.

33 The *Myst.* clearly teach that the Eucharist is a propitiatory sacrifice. But in what sense? Clearly not, as was maintained by F. Clark (*Eucharistic Sacrifice and the Reformation* [Westminster, Md., and London 1960] 256-257, etc.) in the sense that, in the Eucharist, Calvary is *literally* made present, for then the Mass would be neither (5.8A) a "spiritual sacrifice" nor a "bloodless service." St. Thomas Aquinas emphatically rejects any such view; cf. *Sum. theol.* 3.83.1; 3.81.4, (*ad* 1 quite fits this picture) and *passim.* Nor (against Vonier) is a dead Christ offered; in the case of *Christ* the perfect participle has not this connotation, since His death was "once for all" and He is "the Crucified *and Risen* One." But the glorified Christ remains forever the Victim and bears the scars of His Sacrifice on even His glorified Body (John 20.19-29). Priest and Victim are the same (Council of Trent, Denzinger-Schönmetzer, *Enchiridion symbolorum* 1743). See A. A. Stephenson, "Two Views of the Mass," *Theological Studies* (Woodstock, Md.) 22 (1961), 588-609. In the case of any other than Christ, Gk *esphagiasmenon would* imply that the victim was still dead.

Compare Chrys., *Priesthood* 3.4: "When you see the immolated Lord . . . and the High Priest standing and praying over the sacrifice, and the whole congregation empurpled by that precious

in heaven."[34] Oh, the greatness of the mercy of God! To those who had revolted from Him and been reduced to the direst straits He has granted so liberal a pardon for their crimes, He has been so prodigal of His favor, that they may even call Him "Father": "Our Father who art in heaven." They also are a "Heaven" who "bear the likeness of the heavenly man," since God is dwelling in them and mingling with them."[35]

(12) "Hallowed be thy name." God's name is by nature holy, whether we call it so or not. But because it is sometimes profaned among sinners according to the words: "Through you my name is continually blasphemed among the Gentiles,"[36] we pray that the name of God may be hallowed in us: not that from not being holy it becomes holy, but because it becomes holy *in us* when we are sanctified [hallowed] and our actions correspond to our holy profession.

(13) "Thy kingdom come." It is the mark of a pure soul to say without reserve: "Thy kingdom come." For it is the man who has listened to Paul saying: "Therefore do not let sin reign in your mortal body"[37] and has purified himself in action, thought and word, who will say to God: "Thy kingdom come."

(14) "Thy will be done on earth as it is in heaven." God's heavenly, blessed angels do the will of God, as David said

---

Blood . . ." Often, like *Myst.* here, which remarkably anticipates the tone of Late (post-Thomistic) medieval theology, Chrysostom uses very realistic language. Once, however, (fortunately) he explains: "Yes, we offer (the Victim of Calvary), but (only) making the commemoration *(anamnēsis)* of His death . . . We offer, not a different sacrifice (from Calvary), but the same; *or rather, we make the commemoration (anamnēsis)* of that Sacrifice" *(Hom.* 17.3 *in Heb.).* An "anamnesis" is not a "bare commemoration" (Denz.-Schönm. 1753), for in the Sacrifice of the Church the true Priest/Victim is present, and the benefits of the once-for-all Sacrifice are made available.

34 Matt. 6.9-13. The Lord's Prayer seems to have been introduced into the Eucharistic liturgy after *ca.* 375. Only sons can celebrate the Eucharist. With 5.11 compare 5.5; 5.2.

35 Cf. 1 Cor. 15.49; 2 Cor. 6.16; Lev. 26.11-12.

36 Cf. Isa. 52.5, Sept.; Rom. 2.24.

37 Rom. 6.12.

in the Psalm: "Bless the Lord, all ye his angels: you that are mighty in strength, and execute his word."[38] In effect, then, this is what you mean by this petition: "As in the angels thy will is done, so on earth be it done in me, O Lord."

(15). "Give us this day our superessential bread."[39] Ordinary bread is not "superessential"; but this holy bread is superessential in the sense of being ordained for the essence of the soul. Not of this Bread is it said that it "passes into the stomach and so is discharged into the drain";[40] no: it is absorbed into your whole system to the benefit of both soul and body.[41] By "this day" he means "daily," as in Paul's "while it is called to-day."[42]

(16) "And forgive us our debts, as we also forgive our debtors." For our sins are many; we err both in word and in thought, and do many a deed which deserves condemnation. Indeed, "if we say that we have no sin, we are liars," as John says.[43] So we make a bargain with God, begging Him to condone our offenses according as we forgive our neighbours. Bearing in mind, then, the disproportion of this *quid*

---

38 Cf. Ps. 102.20.

39 Whether we translate "superessential" or, with the PGL *(s.v. epiousios)*, "essential" ("substantial"), the general meaning is the same: this Bread is the true Bread, which nourishes the real, inner or noetic self. Cf. 4.5 and Origen *(In Matt.* 85, PG 13.1735): "This Bread . . . is the Word-nourisher of our souls; (it is) the word proceeding from the God-Word." Cf. Origen, *Prayer* 27.1-9, esp. 7-9. The translation depends on whether our author assumed the Platonist or Stoic definition of substance there expounded. Aristotle, followed by Aquinas *(Sum. theol.* 1.66.2), held against Plato that the heavenly bodies were composed of a fifth element (quintessence). For "superessential" cf. *epignōsis* in PGL, *s.v.,* 1. Human soul and body provide a possible analogy for the relation of the Body of Christ to the bread.

40 Matt. 15.17.

41 A close parallel in Origen, *Prayer* 27.9. But what is surprising about the *Myst.,* if John II be its author, is how little it owes to Origen. For the physical assimilation of the Heavenly Bread, cf. *Cat.* 3.3, 4, 12; *Myst.* 3.3, 7A; the unique relation of the sacramental figure to the reality makes it possible to say of the material element (almost) everything that is true of what it signifies.

42 Heb. (3.13), whose Pauline authorship Clement affirmed, Origen hesitated over: cf. R. P. Hanson, in JTS 49.25; Eus. H. E. 6.25.

43 Cf. 1 John 1.8.

pro quo, let us not delay or put off forgiving one another. The offenses committed against us are small, paltry and easily settled; but the offenses we have committed against God are great—too great for any mercy except His. Beware, then, lest, on account of slight and trifling transgressions against you, you debar yourself from God's forgiveness of your most grievous sins.

(17) "And lead us not into temptation," O Lord. Is it this that the Lord teaches us to pray for: not to be tempted at all? How, then, is it said in another place: "A man untempted is a man unproved"?[44] And again: "Esteem it all joy, my brethren, when you fall into various temptations"?[45] But "entering into temptation" could mean being overwhelmed by temptation. For temptation is like a raging torrent which defies the traveller. Some people in time of temptation manage to cross this torrent without being overwhelmed by the raging waters, their prowess as swimmers saving them from being swept away by the tide. But if others who are not of the same mettle enter, they are engulfed: like Judas, who entered into the temptation of avarice and, failing to swim across, was overwhelmed and drowned—physically and spiritually. Peter entered into the temptation of the denial; but, though he entered, he was not drowned, but manfully swam across and was delivered from the temptation. Listen again, in another passage, to a company of triumphant saints giving thanks for their deliverance from temptation: "For thou, O God, hast proved us; thou hast tried us by fire, as silver is tried. Thou hast brought us into a net: thou hast laid afflictions on our back: thou didst let men ride over our heads. We have passed through fire and through water: and thou didst lead us out into a refreshment."[46] You see them celebrating their escape from the trap.[47] And "thou hast brought

44 Cf. Sir. 34.9-10.
45 Cf. James 1.2.
46 Ps. 65.10-12.
47 Touttée's conjecture, accepted by Piédagnel; cf. Ps. 68.15, Sept.

us out," he says, "into a refreshment": their being "brought into a refreshment" refers to their rescue from temptation.

(18) "But deliver us from the Evil One." If "lead us not into temptation" referred to not being tempted at all, He would not have said: "but *deliver* us from the Evil One." The Evil One from whom we pray to be rescued is our adversary, the Devil.

Then, after completing the prayer, you say "Amen," which means, "So be it," thus setting your seal upon the petitions of the prayer which we owe to the divine teacher.

The Communion

(19) Next the priest says: "Holy things to the holy." Holy are the offerings after they have received the visitation of the Holy Spirit; and you are holy after you have been privileged to receive the Holy Spirit.[48] So things and persons correspond: both are holy. Next you say: "One is holy, one is the Lord, Jesus Christ." For truly One only is holy—holy, that is, by nature; yet we also are holy, not, indeed, by nature, but by participation, training and prayer.

(20) After this you hear the chanter inviting you with a sacred melody to communion in the holy mysteries, in the words: "O taste and see that the Lord is good."[49] Entrust not the judgment to your bodily palate, but to unwavering faith. For in tasting you taste, not bread and wine, but the antitypical[50] Body and Blood of Christ.

48 Like much of *Myst.* 5, closely paralleled in Theodore of Mopsuestia.

49 Ps. 33.9.

50 Or "the antitype of the Body"; cf. the anarthrous *Myst.* 3.3. Cf. the Paschal Mass of ApTrad 23.1 (Lat.): ". . . And (the Bishop) shall eucharistize the bread into the representation (Gk. 'antitype') of the Flesh of Christ, and the cup mixed with wine for the antitype (Gk., *homoiōma,* 'likeness') of the Blood. . ."; cf. ApTrad 32.3. Cf. Serapion: "the likeness *(homoiōma)* of the Body of the Only-begotten . . . the likeness of His death"; ApCo 7.25: ". . . for the precious Body . . . and Blood, the representation (antitypes) of which we perform" (Quasten). After *ca.* 430, however, this usage was deprecated, and the Second Council of Nicaea (A.D. 787) equivalently forbade the

(21) Coming up to receive, therefore, do not approach with your wrists extended or your fingers splayed, but making your left hand a throne for the right (for it is about to receive a King) and cupping your palm, so receive the Body of Christ; and answer: "Amen." Carefully hallow your eyes by the touch of the sacred Body, and then partake, taking care to lose no part of It. Such a loss would be like a mutilation of your own body. Why, if you had been given gold-dust, would you not take the utmost care to hold it fast, not letting a grain slip through your fingers, lest you be by so much the poorer? How much more carefully, then, will you guard against losing so much as a crumb of that which is more precious than gold or precious stones!

(22) After partaking of the Body of Christ, approach also the chalice of His Blood. Do not stretch out your hands, but, bowing low in a posture of worship and reverence as you say, "Amen," sanctify yourself by receiving also the Blood of Christ. While It is still warm upon your lips, moisten your fingers with It and so sanctify your eyes, your forehead, and other organs of sense. Then wait for the prayer and give thanks to the God who has deigned to admit you to such high mysteries.

(23) Preserve this traditional teaching untarnished; keep yourselves unsullied by sin. Never cut yourselves off from the fellowship [communion], never through the pollution of sin deprive yourselves of these sacred, spiritual mysteries. "And may the God of peace sanctify you completely, and may your whole spirit, soul and body be preserved blameless at the coming of our Lord Jesus Christ,"[51] whose is the glory now and evermore, world without end. Amen.

---

elements to be called "antitypes" after the consecration (Hardouin, *Acta Conciliorum* [Paris 1714-1715] 4.372A, cf. 369D).

51 1 Thess. 5.23.

SERMON ON THE PARALYTIC

(Homilia eis ton paralytikon ton epi tēn kolymbēthran)

Translated by

ANTHONY A. STEPHENSON

University of Exeter
England

INTRODUCTION

CYRIL'S SINGLE EXTANT sermon is found in only two manuscripts so far edited, B (Bodl. Roe 25, *xi s.*) and R (Paris, B. N. graec. 1447 [Regius 2030; *ca.* 1100]). There is a lacuna in B, but R is apparently entire. The evidence, on balance, strongly favours the Cyrilline authenticity of the Sermon. The silence of the monk Alexander and the Armenian tradition,[1] which know only the Lenten Lectures and the Letter to Constantius, is not very significant, for, unlike the catechetical lectures, the Sermon had no special interest for the Armenian Church and, unlike the Letter, it had no public interest. A comparison with the Lenten Lectures strongly suggests authenticity, for the differences in style between the two works are explained by their different subjects, and the distinction drawn in *Cat.* 13.9 between the method of the Lenten Lectures and the devotional mode of the ordinary sermon (cf. *Procat.* 11), with its mystical/allegorical *(theōretikē,* not "speculative") exegesis, prepares us for exactly what we find in the Sermon. When in the Lenten Lectures Cyril yields to his *attrait,* we find there passages very like the Sermon, notably *Cat.* 13.30-31 and 10.13, which summarizes many of the themes of the Sermon. A difficulty, however, arises from the reference to "our Father's teaching" in chapter 20. Touttée, assuming that on Sundays there were several sermons preached by presbyters in ascending order of seniority, the bishop preaching last, assumed that Cyril was senior presbyter. But Cyril was not ordained presbyter until

1 The Armenian life is published by E. Bihain, *Le Muséon* 76 (1963) 341-48 (cf. 333-38 for Cyril's literary activity). For the monk Alexander, see above p. 145.

after Serdica (A.D. 342), and in the last years before Bishop Maximus' death in 348/9 relations between them were probably strained.[2] But see notes to chapter 20. The Sermon resembles the Lenten Lectures in its anti-Jewish polemic, but its attitude to sex and marriage in chapters 10-12, where the imagery of the Song of Songs is taken to apply to the Passion, is more negative than in *Cat.* 4.24-26.

Cyril's text apparently lacked John 5.4, since there is no reference to the angel, but apparently included verse 3b (cf. ch. 9).

The text of the Sermon, like that of the Mystagogical Lectures, is rather extensively corrupt and presents the translator with many troublesome problems.

For an appraisal of the sermon, see Vol. 1 (FOTC Vol. 61) pp. 6-11.

2 Vol. 1 (FOTC Vol. 61), pp. 21, 22.

SERMON ON THE PARALYTIC

A sermon of our Blessed Father, Cyril, Bishop of Jerusalem, on the Paralytic at the Pool[1]

(1) Wherever Jesus appears, there is salvation. If He sees a revenue officer sitting in his office, He makes him an apostle and evangelist. Laid in the grave, He raises the dead to life.[2] He bestows sight on the blind, hearing on the deaf.[3] When, as now, He visits the public baths, it is not out of interest in the architecture,[4] but to heal the sick.

(2) By the Sheep Market in Jerusalem there used to be a pool with five colonnades,[5] four of which enclosed the pool, while the fifth spanned it midway. Here large numbers of sick would lie (unbelief also was rife among the Jews).[6] The physician and healer of both souls and bodies showed fairness in choosing this chronic sufferer to be the first recipient

1 John 5.2, 3, 5-14. For the absence of verse 4, see above, p. 208. There had also been a reading from St. Paul to the Romans; see below at n. 66.

2 Cf. Matt. 27.53.

3 Cf. ch. 9 *fin.*, and *Cat.* 10.5.

4 As the Greeks specialized in temples, so the Romans' great architectural achievement was their baths. The baths of Caracalla occupied, with their gardens and gymnasia, over thirty-three acres. The five colonnades or porches of John 5.2 suggest that the Pool of the Sheep Market (?) was a public bath.

5 As R has "there was the Sheep Pool," our two MSS reproduce the same divergence as the New Testament MSS. The pool is probably to be identified with the trapezoidal double pool of St. Anna, over a hundred yards long, recently uncovered by excavation in the property of the White Fathers.

6 It is tempting to emend to *astheneia* "(and the Jewish nation was sorely sick)," the spiritual nature of this malady being only implied; B has *apisteiāi* (dative).

of His gift, that he might the earlier be released from his pains. For not for one day only, nor for two, had the poor man lain on his bed of sickness—nor was it now the first month, no, nor the first year—but for eight-and-thirty years. His long-standing illness, rendering him a figure familiar to passersby, now made him ocular evidence of the power of his healer. For the paralytic was known to all by reason of the length of time.[7] But though the master physician gave proof of His skill, He was rebuffed by those who put an unfavourable construction on His work of mercy.

(3) As He walked round the pool, "He saw." He did not elicit the information by asking questions, for His divine power obviated any such need. Not "asking," but "seeing" how long the invalid had lain there; "seeing," He knew; indeed He knew before He saw. For if in the case of secrets of the heart "He had no need to question anyone concerning man, for He himself knew what was in man,"[8] much more was this the case when it was a question of diagnosing diseases with visible symptoms.[9]

(4) He saw a bedridden man weighed down by a sore sickness; for the paralytic's heavy load of sins aggravated the long-drawn agony of disease.[10] A question addressed to the sufferer hinted to him his need: "Wilt thou be healed?" Not a word more; He left him with the question half spoken. For the question was ambiguous; it was because he was sick not only in body but also in soul (compare His later saying: "Behold, thou art cured; sin no more, lest something worse befall thee") that He asked him: "Do you want to be healed?" What mighty power that implied in the physician, making relief depend only on the patient's willing! It is because salvation is from faith that He asked "Do you want to be healed?" that his "Yes" might give Jesus His cue. This "Wilt thou?" is the

7 Is this sentence a gloss?

8 Slightly emending the text which conflates John 2.25 and 16.30, to give the required sense.

9 But Touttée renders: "qui ab exterioribus causis inducuntur."

10 A gloss?

word of Jesus only; it belongs not to doctors who heal the body. For those who treat bodily ailments cannot say to any and every patient: "Wilt thou be healed?" But Jesus grants the will,[11] accepts the faith, and freely bestows the gift.

(5) Once when the Savior was passing by,[12] two blind men were sitting by the roadside.[13] Though their bodily eyes were sightless, their minds were open to the light. The blind men pointed out Him whom the Scribes did not recognize. For the Pharisees who, for all that they had been taught the Law—yes, had studied it from childhood to old age—had neverthe-

---

11 This, as Touttée also remarked, makes nonsense of the whole chapter. The repeated *charizetai* is also highly inelegant. Cyril must have written simply "He accepts the will and bestows the grace," which some medieval scribe changed and interpolated to make Cyril conform to a later, Western orthodoxy, crediting him with: "He grants the will," i.e., the theology of Augustine and the Second Council of Orange. Though Touttée felt obliged to follow the text of the MSS, he thought it incredible; it contradicts the "semi-Pelagian" tenor of the chapter, of the Sermon as a whole and of the Pre-baptismal Lectures. Just above Cyril has said, "putting relief in the power of his will." Cyril's doctrine is clear and consistent. Man needs salvation, and he cannot save himself; only God, through Christ, can save him. But while the Savior offers salvation, our reception of it depends on our willing it. Cyril sometimes inserts a further term, "faith," "believing"; but he holds that believing depends on ourselves. We choose to believe or not; in Cyril's terminology, "choosing, willing" and "believing" are almost synonymous. Cf. *Procat.* 8; "How are my sins blotted out?" "By willing, by believing"; and in *Procat.* 1 Cyril gives a doctrine of election: "Your sincere intention makes you called." Cf. *Cat.* 1.1-5, where "grace" is neither an abstraction nor a quality, but the concrète gift bestowed in baptism, i.e., the forgiveness of sins and the impartation of the Holy Ghost. Salvation is like a race: in *Procat.* as in *Cat.* 1.5 *fin.*, the candidate is "running for his life" (or his "soul"). As *Cat.* 2.5 *(fin.)* and the very emphatic 7.13 show, Cyril is concerned to assert moral responsibility and earnestness against the teaching of certain Gnostics that men are good or evil, saved or lost, by *nature*. Cf. *Cat.* 17.37 *(init.)* and ch. 5 below. If this was the Jerusalem tradition, one can understand why (cf. Introd. to *Myst.*) Pelagius was in 415 acquitted at a diocesan Council of Jerusalem and a Provincial Council at Lydda. Perhaps it was because he knew of this tradition that Pelagius chose Palestine as the place of his exile. It is not, of course, here suggested that Cyril was a Pelagian.

12 Adopting Touttée's conjecture *parēiei* for *periēiei*.

13 Cf. Matt. 20.30-34.

less grown old still uncomprehending,[14] now said: "As for this man, we do not know where he comes from"[15] (for "he came unto his own, and his own received him not").[16] But the blind men kept on crying out: "Son of David, have mercy on us." Those whose eyes did not serve them to read knew Him whom the students of the Law failed to recognize.

Going up to them, the Savior said: "Do you believe that I can do this for you?" and "What will you have me do for you?"[17] He did not say: "What will you have me say to you?" but "What will you have me do for you?" For He was a doer, a maker—a giver of life, too—not now beginning to do for the first time (for His Father works always, and He works with His Father);[18] He was the maker of the whole world at His Father's command.[19] Alone begotten, without intermediary,[20] of the Alone, He questions the blind men, saying: "What will you have me do for you?" Not that He did not know what they wanted, for it was obvious: but He chose to make His gift depend on their answer, that they might be justified out of their own mouths. The reader of hearts could not be ignorant what they would say; but He waited upon their words; now His question was their cue.

(6) He stood by the cripple, the doctor visiting the sick man, nor is it so strange that He condescended to attend the invalid by the pool, for had He not visited us from Heaven? He asked him: "Wilt thou be healed?" by the question leading him on towards the saving knowledge, raising a question in *his* mind. A gift, truly, of grace! No fee was charged; else the patient would not have had the physician coming to him.[21]

14 Cf. Isa. 46.3 (Sept.). Partly missing in R. Cf. *Cat.* 4.2: "studied [the Scriptures] from childhood to old age and nevertheless had grown old still uncomprehending."
15 John 9.29.
16 John 1.11.
17 Matt. 9.28, another account of the healing of two blind men.
18 Cf. John 5.17.
19 A favourite theme of the *Cat.*, e.g. 11.22, 24.
20 Parallels, not verbally exact, in *Cat.* 7.4 and 11.7.
21 In this paragraph Cyril seems to be alluding to the greater cost of

He said to Him: "Yes, sir;[22] for the long duration of my illness makes me desire health; but, desire it as I may, I have no man. . ." Do not lose heart, my good fellow, because you "have no man"; God you have standing by you, One who is at once man and God under different aspects;[23] for both must be confessed. The confession of the humanity without the confession of the divinity is unavailing, or rather earns a curse. For "cursed is he who puts his trust in man."[24] So with us: if, hoping in Jesus, we hope in the man only, not including the divinity, we inherit the curse. But as it is, we confess both God and man, and both truly: in worshipping Him as God truly begotten of the true Father and as man not merely in appearance, but really and truly born, we receive a real and true salvation.

(7) "Yes, I do want to be healed, but I have no man . . ." Maybe it was because of his dire straits that Jesus came to his rescue. For the generality of the sick had relatives,[25] friends too, and maybe other helpers. But the poor cripple, crushed by a literally universal want, utterly destitute, abandoned, alone, found the Son of God, the Only-begotten, coming to his aid.

"Wilt thou be healed?" "Yes, Lord, but I have no man, when the water is troubled, to put me into the pool." No, but you have the spring itself. "For with thee is the fountain of life,"[26] the fountainhead of all fountains. "He who drinks of this water,[27] out of his belly shall flow rivers,"[28] not of the water that flows downwards but of that water that springs

having a visit from the doctor than of receiving treatment at his dispensary *(iatreion)*. *Archiatros* means both a medical officer for the community and, by metaphorical adaptation, "the Supreme Physician."

22 This is Cyril's importation. In John 5 the cripple nowhere makes an act of faith. Odd.

23 For Cyril's Christology cf. ch. 9 below and *Cat.* 4.9 and 11.20.

24 Jer. 17.5.

25 Adopting Milles's conjecture (Oxford 1703), *oikeious* (B has *oikeias)* instead of R's "houses" *(oikias)*.

26 Ps. 35.10.

27 Cf. John 4.14.

28 John 7.38.

up—for the spring inspired by Jesus' draught, unlike man's puny leap which lands him back on earth again, carries us up to the sky;[29] the water "bubbles up unto life everlasting."[30] Jesus is the wellspring of all blessings.

(8) Why, then, fix your hope on a pool? You have Him who walks upon the waters, who rebukes the winds, who holds sovereign sway over the ocean; who not only Himself walked on the sea as on a firm pavement[31] but vouchsafed the like power to Peter. For when the night was black and the Light, though it was there, was not recognized (for Jesus, walking on the waters, passed unrecognized in face and features; it was the characteristic timbre of His voice that betrayed His presence), they, thinking they were seeing an apparition, were frightened until Jesus said to them, "It is I, do not be afraid."[32] Peter said to Him: "If it be Thou whom I know, or rather whom the Father revealed to me, bid me come to thee over the waters"; and Christ, generously sharing what was His own, said: "Come."

(9) There stood by the waters of the pool the Ruler and Maker of the waters. To Him the cripple said: "I have no man, when the water is troubled, to put me into the pool." The Savior said to him: "Why do you await the troubling of the water when you can be cured with no trouble at all? Why wait for the movement that is seen? More swiftly is the mind's command performed by the word. Only look down into the swirling power of the spring[33] and glimpse there

29 Cf. *Letter to Constantius* 2.
30 John 4.14.
31 In *Cat.* 13.9 Cyril quotes "Thy way is in the sea" (Ps. 77.19).
32 Matt. 14.27.
33 A combination of some of the following ideas: (a) *Cat.* 14.5 *fin.*: "But who is the 'sealed fountain' (Cant. 4.12), the 'well of living water' (Cant. 4.15)? It is the Saviour Himself . . . ." (b) Since to know two of three proportionally related terms is to know the third (2:4 :: 4:?), the image in the pool of "the image of the invisible God" (Col. 1.15) is the clue to the supreme and saving knowledge, that of the Father. (c) As being relatively immaterial, the fleshless reflection of Christ in the pool is more like the Word than is His bodily form. (d) The water welling up from the depths of the spring symbolizes the Son streaming forth from the fountainhead *(pēgē)* of Deity.

God clothed in flesh; consider not the man whom your eyes see, but the invisible God who works through Him whom you see."[34]

"I have no man, when the water is troubled, to put me into the pool." He said to him: "Why set such narrow bounds to hope, intent on some poor water-cure? Arise: He who commands it is the Resurrection."

Everywhere the Savior becomes "all things to all men";[35] to the hungry, bread; to the thirsty, water; to the dead, resurrection; to the sick, a physician; to sinners, redemption.

(10) "Rise, take up thy pallet and walk." But first rise, cast away your sickness; afterwards you can put muscle on faith. Exert your strength first upon the bed that used to carry you; learn to carry away on a wooden stretcher those passions by which you were for so long carried away.[36] He was ordered to carry his wooden litter by that Savior of whom it was said: "The King hath made him a litter of the wood of Lebanon. The pillars thereof he made of silver, the seat of purple, the inside paved with mosaic."[37] The imagery represents the Passion, this imagery reserved in the Song of Songs for sober and chaste bridals.

For you must not, accepting the vulgar, superficial interpretation of the words, suppose that the Canticle is an expression of carnal, sexual love. No; it is the language of bridals with an immortal Lover,[38] bridals pure and chaste. If you do not divine the sense of the Canticle, go to the Book of Proverbs. Make an indirect approach, mounting by

---

34 Cf. the Bethlehem passage in *Cat.* 11.20; also 4.9.

35 Cf. 1 Cor. 9.22. Cf. ch. 1 above and *Cat.* 10.5, though there the list is mostly different.

36 Adopting Touttée's first conjecture, *se bastasanta.*

37 Cant. 3.9, 10.

38 While in classical Greek *nymphikos* means simply "bridal," sometimes in the Fathers it is a mystic word; cf. Greg. Nyss., *Hom. 1 in Cant.* (PG 44.772B) and (?) Basil of Ancyra, *De virg.* 50 (PG 30.768C). Here the word not only does not imply but positively excludes any idea of sex; cf. English "nympholept" and (biological) "nymph." By an extension of this mode of thought Cyril reads the passionate imagery of the Canticle as referring to the Passion of Christ.

degrees to the Canticle. "Wisdom hath built herself a house," it says, as though speaking of a woman, "and hath sent her servants."[39] Elsewhere it says: "Love her, and she will protect thee."[40] This is not the love of woman, but of wisdom, which drives out carnal love. For where wisdom is stored, there carnal love is banished; not passions but wise thoughts house with wisdom. "They are become as stallions frenzied in heat":[41] an urge unworthy of reason. If, then, in the Canticle you hear talk of a bride and a bridegroom, do not read into such language a reference to sexual passion (that would be to fall back to earth),[42] but sublimate the passions by the passionless.

(11) Meditate on the heavenly lessons of the Song, a Song that breathes chastity and tells of the Passion of Christ. In describing the Passion of the Savior, it even names the place: "I am come into my garden,"[43] referring to the Garden of His burial. It mentions the spices too: "I seized aromatic spices in handfuls";[44] for the divine purpose reached its fulfillment. After His resurrection He said: "I have eaten my bread with my honey."[45] For "they gave him honey from the honey-comb."[46] Again, referring to the wine mingled with myrrh, the Canticle says: "I will give thee a cup of spiced wine."[47] Of the perfume poured over His head it says elsewhere: "While the King was at his repose, my spikenard sent forth the odor thereof";[48] for "when he was reclining at table in the house of Simon the leper, a woman came in and broke an alabaster box of ointment of precious spikenard, which

39 Prov. 9.1, 3.
40 Prov. 4.6.
41 Cf. Jer. 5.8.
42 For this expression cf. *Cat.* 11.7 and ch. 7 above.
43 Cf. Cant. 5.1. Following Touttée's suggestion, I have changed this and the next quotation to the first person. Cf. *Cat.* 13.32 *init.;* 14.5 *init.,* 11.
44 Cf. Cant. 5.5?
45 Cant. 5.1 (Sept.).
46 Luke 24.42 (omitted in most modern texts). *Cat.* 14.11 *fin.*
47 Cant. 8.2., *Cat.* 13.32.
48 Cant. 1.11 (12).

she poured over his head."[49] So of the Cross: ". . . a litter of wood"—the wood of the cross which carried Him—"the pillars thereof he made of silver." The commencement of the cross was silver, the betrayal.[50] For as a beautiful chamber is crowned with a golden roof, the whole structure soaring upon pillars, so of both the crucifixion and of the resurrection of Christ the beginning was silver.[51] For if Judas had not betrayed Him, He would not have been crucified. Therefore it was, as symbolizing the beginning of His famous Passion, "the pillars thereof he made of silver."

(12) "The coverings of purple." Therefore they also "clothed Him in purple":[52] in mockery, of course, but fulfilling the prophecy; doing it under inspiration, for He *was* a King. However much they did it in a spirit of derision, still they did it; His royal dignity was emblematically heralded. So, likewise, though it was with thorns they crowned him, it was still a crown. And it was soldiers who crowned Him; kings are proclaimed by soldiers.[53] "The covering of purple, the inside paved with mosaic":[54] the devout children of the Church know Lithostrotos or "Gabbatha" in Pilate's palace.

(13) But this is a digression; when on the subject of the pallet, I was led on to speak of the litter in the Canticle.

He said, therefore, to him: "Rise, take up thy pallet and walk." The disease was long-standing, the remedy swift. The paralysis had lasted for years; the strengthening of the sinews was instantaneous. For the creator of the sinews, He who provided a variety of remedies for the blind, He who gave that incongruous salve by anointing with clay (for a plaster of clay, applied to sound eyes, deprives them of sight, but

49 Mark 14.3.
50 Cf. *Cat.* 13.9-10.
51 Apparently the glorification (Cross and Resurrection) of Jesus is symbolized by the golden canopy over the daïs or by the golden roof of the throne room. Cf. *Cat.* 13.6, 22, where the Passion is a coronation.
52 Mk. 15.17.
53 Close parallels in *Cat.* 13.17.
54 Cant. 3.10 (Sept. *lithostrōtos*).

Jesus by means of clay bestowed sight upon the blind). . . His power reached others by yet other means.[55]

Where He simply said: "Rise, take up thy pallet and walk," what astonishment, do you think, seized the beholders! Yet, marvellous as the sight was, it was the faithlessness of the onlookers that was really strange. A years-old disease is healed, but an obstinate incredulity was not healed. Instead the Jews' malady persisted; they did not want a cure.

(14) If they were right to be amazed by the incident, they should have gone on to adore the healer of bodies and souls. But they murmured; for they were the children of murmurers, of those who twisted good into evil, calling bitter sweet and sweet bitter. It was quite in accordance with the divine "economy"[56] that Jesus worked on the sabbath, performing deeds transcending the sabbath, that the deed might convince. It was because an assertion can be met by a counter-assertion, while there is no answer to the deed,[57] that He used to heal on the sabbath; the lesson is, instead of relying on arguments, which only provoke counterarguments, to let deeds convince the onlookers.

(15) They said to him: "It is the Sabbath; it is not lawful for thee to take up thy pallet." The Lawgiver was present, and another says: "It is not lawful for thee"? "Appoint, O Lord, a lawgiver over them":[58] it was spoken of the Savior. The man who had just been cured both in soul and body immediately retorts with a wise word from Wisdom.[59] Unable to give a legal answer, he makes a brief one: "You all know," he says, "my long-standing sickness and the long years I was

55 The text and construction are hereabouts a little uncertain.

56 "Economy": a technical word: the divine plan or strategy; cf. John 5.17. Probably Cyril is playing on the word. Instead of empty talk, Jesus acts; and His action is economical, since He heals by the one word "Arise." Similarly in ch. 15 Cyril praises the paralytic's economy of words. Or else translate: "It was quite deliberately that. . . ."

57 In *Cat.* 13.8 arguments are met by counterarguments, while the fulfillment of prophecy convinces.

58 Ps. 9.21 (Sept.).

59 The invalid's spiritual cure implies enlightenment and the gift of wisdom.

bedridden, my destitution in my distress. Not one of you ever took pity on me, taking me and putting me first into the pool that I might be cured. Yet, when then you showed no pity, how have you now assumed the office of lawgivers, saying: 'You're not allowed to take up your pallet'? My answer, then, in a nutshell is this: 'I did it at the command of Him who cured me.' However little account you make of me, yet the deed should impress you. He applied no salve; He employed none of the expedients or remedies known to medicine. He spoke a word, and the work followed; He commanded, and I executed His command. I am only obeying the command of Him who by his command healed me. For if He who commanded had been powerless by His command to cure me, I should not be obliged to obey His commands. But now that His word of command has caused a palpable and inveterate illness to disappear, I have every right to listen to Him to whom my disease listened and, listening, was ended. He who made me well, he it was who said to me: 'Take up your bed.' "

(16) The *miraculé* did not know the identity of his healer. We have here a striking instance of our Savior's shunning of vaingloriousness. For after working the cure He turned aside to avoid receiving recognition for the cure. We do just the opposite. If we are fortunate enough to have a vision in a dream or to succor someone by the imposition of hands or to drive out a devil by invoking the Lord,[60] so far are we from hiding our little triumph that, even unprompted, we boast about it. Jesus gives us an object lesson in not talking about oneself. After the cure He immediately turned aside to avoid recognition.[61] He comes and goes as the occasion calls. When it was proper to prevent the acclaim of the achievement, He withdraws; only when the crowds had gone did He re-

60 For these charismata characteristic of the early Church, cf. *Cat.* 1.5; 5.9, 11; 17.37.

61 Cf. John 5.13.

appear to add spiritual to physical healing,[62] saying: "Behold, you are well: sin no more."[63]

(17) He is a versatile doctor, sometimes healing the soul first, and then the body, sometimes following the reverse order. "Leave your sinful ways, lest something worse befall you," He says, through one teaching many. For the warning is addressed not alone to the man in the Gospel, but to all of us. For if ever we find ourselves afflicted by sickness, grief or trouble, let no one lay it to God's charge: "for God cannot be tempted by evil, and himself tempts no man."[64] Each of us is scourged, "fast bound with the ropes of his own sins."[65]

"Sin no more, lest something worse befall you." Listen to the saying, Everyman. Let him who before was a fornicator slough off his lust; let him who before was avaricious become generous in almsgiving; let the thief pay heed: "Sin no more." Great is God's forbearance, lavish His grace. But let not His exceeding patience breed contempt. Do not make God's long-suffering a pretext for continuing in sin. Take the cure for your carnal passions, so that you too can say, in the words of the lesson so appropriately read: "For what time we were in the flesh, the sinful passions, which were aroused by the law, were at work in our members."[66] If the Apostle says, "What time we were in the flesh," he was not speaking of our mortal envelope of flesh but of the deeds of the flesh. He was himself, indeed, still clad in the flesh when he said,

62 Cf. *epagagēi* in *Cat.* 10.13. In 10.13 the paralytic's soul is cured first. As evidence against identity of authorship this is counterbalanced by the common interest in the question of the order of healing in *Cat.* 10.13 and chs. 16-17 of the present sermon. In *Cat.* 10.13 Cyril, perhaps using a classified collection of miracle stories, may have been misled by the order of events in the cure of the different paralytic in Mark 2.2-12, where the soul is cured first. Moreover there is quite a strong case, from text and context, for translating here: "to let the man know that his soul had been cured along with his body"; the cripple's soul has already been cured in ch. 15 *(init.)*.

63 John 5.14.

64 James 1.13.

65 Cf. Prov. 5.22.

66 Rom. 7.5.

"What time we were in the flesh." It is in the sense in which, when the deluge was preparing, God said: "My spirit shall not remain in these men, because they are flesh"[67] (the spirit being perverted to fleshly appetite), that the Apostle says: "When we were in the flesh."

(18) Let no one, then, be "in the flesh"; but, being in the flesh, let him not walk according to the flesh. The Apostle does not mean that, to avoid sin, we should withdraw altogether from the world, but that, being in the flesh, we should make the flesh our servant and not be ruled by it. Let us not be slaves, but masters, in our own house. Let us be moderate in our eating, not allowing ourselves to be carried away by gluttony. So, bridling our appetite, we shall govern also its henchman, lust. Let the soul rule the body and not be at the beck and call of animal instinct.

"Sin no more, lest something worse befall you." It is a warning to all; God grant that all ears may hear it. For it is not always that the fleshly ear, when it receives a message, transmits it to the mind. That is why the Savior, when addressing those who had "ears of flesh," said, "If you have ears that can hear, then hear."[68]

(19) Let everyone, then, give ear to Jesus and "sin no more." Let us, rather, hasten to the great Pardoner. Are we ill? Let us have recourse to Him. Is it a sickness of the soul that ails us? Let us become disciples of the physician of knowledge. Are we hungry? Let Him give us bread. Are we dead? Let Him raise us to life. Have we grown old in ignorance? Let us beg wisdom of Wisdom.

Version (a)[69]	*Version (b)*[69]
(20) But our argument has led us to protract our dis-	(20) But my sermon has betrayed me into wordiness,

67 Gen. 6.3.

68 Matt. 11.15.

69 After the first sentence the two MSS differ markedly. Version (a) following the *textus receptus,* that of Touttée and Reischl-Rupp, which follows B with Touttée's emendation of *lalei* to *kalei* ("summons").

course, and maybe we are standing in the way of our Father's teaching. The hour summons us to attend to mightier words than mine that, aided by mightier works, we may by those works send up our praise to God, to whom be the glory now and forever, through all eternity. Amen.

and I am, maybe, standing in the way of its practical lesson. God grant that all of us may heed the Savior's words, that, aided by mightier works, we may send up, *etc.*

The "father" is then presumed to be the bishop, due to preach last. But "mightier words" then seems fulsome and after the mounting emphasis, since ch. 14, on the contrast between words and deeds the announcement that the sequel is to be yet another sermon seems an anticlimax, all the more odd when the words/deeds contrast is continued in ch. 20 itself. One would expect the "mightier words" to be some quoted words of the Savior, as in fact R represents them: presumably the words "Sin no more," i.e., the practical lesson of the Sermon. So version (b) follows R but emends *patrikēs didaskalias* ("Father's teaching") to *praktikēs didaskalias,* "practical lesson, "moral." In the Origenist tradition the comparative importance of *theōria* and *praxis,* contemplation or study and action or conduct, was a regular question. The (b) version is compatible with a number of possibilities, single or combined: some form of confession of sins, the Eucharist, Christian living in the world.

If *patrikēs* is wrong, the Sermon could have been preached by Cyril any time up to 386.

LETTER TO CONSTANTIUS

(Epistolē pros Kōnstantion)

Translated by

ANTHONY A. STEPHENSON

University of Exeter

England

INTRODUCTION

IN THIS LETTER to the Emperor Constantius II,[1] written shortly after his accession to the see of Jerusalem,[2] St. Cyril announces the appearance of a luminous cross (perhaps actually a parhelion) in the sky over Jerusalem. The genuineness of the letter, although not entirely unchallenged, is incontestable, apart from the concluding sentences, which, with their *homoousion* ("consubstantial") and repetitiousness, are obviously spurious.[3]

Cyril is known as the author of such a letter by Sozomen, Theophanes and the Armenian tradition. Moreover, the event which occasioned the letter unquestionably occurred, being attested by Sozomen[4] and Philostorgius.[5] The rococo style is certainly rather different from Cyril's ordinary manner, but Cyril could be ornate, and it is easy to imagine him producing this effusion after an evening browsing over the imperial correspondence in the Jerusalem chancery, to which he had just gained access. In those archives he would no doubt have found the original of Constantine's elaborate letter to Macarius.[6] If Cyril took that letter as supplying the model for his own *stylus curiae,* it would explain why, amid the high-flown phraseology and elusive, breathless syntax of his

1 See Telfer's valuable notes.
2 "Epistolary firstfruits," chs. 1 and 7.
3 As J. Quasten, *Patrology* III (Utrecht etc. 1960) 368, and others have pointed out, the Nicene doxology was presumably added by a scribe bent on edification: an unnecessary attempt to vindicate Cyril's orthodoxy.
4 H.E. 4.5.
5 Philostorgius (H.E. 3.26), while aware that the apparition occurred at Jerusalem, unaccountably speaks of it as being seen in the field of battle at Mursa.
6 Reproduced by Eusebius, *Vita Constantini* 2.29-31.

own epistle, it is sometimes so difficult to discover what is actually being said. If the letter were not genuine, it must be either a forgery or a medieval rhetorical exercise, but it would defy the highest skill of forger or student to catch so well the distinctive Cyrilline theological interests, the historical moment and the *exalté* style so natural to the occasion. In spite of one or two puzzles, therefore, the authenticity of the letter must be accepted. It is at first sight surprising that the apparition of the Cross at Jerusalem does not lead Cyril to mention the comparable vision of the Cross by Constantine in 312. But to have done so would have been tactless, as Constantius had not himself been privileged to see the Jerusalem apparition; nor do the Lenten Lectures mention Constantine's vision; a forger would probably have mentioned it. Cyril shows himself the more accomplished courtier by comparing (ch. 3) the discovery of the Jerusalem holy places on *earth* during Constantine's reign with the recent apparition of the holy Cross in the heavens.

Cyril's letter, written in 350 or 351, perhaps on May 7, is closely related to the political situation and the greatest military crisis of Constantius' life. From 18 January 350, when the usurper Magnentius was proclaimed emperor at Autun, until his decisive defeat at Mursa (Essek) 28 September 351, Constantius was faced with a very dangerous situation. The revolt was swiftly followed by the murder of the Western Emperor, Constantius' brother Constans, and the West immediately aligned itself solidly behind Magnentius. Italy and Africa soon rallied to the usurper, and Vetranio, proclaimed Illyrian Emperor 1 March 350, though at first pledging loyalty to Constantius, was by May feigning (probably) alliance with Magnentius. About June an embassy from Magnentius and Vetranio proposed to Constantius, now freed from the war on the Persian frontier, that he recognize Magnentius as co-Augustus in the West, at the same time giving his sister Constantia in marriage to Magnentius and himself wedding Magnentius's daughter. Though anxious to avoid the fearful bloodshed of a civil war, Constantius did not feel free to raise his brother's murderer to his throne. He rejected the proposals. In December 350 Constantius and Vetranio met in the presence of their armies. When the latter's troops declared for Constantius, Vetranio surrendered his diadem to him. It is perhaps to this that Cyril alludes in chapter 2, though various cities also seem to have offered Constantius crowns, as a pledge of their loyalty, in the course of his progress westward to confront Magnentius.

After the murder of Constans, Constantius proclaimed himself sole Emperor; and, concerned for the dynastic succession, in March 351 he elevated his nephew Gallus to the rank of Caesar, changed his name to Flavius Claudius Constantius, and married him to his sister Constantia, thus making him *frater Augusti*.[7]

Magnentius was a barbarian and a pagan but, as soon as he appreciated the numerical strength and commitment of pro-Nicene Christianity in the West, he proclaimed himself a champion of Nicene Christianity. Hoping to win Egypt, he made overtures to St. Athanasius, who received his ambassadors and was almost certainly in sympathy, and perhaps in secret correspondence, with him. It is all the more interesting, therefore, to see St. Cyril addressing Constantius in terms of cordial, even flattering, respect and hinting (chs. 2 and 3) that he surpasses the great Constantine in *eusebeia* (piety, orthodoxy). For Constantius has been commonly described by ancient and modern Church historians as "arianizing," though Sozomen was probably right in classing him as a homoeousian.[8] If so, his views on the Trinity were much the same as Cyril's own—and equally far from Arianism. Cyril may even have been right (he was well placed to know) in implying (ch. 2) that the Emperor was something of a

7 N. H. Baynes, in *Cambridge Medieval History* 1 (New York 1911) 60.
8 Sozomen, 3.18.103. See Vol. 1, p. 52.

theologian; briefed by his theological *periti* (it was only from late 351 to 360 that Valens and Ursacius monopolized this role), he may have understood the *Problematik* of the Trinitarian question better than some later theologians. Socrates is probably antedating events by a year or two when he says (cf. H.E. 2.26, 27) that it was at this time that Constantius "in an ungovernable fury commanded [Athanasius] to be put to death wherever he might be found" and that the war between Constantius and Magnentius was paralleled by the ferocity of the war between the pro-Nicene and anti-Nicene Christians. But it is certain that from about the summer of 350 Constantius suspected Athanasius of conspiring with Magnentius against him, and the Eastern bishops were meditating the overthrow of Athanasius, who had only owed his restoration to the influence of Constans. The letter is, therefore, an important source for the biography of Cyril. It must, however, be remembered that by 355 Cyril was at loggerheads (but over what—theology or cathedral rivalries?) with Acacius, who had Constantius confirm his deposition in January 360.

Why did Cyril assume that the apparition of the shining Cross was an omen of victory for Constantius? Because it appeared during Constantius' reign? Because it appeared in the East? Because Magnentius was a pagan? Even this last consideration, however, is too general to be altogether satisfactory. It would make much better sense—it would be more specific and pointed in view of the heavily underlined and repeated insistence (ch. 4) that the brilliance of the Cross outshone and "conquered" the *sun*—if, while the troops of Constantius marched under Constantine's Christian standard, the Chi-rho or labarum, Magnentius had at some period adopted some emblem of paganism, now synthetically represented by the Sun-God, *Sol Invictus*. But the epigraphic and numismatic evidence so far available is against this. While some of the titles of Magnentius found in inscriptions might be construed as an appeal to antique, pre-Christian *Romanità,* it is certain that he issued some coins with a Christian, anti-Arian symbol. By no means all, however, of the relevant numismatic evidence has as yet been published; when the long-awaited eighth volume of *Roman Imperial Coinage* appears, it may throw some further light on this question and at the same time establish the date of Cyril's letter. The present state of the evidence points, on the whole, to 351, although Cyril's description of his letter as his "epistolary firstfruits" favours 350.

Probably the letter also contains an urgent, though diplomatically veiled, invitation to Constantius to receive Baptism, preferably (ch. 7) at Jerusalem, to avoid the risk of dying unbaptized either in battle or on the Last Day. For Cyril relates the heavenly apparition to the sign of the Son of Man in the eschatological discourse in Matt. 24, where it presages the coming of Antichrist and the End (Matt. 24.30). How else explain the passage[9] where Cyril implores the Emperor to read and re-read, for his soul's good, the whole context, and especially the sequel, of Matt. 24.30? Almost half of the letter is meaningful only within Cyril's view of baptismal illumination as converting *pistis* (faith) into *gnōsis* through the demonstration of the Christian verities by miracle and, especially, the fulfillment of prophecy. Cyril tells the Emperor, already quite an adept owing to his private studies (ch. 2), that for him the shining Cross, both as miracle and fulfillment of prophecy, supplies the demonstration which ordinary catechumens received in the Lenten Lectures.[10] The Emperor is qualified to receive baptism. Within this pattern the exhortation (ch. 5) to "build knowledge upon faith" hints that the sacramental counterpart of the "gnosis" supplied by the demonstration is baptism, while the "salvation wrought in Jerusalem" (ch. 7) was, in Cyril's view, mediated by baptism,

---

9 Ch. 6.

10 *Letter,* chs. 1, 2, 4 (end), 6. See Vol. 1, Introd., pp. 6-9.

which he held[11] to be an indispensable means of salvation. Nor does this theme in the letter contradict Cyril's statement that in the portent in the skies Heaven had manifested its favour towards Constantius. For there was no law about the time for baptism; only the danger of death in which Constantius now stood and the imminence of the End introduced a new element into the situation. In the event Constantius did not take Cyril's advice; he was, like his father, baptized on his deathbed by an Arian. But he took no risks either. At Mursa, instead of plunging at the head of his knights into the thickest of the fray he stayed in the town, awaiting news of the outcome, attended by Valens, the local ordinary, no doubt with a pitcher of water handy.[12]

11 *Cat.* 3.4, 10.

12 Theodoret (H. E. 3.1) relates that on the eve of one of the battles in the war against Magnentius, Constantius mustered his troops and urged them to be baptized before the battle.

THE LETTER TO CONSTANTIUS

Letter of the Blessed Cyril, Archbishop of Jerusalem, to the most godly Emperor Constantius, the seventh of May, concerning the sign of the luminous Cross which appeared in the heavens and was seen at Jerusalem.[1]

(1) From Cyril, Bishop of Jerusalem, to the most Sacred and Godly Emperor Constantius Augustus—Greetings in the Lord.

This, my first letter from Jerusalem, I send as firstfruits to your Sacred Majesty, a tribute which it befits you to receive and me to offer. Herein your Majesty will find no effusive compliments, no appeals to credulity tricked out in rhetoric's finery, but the straightforward report of a supernatural, heavenly vision, a vision which guarantees to your Majesty the truth of the predictions contained in the Holy Gospels[2] and now fulfilled by the event.

(2) Let those who have the means crown your Majesty's precious head, bringing many a golden diadem studded with gleaming jewels; we offer you no earthly crown (nay, to the earth earth's gifts return), but hasten to bring your Reverence knowledge of the marvels which, in your sacred reign, God has wrought in the heavens. If I speak of "knowledge," it is no first introduction to divinity I mean (rather is your piety[3] a lesson to others) but only the certification of what you have this long time known. So may you, who already

1 The title is from the manuscripts, but is not part of Cyril's text.
2 Matt. 24.30; cf. ch. 6 below.
3 Or "orthodoxy" *(eusebeia)*.

sit upon the throne of your great father, both face the foe with livelier confidence when apprised of the more dazzling diadems with which Heaven has adorned you and, as befits the hour, now more than ever give thanks and praise to the King of Kings, who, by showing forth these marvels in your reign, has given concrete proof of his benevolence towards your Majesty.

(3) For if in the days of your Imperial Father, Constantine of blessed memory, the saving wood of the Cross was found in Jerusalem (divine grace granting the finding of the long hidden holy places to one who nobly aspired to sanctity), now, Sire, in the reign of your most godly Majesty, as if to mark how far your zeal excels your forebear's piety, not from the earth but from the skies marvels appear: the trophy of the victory over death of our Lord Jesus Christ, the Only-begotten Son of God, even the holy Cross, flashing and sparkling with brilliant light, has been seen at Jerusalem.

(4) During these holy days of the holy Paschal season, [on the Nones of May][4] at about nine in the morning, a gigantic luminous cross was seen in the sky above holy Golgotha, extending as far as the holy Mount of Olives; not seen by one or two only, but clearly visible to the whole population of the city; nor, as might be expected, quickly vanishing like an optical illusion, but suspended for several hours above the earth before the general gaze and by its dazzling splendor conquering[5] the sun's rays; for clearly, conquered[5] by them, it would have been obscured—had not its own more powerful blaze eclipsed the sun. Immediately the whole population, overcome with joy mingled with fear of the heavenly vision, hastened to the Holy Church: young and old, people of both sexes and every age, even to the maidens closeted in their

4 Missing from about half the manuscripts.

5 *Nikēsas, nikōmenos:* the cross seen by Constantine in the skies carried the inscription "By this, conquer." Did Magnentius at some period adopt the symbol of the Sun God on arms, standards, or coins? See Introduction.

homes, local and foreign Christians, as well as visiting pagans —all with one accord, and as with a single voice, extolling Christ Jesus our Lord, the Only-begotten Son of God, the worker of wonders. For were they not the sensible recipients of an object lesson that the holy doctrine of the Christians "is not in the persuasive words of wisdom, but in the demonstration of the Spirit and of power,"[6] a doctrine not announced only by men, but now attested by God from Heaven?

(5) We citizens of Jerusalem, therefore, eyewitnesses of this astonishing miracle, have paid, and shall further pay to God, the Universal King, and to the Only-begotten Son of God, fitting adoration joined to thanksgiving. We have offered, and will continue to offer, fervent prayers in the holy places on behalf of your Sacred Majesty. Since, rather than bury in silence this heavenly vision, it is our duty to announce the good news to your godly Majesty, we have immediately made haste to do so in this letter, to the end that, rearing upon the sound foundation of your previous faith the knowledge afforded by this fresh demonstration[7] from on high, with unshakable confidence in our Lord Jesus Christ and filled with all your customary courage as one who has God himself for an ally, you may boldly advance the standard of the Cross, riding with the very banner that streamed in the skies, glory's own device, the badge which redoubled Heaven's exultation upon the manifestation of even its semblance to mankind.

(6) In this miracle, your most Sacred Majesty, testimonies of the Prophets and the holy words of Christ contained in the Gospels find their fulfillment—though they will be more amply fulfilled hereafter.[8] For in the Gospel according to

6 1 Cor. 2.4.

7 *Pistis, gnōsis, epideichthentōn*/.; cf. *apodeixis* ("demonstration") above, ch. 4.

8 Does this mean that the present vision is only a preliminary rehearsal of what will in the future be enacted on a grander scale (the eschatological sign itself) or that the appearance of the Cross is

Matthew, the Savior, imparting the knowledge of future events to his blessed Apostles, and through them to later generations of Christians, declared plainly beforehand: "And then will appear the sign of the Son of Man in heaven."[9] When you take in your hands, according to your wont, the sacred book of the Gospels, you will find written there the predictions of this prodigy. I urge you above all men, Sire, to peruse this prophecy with the more anxious attention on account of the whole context of the passage; for the predictions of our Savior demand the most reverent study if we are to escape injury at the hands of the opposing Power.

(7) These epistolary firstfruits I offer to your most Sacred Majesty. This, my first utterance from Jerusalem, I address to you, my true and devout fellow worshipper of Christ, the Only-begotten Son of God, our Savior—of Him who, in accordance with the divine Scriptures, wrought the salvation of the world in Jerusalem, here trampling upon death, by His own precious blood blotting out the sins of men and making available life, immortality and the spiritual, heavenly grace to all who believe.[10] May His power and His grace gladden and preserve you, distinguished by ever greater and more brilliant advances in holiness and proudly rejoicing in noble scions[11] of your royal line. May God Himself, the King of

---

the first scene in the eschatological drama, the remainder of which is now due to unfold? See Matt. 24.15-51.

9 Matt. 24.30.

10 Note the baptismal phraseology.

11 In the summer of 350 the usurper Magnentius offered peace to Constantius on condition that the Emperor recognize him as co-Augustus in the West, at the same time giving his sister Constantia in marriage to Magnentius and himself wedding Magnentius' daughter. Constantius rejected these terms. Telfer (p. 198) has pointed out that Magnentius' proposals imply that Constantius' first wife was dead by summer 350, when Constantius would consequently have been a childless widower. Some years later Constantius married Aurelia Eusebia, and Telfer suggests that at the time of Cyril's letter the Emperor had already announced his intention to marry again, and that this explains Cyril's reference to "royal scions." This ingenious suggestion is the likeliest explanation. Yet if (as Telfer seems to allow) the Emperor was probably not yet betrothed to Eusebia, Cyril would hardly have wished children upon him. Two alternative possibilities

Kings, the bestower of all goodness, guard and keep you, with all your House, for many a long peaceful year to be the glory of Christians and the world.

(8) May the God of all vouchsafe to us your most Sacred and August Majesty in good health, together with all your House, for many a long and peaceful year, adorned with every virtue, displaying your customary solicitude for the holy churches and for the Roman Empire, illustrious for ever more brilliant feats of godliness, ever glorifying the Holy [and Consubstantial] Trinity,[12] our true God, to whom is due all glory forever and ever. Amen.

suggest themselves. Perhaps—an hypothesis concerning which there is no evidence either way—Constantius's first wife in May 350 was expecting a child but died soon afterwards in childbirth. Alternatively, when (March 351)), marrying his nephew Gallus to his sister and bestowing upon him the imperial rank and name, Constantius may have announced that he would regard any children of the union as his own. *Enabrynomenon* ('proudly delighting'), however, and the fact that in 351 the Emperor was only thirty-nine tell against this hypothesis.

12 'Consubstantial' is certainly an interpolation. Probably most or all of this last chapter is spurious. Several of its phrases are repeated from ch. 7, the doxology seems inappropriate in a letter of this sort, and ch. 7 would provide a good conclusion. The repetitions are odd; conceivably ch. 8 is, apart from the "consubstantial," an alternative draft of his conclusion by Cyril himself.

THE FRAGMENTS

Translated by

ANTHONY A. STEPHENSON

University of Exeter

England

THE FRAGMENTS

Four fragments that have been attributed to Cyril come purportedly from his sermons or homilies, of which the only complete and genuine example is the *Sermon on the Paralytic.* (The sermon on the feast of the Purification [Hypapante] is complete but spurious.)[1] Even the three sermon-fragments printed below appear to be spurious;[2] and a fourth fragment, which is generally rejected, has been omitted.[3]

Fragment 1

[St. Cyril of Jerusalem: from a sermon on that passage in the Gospel where the Lord changed the water into wine.]

He was desirous neither wholly to manifest His divinity nor altogether to conceal it (not to manifest it, on account of His contemporaries, not to conceal it, on account of those who would come after), but to underline the operations of both His divinity and His humanity, lest either the divine power be obscured or the human nature be disbelieved. For since that heresy would emerge which says that the body was a phantom come down from heaven (since the incorruptible nature would not have taken the mortal body's flesh or have admitted uncleanness, stain or spot), God, in order to convince the human race that He had truly become what

1 On this and other spuria, see the bibliography in Quasten, *Patrology* III 369, and PG 33.1183-1210.

2 Everything in these fragments points to a later time, that of St. Cyril of Alexandria and the Two Natures controversy: the subject matter, the dense, schematic, paragraphed argument, and the technical terminology. But cf. Quasten, *loc. cit.*

3 Published by F. Diekamp, *Analecta patristica* (Orientalia christiana analecta 117; Rome 1938) 10-12; cf. Quasten, *loc. cit.*

we are while remaining what He was, allowed His flesh to suffer what belongs to the flesh.

Fragment 2

[The Same: from the same discourse.]

He worked miracles, He displayed His double operation, the same Christ suffering as man and acting as God—not different subjects, though diverse modes of operation.

Fragment 3

[Cyril of Jerusalem: on the text: "I go to My Father."[1]]

That the distinction of natures appears from the difference of the things said of Him.

1 Cf. John 14.13, 28.

INDICES

GENERAL INDEX FOR

LENTEN LECTURES 13–18

GENERAL INDEX FOR THE MYSTAGOGICAL LECTURES, SERMON ON THE PARALYTIC, AND LETTER TO CONSTANTIUS

INDEX OF HOLY SCRIPTURE

(Books of the Old Testament)

(BOOKS OF THE NEW TESTAMENT)

THE FATHERS OF THE CHURCH SERIES

(A series of approximately 100 volumes when completed)

VOL. 1: THE APOSTOLIC FATHERS (1947)
- LETTER OF ST. CLEMENT OF ROME TO THE CORINTHIANS (trans. by Glimm)
- THE SO-CALLED SECOND LETTER (trans. by Glimm)
- LETTERS OF ST. IGNATIUS OF ANTIOCH (trans. by Walsh)
- LETTER OF ST. POLYCARP TO THE PHILIPPIANS (trans. by Glimm)
- MARTYRDOM OF ST. POLYCARP (trans. by Glimm)
- DIDACHE (trans. by Glimm)
- LETTER OF BARNABAS (trans. by Glimm)
- SHEPHERD OF HERMAS (1st printing only; trans. by Marique)
- LETTER TO DIOGNETUS (trans. by Walsh)
- FRAGMENTS OF PAPIAS (1st printing only; trans. by Marique)

VOL. 2: ST. AUGUSTINE (1947)
- CHRISTIAN INSTRUCTION (trans. by Gavigan)
- ADMONITION AND GRACE (trans. by Murray)
- THE CHRISTIAN COMBAT (trans. by Russell)
- FAITH, HOPE, AND CHARITY (trans. by Peebles)

VOL. 3: SALVIAN, THE PRESBYTER (1947)
- GOVERNANCE OF GOD (trans. by O'Sullivan)
- LETTERS (trans. by O'Sullivan)
- FOUR BOOKS OF TIMOTHY TO THE CHURCH (trans. by O'Sullivan)

VOL. 4: ST. AUGUSTINE (1947)
- IMMORTALITY OF THE SOUL (trans. by Schopp)
- MAGNITUDE OF THE SOUL (trans. by McMahon)
- ON MUSIC (trans. by Taliaferro)

ADVANTAGE OF BELIEVING (trans. by Sr. Luanne Meagher)

ON FAITH IN THINGS UNSEEN (trans. by Deferrari and Sr. Mary Francis McDonald)

VOL. 5: ST. AUGUSTINE (1948)

THE HAPPY LIFE (trans. by Schopp)

ANSWER TO SKEPTICS (trans. by Kavanagh)

DIVINE PROVIDENCE AND THE PROBLEM OF EVIL (trans. by Russell)

SOLILOQUIES (trans. by Gilligan)

VOL. 6: ST. JUSTIN MARTYR (1948)

FIRST AND SECOND APOLOGY (trans. by Falls)

DIALOGUE WITH TRYPHO (trans. by Falls)

EXHORTATION AND DISCOURSE TO THE GREEKS (trans. by Falls)

THE MONARCHY (trans. by Falls)

VOL. 7: NICETA OF REMESIANA (1949)

WRITINGS (trans. by Walsh and Monohan)

SULPICIUS SEVERUS

WRITINGS (trans. by Peebles)

VINCENT OF LERINS

COMMONITORIES (trans. by Morris)

PROSPER OF AQUITANE

GRACE AND FREE WILL (trans. by O'Donnell)

VOL. 8: ST. AUGUSTINE (1950)

CITY OF GOD, Bks. I-VII (trans. by Walsh, Zema; introduction by Gilson)

VOL. 9: ST. BASIL (1950)

ASCETICAL WORKS (trans. by Sr. M. Monica Wagner)

VOL. 10: TERTULLIAN (1950)

APOLOGETICAL WORKS (vol. 1), (trans. by Arbesmann, Sr. Emily Joseph Daly, Quain)

MINUCIUS FELIX

OCTAVIUS (trans. by Arbesmann)

VOL. 11: ST. AUGUSTINE (1951)

COMMENTARY ON THE LORD'S SERMON ON THE MOUNT WITH SEVENTEEN RELATED SERMONS (trans. by Kavanagh)

VOL. 12: ST. AUGUSTINE (1951)
LETTERS 1-82 (vol. 1), (trans. by Sr. Wilfrid Parsons)

VOL. 13: ST. BASIL (1951)
LETTERS 1-185 (vol. 1), (trans. by Deferrari and Sr. Agnes Clare Way)

VOL. 14: ST. AUGUSTINE (1952)
CITY OF GOD, Bks. VIII-XVI (trans. by Walsh and Mother Grace Monahan)

VOL. 15: EARLY CHRISTIAN BIOGRAPHIES (1952)
LIFE OF ST. CYPRIAN BY PONTIUS (trans. by Deferrari and Sr. Mary Magdeleine Mueller)
LIFE OF ST. AMBROSE, BISHOP OF MILAN, BY PAULINUS (trans. by Lacy)
LIFE OF ST. AUGUSTINE BY POSSIDIUS (trans. by Deferrari and Sr. Mary Magdeleine Mueller)
LIFE OF ST. ANTHONY BY ST. ATHANASIUS (trans. by Sr. Mary Emily Keenan)
LIFE OF ST. PAUL, THE FIRST HERMIT; LIFE OF ST. HILARION; LIFE OF MALCHUS, THE CAPTIVE MONK (trans. by Sr. Marie Liguori Ewald)
LIFE OF EPIPHANIUS BY ENNODIUS (trans. by Sr. Genevieve Marie Cook)
A SERMON ON THE LIFE OF ST. HONORATUS BY ST. HILARY (trans. by Deferrari)

VOL. 16: ST. AUGUSTINE (1952)—Treatises on Various Subjects:
THE CHRISTIAN LIFE, LYING, THE WORK OF MONKS, THE USEFULNESS OF FASTING (trans. by Sr. M. Sarah Muldowney)
AGAINST LYING (trans. by Jaffee)
CONTINENCE (trans. by Sr. Mary Francis McDonald)
PATIENCE (trans. by Sr. Luanne Meagher)
THE EXCELLENCE OF WIDOWHOOD (trans. by Sr. M. Clement Eagan)
THE EIGHT QUESTIONS OF DULCITIUS (trans. by Mary DeFerrari)

VOL. 17: ST. PETER CHRYSOLOGUS (1953)
SELECTED SERMONS (trans. by Ganss)
ST. VALERIAN
HOMILIES (trans. by Ganss)

VOL. 18: ST. AUGUSTINE (1953)
LETTERS 83-130 (vol. 2), (trans. by Sr. Wilfrid Parsons)

VOL. 19: EUSEBIUS PAMPHILI (1953)
ECCLESIASTICAL HISTORY, Bks. 1-5 (trans. by Deferrari)

VOL. 20: ST. AUGUSTINE (1953)
LETTERS 131-164 (vol. 3), (trans. by Sr. Wilfrid Parsons)

VOL. 21: ST. AUGUSTINE (1953)
CONFESSIONS (trans. by Bourke)

VOL. 22: ST. GREGORY OF NAZIANZEN and ST. AMBROSE (1953)
FUNERAL ORATIONS (trans. by McCauley, Sullivan, McGuire, Deferrari)

VOL. 23: CLEMENT OF ALEXANDRIA (1954)
CHRIST, THE EDUCATOR (trans. by Wood)

VOL. 24: ST. AUGUSTINE (1954)
CITY OF GOD, Bks. XVII-XXII (trans. by Walsh and Honan)

VOL. 25: ST. HILARY OF POITIERS (1954)
THE TRINITY (trans. by McKenna)

VOL. 26: ST. AMBROSE (1954)
LETTERS 1-91 (trans. by Sr. M. Melchior Beyenka)

VOL. 27: ST. AUGUSTINE (1955)—Treatises on Marriage and Other Subjects:
THE GOOD OF MARRIAGE (trans. by Wilcox)
ADULTEROUS MARRIAGES (trans. by Huegelmeyer)
HOLY VIRGINITY (trans. by McQuade)
FAITH AND WORKS, THE CREED, IN ANSWER TO THE JEWS (trans. by Sr. Marie Liguori Ewald)
FAITH AND THE CREED (trans. by Russell)
THE CARE TO BE TAKEN FOR THE DEAD (trans. by Lacy)
THE DIVINATION OF DEMONS (trans. by Brown)

VOL. 28: ST. BASIL (1955)
LETTERS 186-368 (vol. 2), (trans. by Sr. Agnes Clare Way)

VOL. 29: EUSEBIUS PAMPHILI (1955)
ECCLESIASTICAL HISTORY, Bks. 6-10 (trans. by Deferrari)

VOL. 30: ST. AUGUSTINE (1955)
LETTERS 165-203 (vol. 4), (trans. by Sr. Wilfrid Parsons)

VOL. 31: ST. CAESARIUS OF ARLES (1956)
SERMONS 1-80 (vol. 1), (trans. by Sr. Mary Magdeleine Mueller)

VOL. 32: ST. AUGUSTINE (1956)
LETTERS 204-270 (vol. 5), (trans. by Sr. Wilfrid Parsons)

VOL. 33: ST. JOHN CHRYSOSTOM (1957)
HOMILIES 1-47 (vol. 1), (trans. by Sr. Thomas Aquinas Goggin)

VOL. 34: ST. LEO THE GREAT (1957)
LETTERS (trans. by Hunt)

VOL. 35: ST. AUGUSTINE (1957)
AGAINST JULIAN (trans. by Schumacher)

VOL. 36: ST. CYPRIAN (1958)
TREATISES (trans. by Deferrari, Sr. Angela Elizabeth Keenan, Mahoney, Sr. George Edward Conway)

VOL. 37: ST. JOHN OF DAMASCUS (1958)
FOUNT OF KNOWLEDGE, ON HERESIES, THE ORTHODOX FAITH (trans. by Chase)

VOL. 38: ST. AUGUSTINE (1959)
SERMONS ON THE LITURGICAL SEASONS (trans. by Sr. M. Sarah Muldowney)

VOL. 39: ST. GREGORY THE GREAT (1959)
DIALOGUES (trans. by Zimmerman)

VOL. 40: TERTULLIAN (1959)
DISCIPLINARY, MORAL, AND ASCETICAL WORKS (trans. by Arbesmann, Quain, Sr. Emily Joseph Daly)

VOL. 41: ST. JOHN CHRYSOSTOM (1960)
HOMILIES 48-88 (vol. 2), (trans. by Sr. Thomas Aquinas Goggin)

VOL. 42: ST. AMBROSE (1961)
HEXAMERON, PARADISE, AND CAIN AND ABEL (trans. by Savage)

VOL. 43: PRUDENTIUS (1962)
POEMS (vol. 1), (trans. by Sr. M. Clement Eagan)

VOL. 44: ST. AMBROSE (1963)
THEOLOGICAL AND DOGMATIC WORKS (trans. by Deferrari)

VOL. 45: ST. AUGUSTINE (1963)
THE TRINITY (trans. by McKenna)

VOL. 46: ST. BASIL (1963)
EXEGETIC HOMILIES (trans. by Sr. Agnes Clare Way)

VOL. 47: ST. CAESARIUS OF ARLES (1964)
SERMONS 81-186 (vol. 2), (trans. by Sr. Mary Magdeleine Mueller)

VOL. 48: ST. JEROME (1964)
HOMILIES 1-59 (vol. 1), (trans. by Sr. Marie Liguori Ewald)

VOL. 49: LACTANTIUS (1964)
THE DIVINE INSTITUTES, Bks. I-VII (trans. by Sr. Mary Francis McDonald)

VOL. 50: OROSIUS (1964)
SEVEN BOOKS AGAINST THE PAGANS (trans. by Deferrari)

VOL. 51: ST. CYPRIAN (1965)
LETTERS (trans. by Sr. Rose Bernard Donna)

VOL. 52: PRUDENTIUS (1965)
POEMS (vol. 2), (trans. by Sr. M. Clement Eagan)

VOL. 53: ST. JEROME (1965)
DOGMATIC AND POLEMICAL WORKS (trans. by John N. Hritzu)

VOL. 54: LACTANTIUS (1965)
THE MINOR WORKS (trans. by Sr. Mary Francis McDonald)

VOL. 55: EUGIPPIUS (1965)
LIFE OF ST. SEVERIN (trans. by Bieler)

VOL. 56: ST. AUGUSTINE (1966)
THE CATHOLIC AND MANICHAEAN WAYS OF LIFE (trans. by Donald A. and Idella J. Gallagher)

VOL. 57: ST. JEROME (1966)
HOMILIES 60-96 (vol. 2), (trans. by Sr. Marie Liguori Ewald)

VOL. 58: ST. GREGORY OF NYSSA (1966)
ASCETICAL WORKS (trans. by Virginia Woods Callahan)

VOL. 59: ST. AUGUSTINE (1968)
THE TEACHER, THE FREE CHOICE OF THE WILL, GRACE AND FREE WILL (trans. by Russell)

VOL. 60: ST. AUGUSTINE (1968)
THE RETRACTATIONS (trans. by Sr. Mary Inez Bogan)

VOL. 61: ST. CYRIL OF JERUSALEM, VOL. 1 (1969)
INTRODUCTORY LECTURE (trans. by Stephenson)
LENTEN LECTURES 1-12 (trans. by McCauley)

VOL. 62: IBERIAN FATHERS, VOL. 1 (1969)
MARTIN OF BRAGA, PASCHASIUS OF DUMIUM, LEANDER OF SEVILLE (trans. by Barlow)

VOL. 63: IBERIAN FATHERS, VOL. 2 (1969)
BRAULIO OF SARAGOSSA, FRUCTUOSUS OF BRAGA (trans. by Barlow)

VOL. 64: ST. CYRIL OF JERUSALEM, VOL. 2 (1970)
LENTEN LECTURES 13-18 (trans. by McCauley)
MYSTAGOGICAL LECTURES (trans. by Stephenson)
SERMON ON THE PARALYTIC (trans. by Stephenson)
LETTER TO CONSTANTIUS (trans. by Stephenson)